British Post War Military Campaigns

A Soldier's Story

A Bundle of a Series of Four Books
The Early Years - Square Bashing
Cyprus – Fighting the EOKA
The Bloody War of Aden
The African Affair

INTRODUCTION

As the reader, if you are expecting this to be a story you will not be disappointed. If you are expecting a history lesson, you will not be disappointed. If you are expecting a diary or a journal, again, you will not be disappointed.

This is a compilation of four books describing one man's fascinating life in the British Military based on his memoirs, and told in a style between these genres. This book describes the early years of our soldier's training, who later went on to take charge of many Special Ops and lead an amazing and sometimes bizarre career in various theatres of military operation around the world.

Due to the clandestine nature of some of his exploits, the UK government gave our soldier a brand new identity on two occasions.

In the first book, you will meet our hero as a young man, whom the author has decided to name Mark 'Mac' Hudson. Through Mac, we are privileged to an inside glimpse into many of the personal encounters experienced by the author, who due to still having contracts on his head three decades later, wrote under the pen name of Ken Johnston.

In this poignant, sometimes silly, often humorous and at other times extremely real and hard-core series of recollections written by someone who lived through them; you, the reader, will be drawn into the world of the challenges, struggles, victories, and defeats shared by the brave men who fought in Britain's small wars.

Contents

BOOK ONE - SQUARE BASHING

CHAPTER 1

Squeaky Boots Jordan

Stories about Drill Instructors are always plentiful in service and ex-service men's conversations. Some are true, some are exaggerated by varying degrees, some are vastly distorted after being spread about here and there, and some are a collection of downright lies. However, all these stories, whatever their description, have one thing in common – a squaddie type of humour, which will often make a person serving in the military howl with laughter, even when he or she is serving in very miserable and adverse conditions.

Our hero, Mark Hudson, or 'Mac' to his friends, has his share of stories about drill instructors he met during his military service, and Squeaky Boots Jordan is at the top of his list. Squeaky Boots achieved his nickname because his boots actually squeaked when he walked. Constant cleaning and bulling up with a deluge of polish and spit, and hour after hour, making minute circles on the leather with a clean cloth, made them gleam up to, and including the fifth lace hole. This dedicated attention caused them to creak and squeak like crazy when he walked. When his sacred parade ground drills began, one would hear the noise increase and sound somewhat like out of tune clarinets warming up before a concert, finally playing the Poet and Peasant Overture as a centrepiece as he banged and stomped his feet.

Squeaky's dress was always immaculate in every way. You could not see his eyes, because his cap peak hid them. This peak was so brilliantly polished that your own reflection jumped out of its surface right back at you. His highly pressed uniform had creases so sharp they looked like they would cut if one inadvertently got close enough to

Squeaky. However, this would rarely happen, as young soldiers would run and hide behind barrack blocks rather than walk past him and incur his wrath that would surely befall them for any obscure reason.

Unfortunately, this was something that Mac had managed to do on many occasions, without intentionally trying. Squeaky would find fault, even when one felt near perfect in one's dress and carriage.

Mark 'Mac' Hudson was one of the few servicemen who, unlike Squeaky Boots, didn't have a nickname that somehow reflected his character. Mac seemed to be the most creative the men could find. Mac took the fact as a compliment, assuming to himself that he'd never screwed up bad enough to warrant a mocking name to begin with. Mac had climbed the ranks quickly; he was extremely fit and a fast learner and passed courses and promotion examinations in rapid succession.

Mac was also an excellent soldier; a natural leader, who led his men from the front and never asked them to perform any task he could not or would not handle himself. He received high decorations for his work and reached Senior Commissioned Rank. Our story will lead us through many adventures and memoirs of Mac, but at this point in the story, we find Mac still a trainee Branch Commission Officer, wet behind the ears, and under Squeaky's influence and command. This background will give an idea of how Squeaky affected Mark 'Mac' Hudson's life, and still does to this day.

On one blustery day, a hardy band of fellows, Mac included, actually saw Squeaky Boots scolding some daffodils and hyacinths at the side of the Catterick camp road, because he had no humans around whom to punish.

"Stand still! You yellow, sickly looking crap hats. How dare you wave about in the wind when I'm walking past you?" He was shouting at the top of his considerably resonant voice.

"You bow your head in submissive subservience when I am in the vicinity, do you understand?"

With this question, he stabbed at the offending blooms with his varnished and brass-tipped pace stick, which was magical and with a mind of its own. Often, Mac would recall how he and his follow officer trainees had been subject to sudden pain when that stick had jumped out of Squeaky's hand and hit them on the funny bone if their arms were not swinging high enough or straight enough for the shoulder height demand. When this pain occurred, Squeaky would discipline the monstrous stick in a very loud voice.

"Now stick, none of that. You are not allowed to hit budding Officers and Gentlemen. They are the cream, Stick! The bloody cream! I know you think they are useless; you don't have to tell me. I can see they are... useless is not a good way to describe them. Pathetic is better. You only want to hurt them to make them better. Of course you do, I feel the same way!"

Amazingly, this farce always made Mac and the other men laugh, and they all worked harder trying to please the stick. The stick was human, and in charge, and had far more experience than the lowly little band of trainees, commonly known as sproggs, crows or smurfs, special handles for the armed forces recruits as they were often referred to by others in more exalted positions in life.

Mac knew, all too well, that sarcastic humour was a trained, standard asset of the drill instructor. "Am I hurting you, soldier? I should be. I'm standing on your bloody hair," type syndrome.

This ability to belittle fellow human beings under training is a carefully rehearsed skill.

Mac fondly recalls how Squeaky would practice the stance he used when giving orders in front of a full-length mirror in the barrack block entrance. Thick skin is required to make other people shrink in mental and physical abeyance when orders are given, and techniques are passed on from instructor to instructor.

The purpose is to channel massed formations of individual characters into a conforming bunch of instinctively disciplined men with good morale (mainly due to their friendship for each other) then turn them into a crew of non-thinking automatons who can be molded into whatever performing tool the Government may require.

Once achieved, the men can then be trained to meet any operations that may be essential during distinct developments of a war situation. Performing this important task necessitates the Drill

[16]

Instructor (DI) should have brains to a limited degree, and understand an overall picture of the military situation. He needs to be politically shrewd and have a heart for the individuals whose lives he makes a misery. He must have the personal courage to make himself a revered image of ridicule of thousands of men under training and carry this with grace. A difficult job, and one only a precise species of man can successfully carry off.

Mac's instructor Squeaky's personality fitted this overall picture, but with one added distinction. Squeaky had a dictionary of his own in his head, and the very original instructions Squeaky offered came from his very varied experiences and was not copied from others.

Usual drill instructor humour, often used by Squeaky, is all said in a very regimented voice and stance, and more often than not directed at a recruit who has performed in an incorrect way.

Looking back over the years, Mac could often reflect on the times he spent under Squeaky's command with a good chuckle. Some of Mac's favourites are:

"If you had another brain, Sir, you would possess an aggregate total of one."

"Your mother obviously picked the wrong gene pile."

"I've studied your movements, Sir. Have you got your knickers stuck half way up your arse? You haven't? Then you had better come to my room at seven this evening for a hip replacement."

"To cough is a military test to see if you have a pair of balls, stop trying to prove yourself and impress me. The next time you cough, I'll cut them off."

After a plea of innocence from the victim, "OK the cough is a cold, colds are allowed between 0001 hours and 0500 hours, after that time, any cough warrants a de-rollicking, understood?"

"Yes, Sir."

"DO NOT call me Sir. I'm too intelligent to be a bloody officer, understood?"

"Yes, Sgt"

"Good! Now we are showing a modicum of intelligence, aren't we? Well done!"

"It will take you years of practice to become thick officers Gentlemen."

Mac recalls some comments during planning a training exercise:

"What is the most dangerous thing you can meet on this operation, Gentlemen?"

"Rebel tribes working outside of the Geneva Convention?"

"No."

"Blow pipes and poison darts?"

"No."

"Snakes?"

"No."

"Anopheles Malaria bearing mosquitoes?"

"Dangerous, but not the most dangerous."

"Vampire bats and Leeches?"

"No."

"Calked Magalia flies and grubs incubating inside us?"

"No, Smart Arse,"

"Tse flies and sleeping sickness?"

"No, well done. You tried Gentlemen, and you came up with some good ideas, however you forgot that Captain Simons is coming with us on this exercise as umpire. In this capacity, it will be necessary for him to carry a map and a whistle. That, Gentlemen, is the most dangerous thing you will ever see or meet in your career, an officer with a map, Gentlemen! A bloody officer with a map! Remember that always. Do you see now, Gentlemen, what dangerous animals you are going to become when I've finished training you? You will be feared, Gentlemen, feared by all. Pick up a map and your soldiers will tremble with unadulterated fear!

"Fear is your major weapon as officers, show intelligence and you could start a mutiny, let your Senior NCO think they are running the show!

"Sit down. Shut up. Listen in; I've heard something on the grapevine. In other words, it has been officially leaked that you have all passed your course, and as of Friday this week, you will receive the

Queen's Commission. God help the Nation. Five days left for me to honour Her Majesty and try to make something resembling an officer out of you. I need your help! I can only do so much myself! The rest must come from you! Are we on the same wavelength?"

"Yes, Sgt!"

Mac fondly recalls what a cunning fox he was; he had the men sweating their cobs off for a whole week and on top of it they thought he was doing them a favour. Mac and the majority of the men did receive their Queen's Commission. When Squeaky had finished training Mac, he officially became an Officer and Gentleman, but Mac still felt that he was one of Squeaky Boot's toys to play about with at his will.

Was that Squeaky's intention? Or was Mac paranoid?

CHAPTER 2

Squeaky Boots' Legacy

Over the following years of service, in different parts of the world, Squeaky Boots was often the subject of conversation in the Officer's Mess. Just as students tend to remember the important teachers from their school days, so Mac remembered his military mentors. Squeaky Boots did very well in the promotion field, and it seemed to Mac that he had made exceptionally rapid progress to the ultimate rank of Warrant Officer. Upon reflection, it was, in fact, about five years, which was the normal expected progression for his trade group.

With this increase in rank, Squeaky received more power and command responsibility, and he developed an even keener sarcastic sense of bizarre humour and urine extraction of his students, if their stories filtering back to Mac were anything to go by.

One evening in a pub, Mac recalls overhearing this example of a Squeaky Incident. The story went something like this:

"Have you ever farted, Sir? Have you ever heard an Officer and a Gentleman fart, Sir?"

"No, Warrant Officer."

"Why do you think that is, you intelligent lump of shit?"

"I don't know, Warrant Officer."

"Because from birth, officers are born with a silencer stick up their arses, in case they inadvertently say anything intelligent or disturb their mama and papa shagging. Understood?"

"No Warrant Officer. What is shagging?"

"Shagging, Sir, is when a man and a woman make love to each other and make babies with no brains, like you boy! Have you ever had a shag?"

"No, Warrant Officer."

"Corporal Knowles! Bring out the rubber doll, gather all the unit virgins together, and we will have a shagging class at 14:00 hours. I don't want any man in my command going into action to die for Queen and Country still a virgin. If he's thinking about what it's like, he's dead; his mind is not on killing. Expedite immediate, MOVE!"

Mac had to chuckle again when he overhead this story, realizing that Squeaky had not changed all that much. Mac was sure that hundreds more episodes in a similar sort of vein were still floating around. Some would be funny, some very funny, and some even quite sick, but Mac knew that they would all carry the Squeaky Boots hallmark.

One Officer who joined Mac in the Middle East had fallen foul of Squeaky Boots, as Mac once had, and when Mac and this man began chatting, he had Mac in hysterics with narratives of the psychological torture used on him by the drill square vampire, whom Mac remembered so well.

"Go to the supply stores, Sir. Give the store's Warrant Officer my regards, and tell him I've sent you to collect a KD overcoat for yourself, a tin of striped paint for me, and a long wait. Understood?"

Now, here is the madness of that order. KD means Khaki Drill, and is a uniform issue for Middle East and Far East hot climates, so no KD overcoat exists. On cold nights in these places, one uses the standard UK issue overcoat. Number two; have you ever seen striped paint? Number three, the long wait is a routine played by different Unit Heads of Department to see how long our trainee takes to realize he has been taken for a ride and do something about it.

Mac listened while his companion told the following story. Upon arriving at the stores, and finding the store Warrant Officer the following conversation ensued:

"Mr. Jordan's compliments, Sir!"

"Thank you for delivering them, Cadet Sir. Thank him for me when you return. Now, what can I do for you?"

"Mr. Jordan says I'm to fetch a KD overcoat for myself, a tin of striped paint for him, and a long wait, Warrant Officer."

[21]

"Good, that seems quite reasonable, let's see what we can do for you, what week of training are you on, son?"

"Second week, Warrant Officer."

"Are! Then you haven't been measured for clothing here before have you?"

"No, Warrant Officer."

"No problem, we'll sort you out in no time, but first I'd like you to go back to WO Jordan and ask him which stripe colours he wants for his paint. We have broad white and narrow black or narrow yellow and broad black with just a hint of deep red on the edges. Away you go, there's a good chap."

A confused Officer Cadet rushes away, because God in the form of a Warrant Officer has spoken. He knows something is wrong, but can't quite put his finger on it, running such high power messages between such high powered people has blown his mind; it's not functioning correctly.

"You're back. That was quick, and how did you go on, Sir?" quipped Squeaky Boots.

"Fine, Warrant Officer, the stores WO says thank you for your compliments. He's going to measure me for my overcoat when I get back. He wants me to find out what colour of the striped paint you want. Black and white, or black and yellow, and stripe widths, and do you want a hint of red on the borders? And if you do, he'll do it for you when I tell him what you say."

"Steady on lad, take it easy. You'll blow your arse out of its socket if you rush about and babble on like that. Now let's see, tell the stores WO I would like yellow and black in the bottom half of the tin, and black and white in the top half. I'll leave the widths to his judgment, and I'll have a slight tint of red in the top half. What do you think, Sir? That should look good on the curb stones shouldn't it?"

"Yes, Warrant Officer."

"Off you go then! Schnell!" Away goes one even more confused Cadet, turning rapidly to his left, when he hears a blood-curdling scream from Squeaky:

"Do not walk on my Parade Square, you stupid little bastard!"

[22]

Back at the stores, the WO is very understanding, and is even quite pleasant and jovial, compared to Squeaky Boots. Mind you, no one would have a problem appearing more jovial than that manic parade ground fanatic.

"Well done, boy. That didn't take you long, and rest assured I will sort out Warrant Officer Jordan's order, whilst you are having your measurements taken for your overcoat. Go over to the cubicle, pull the curtains, and have a rest after all that errand running. The tailor will be with you shortly."

Away goes one relieved Cadet, thinking to himself what a tremendously kind person the store's WO was.

Three hours later, the Cadet starts anxiously looking around the corner of the curtain. No one seems to be heading his way. Should he remind somebody he's still here? No, he'd better not. The store WO had been nice to him and he didn't want to upset him, and after all it is a training camp, and they deal with hundreds of men like him every day, so they must know what they are doing. Patience is golden, his mother used to say. Another two hours, still no action. Suddenly, our Cadet has a brainwave at last. He will ask one of the soldiers he can see working on the counter if he'd been forgotten. That way, he wouldn't upset the nice Warrant Officer. Go for it, take a deep breath, and go for it. Two hours later, he plucked up courage and went for it.

Hundreds of Cadets have fallen for the long wait; and our Cadet did not do too badly. He came away after seven hours, when the record, we have been informed, stands at eighteen hours, and the training staff is sure that one day they will find someone stupid enough to beat that score. The soldier at the counter was sympathetic.

"Yes, Sir? May I help you?" said with a sincere, genuine look on his face and oozing innocence.

"Yes, please. I've been waiting to be measured for my KD overcoat for six hours, and I wondered if I'd been forgotten."

"No, Sir. You haven't been forgotten. You are having the piss taken out of you on what is commonly termed 'the long wait'. The store's staff has been taking bets on how long it would take you to ask somebody what was going on. I'm in with a chance of winning fifty quid, because I said you looked intelligent, compared to most, and would possibly question someone in less than seven hours, so I'm in with a chance. Any questions?"

"Yes. What do I do now?"

"Go back to your barrack block, have a shower, go for your tea, and laugh about it. You are not the first twat and you won't be the last, so don't worry about it."

"What about the tin of striped paint for the drill Warrant Officer?"

"Tell him we've given it to a zoo to smarten up the zebra and tiger cages. He won't say a word, I assure you."

"Can I have your name in case he wants to talk to you himself?"

"You can't ask intelligent questions like that. You're letting your side down. Stay stupid. Now, piss off."

Back to the real world scurries our little cadet, but not to ridicule, his peers thought him brave that he dare ask questions after following orders from a Warrant Officer – and Squeaky Boots didn't utter a word.

CHAPTER 3

Squeaky Boots' Downfall

The mid 1960s saw the start of the second major British military re-organisation since the significant post-war changes in the early 1950s. These changes were introduced over a period of two years. Tremendous cuts took place in the structure and personnel manning, plus there was an increase in the work amalgamation of military trade groups. This was a cost cutting exercise, which affected all the services. Job descriptions, workload, responsibility, and tasks increased out of all recognition to previous work schedules. The changes carried no rank increase or pay rise.

This change was to be a masterpiece of money saving. Manpower management decisions were taken by the powers that be in the Ministry of Defence. A few senior officers received a knighthood at the expense of thousands of rank and file, previously dedicated, military personnel. After the shakeup, most people found they had to sacrifice high standards and efficiency for a far lower, mediocre, final result in their work. It was not a satisfying situation.

How did this shake up affect Squeaky Boots?

Before the changes, Squeaky trained drill, turn out, military law, and general standards to the good order and discipline of the Queen's Military regulations and Geneva Convention. He also dealt with general administration, pay, ration returns, leave, sick parades, church parades, dental parades, etc. Altogether, it was a steady fourteen-hour day to achieve the best results for his men and the service.

Under the new rules, the trade of Drill Instructor was one small part of a job description entitled 'Ground Combat Training Instructor' (GCTI) for Army Personnel, and 'Ground Defence Training Instructor' (GDTI) for Royal Air Force men. Each instructor would be required to teach drill, first aid, fire protection, light rescue from buildings (heights and basements), nuclear, biological and chemical warfare, which included respirator fitting and testing in a gas chamber. On top of that, weapons training on all small arms, conduct range-firing exercises, map reading, signal procedure, as well as looking after their recruit's normal administration and welfare were added to this list. In addition, leadership training was a big part of their responsibilities. Reliability and initiative training, survival training, field hygiene and living in a tented camp should also be added to this inventory. It's obvious that something had to suffer, and indeed it did, the outcome was inferior results across the board and less efficient servicemen and women.

Courses were in abundance to prepare an instructor to fulfil the task set under the new policy. Cross service training became the vogue. Army, Navy, and RAF all attended the same courses in quick succession, and having completed training, the men and women entered a teaching pool for allocation of postings. Cross service teaching was common, especially with the RAF Regiment, which had been using this policy for years, and had positioned GDTIs on every RAF station and recruit training school. With this established structure, it was easy for the RAF to include Army and Navy units to its instructor postings; after all, they all did the same courses.

As a little trip down memory lane for ex-GCTIs and GDTIs, the compulsory courses to attend one after the other were as follows:

The qualifications required before starting training, were Substantive Corporal, five years' service, Drill Instructor's course with the Brigade of Guards, and eight weeks at Pirbright. The courses to complete were the First Aid Course; three weeks at RAF Freckleton; Nuclear, Biological, and Chemical Warfare; three weeks at Winterbourne Gunner; Light Rescue Instructor; four weeks at RAF Sutton on Hill; Small Arms Weapons Instructor; eight weeks at Hythe School of Infantry; Man Management and Youth Leadership; six weeks at the Army School of Education at Beaconsfield; Survival, Reliability and Initiative training; plus Escape and Evasion and Resistance to Interrogation. In addition, there were SAS, Para, Marine instructors and two weeks on the Brecon Beacons.

[26]

A pass in all these courses, and then an allocation of a teaching post, denoted automatic promotion to Sergeant. Occasionally a serviceman would start the course as a Sergeant and remained a Sergeant on completion. "Hard luck mate," was the friendly cry.

Women had shown their worth in war-type situations throughout the Battle of Britain. They skillfully worked as photo interpreters, map plotters, forwards air controllers, radar operators, signalers, parachute packers, caterers, stores organisers, drivers, and the lesser known position of aircraft ferry pilots. Thanks to their efforts all types of aircraft were kept flowing to the squadrons by road and air.

Women had been one of the deciding factors in fighter command winning the battle. The new defense white paper gave a priority to increase the women's force in all three services, and this inevitably increased the number of female officers to train. Squeaky Boots was chosen to teach the Women's Combined Services Officer course at RAF Henlow.

Teaching women can be a very rewarding job, as they are keen to impress a male instructor and show they can be superior to men. Their efforts are therefore greater than their male counterparts, and with the exception of the physical strength comparison, they normally finish the course with higher overall results than men. Because they are so keen, everything they do is treated very seriously; there is little room for fun and virtually no sense of humour. Squeaky Boot's style was doomed from the start.

Many tales were repeated to Mac and the other men in relation to the way the women ganged up on Squeaky Boots, and they had no reason to disbelieve these stories, as the same stories came from many different sources.

On one occasion, Squeaky was teaching a first aid class, the subject being how to pick someone up in a fireman's lift and carry them to a safe place. Squeaky had the class seated in the front rows of the station cinema, and he placed two girls on the stage as demonstrators. With one of the girls lying down on her back acting as a casualty, Squeaky began to demonstrate his actions, discussing each move he performed.

[27]

"Now then, my lovelies, this bird on the floor has been knocked unconscious by falling bricks during a bombing. The building is in danger of collapse, so it is imperative we move her to safety. There is nobody to help you; she is bigger and heavier than you are, but you can move her by following my demonstration. Any questions?"

This was the standard introduction of the lesson if he had been teaching men; he was soon to find out that it is different when dealing with women.

"Good. To continue, bend down on one knee, keeping the knee close to the top of her head as you do so. Now put your fingers in her mouth and ensure there are no obstructions to her breathing and that her tongue has not fallen back into her throat, a very common occurrence with comatose casualties."

Squeaky followed his own instructions.

"Now, place both arms down to her sides, keeping them as close to her body as you can. Move down to her feet and cross one leg over the other like so." Again, he provided a detailed demonstration.

"Are we all clear so far? Good, let's continue. Position yourself back at her head, on one knee like before, and note this is the tricky bit, you see I've crossed her left leg over her right. This means I'm going to roll her onto her stomach to the left. Now watch closely - I place my left hand on top of her left chest and my right hand under her right shoulder, and then spin her to the left like this." With one easy flowing move, Squeaky spun the girl over onto her stomach with such ease he brought a gasp of surprise from the students.

"Fine. Now the lift itself. Keep yourself positioned at the casualty's head and place both your arms underneath her armpits. Clasping your hands firmly together behind her back, pull her up into a half-upright position resting her on your knee so that you can move your hand position for the final lift. Are we clear so far? Good. Now, watch carefully. Stand up yourself, and pull the casualty into an upright stance, with her weight leaning against you. Take her right wrist with your left hand. Bend down, so her body folds over your back. Put your right arm all the way through her legs and lift her up on your shoulders." Squeaky made the smooth transition from supporting the body to carrying it in one easy move.

"Have we all seen and understood that move? Well done. All we have to do now is change over the handgrips, and clasp her right wrist with your right hand. Good, that lets you carry the patient, leaving our left hand free for climbing ladders or opening doors. It's easy when you know how, isn't it?"

Squeaky then organised the women into two person teams to practice. The students worked hard at their practice, carrying the casualties through doors, upstairs, down the air raid shelter slope, and up and down fire escapes.

As the lesson progressed the students learnt to use the lift and negotiate hazards with an unconscious person on their back. The aim of the lesson had been achieved. That would be considered a success in a man's world, but not in the world of teaching women.

"That concludes this lesson, ladies. Are there any questions?

"Yes, Warrant Officer." This question was asked by a huge blonde sumo wrestler-type from the back of the class.

"Yes, young lady, what's your question?

"The demonstration you gave used a woman as a victim, we practiced with other women, how would we fare with a man your size, you know, someone who is bigger and heavier?"

"A good point, well the proof is in the pudding and so on. Come up here and use me as the casualty, show the class what you can do."

Out of her seat came our student, rolling down the aisle and slowly climbed up to the stage, which was at least six feet off the ground.

"Right, young lady, you carry out a demonstration on me slowly, so all the class can confirm in their minds what to do."

Mayhem followed, as every deliberate move the girl made was greeted with loud screams, whistles, and yells of 'sock it to him' and similar suggested tortures. It was exquisite, epically stupendous, hilarious chaos. The crescendo came when our monstrous female cadet stood at the front of the stage with Squeaky draped captive over her shoulders, ecstatic at the calls and screams of 'Throw him off!' She

[29]

did just that. Turning to one side and dropping her shoulder, she threw Squeaky, not dropped him... but threw him off the stage. His hip was somewhat badly bruised, not helping his regimental smartness when he moved.

The outcome of this episode for Squeaky did not help his position at the school at all. Unfortunately for him, the three senior female officers in charge of the training wing were having a walkabout. Hearing what sounded like a rugby crowd at Twickenham screaming from the cinema, they peered in to investigate the noise, arriving just in time to see Quasimodo II posing on the edge of the stage with Squeaky draped over her shoulders, directly before throwing Squeaky off the stage.

Later, they questioned the women cadets about the incident and drew conclusions from their replies that resulted in Squeaky being called up in front of a disciplinary hearing. A hearing of this nature fell short of being a charge (a service summons by service law), its purpose was to decide whether an offense had been committed. If not, advice was given to avoid an individual coming close to the mark again and to act as a recorded warning. If the panel of three women officers, one from each branch of service (nicknamed 'The Three Witches' by the rank and file) decided an offense had been committed, the offender was formally charged and the normal military path of discipline would follow.

The complaints against Squeaky were very petty, nitpicking issues, but serious enough for the hearing to take place simply because the students were women. Squeaky had addressed the cadets as 'lovelies'. To Mac's mind, by the looks of some of these women, they should have been flattered.

Squeaky had called the demonstrator a bird. Perhaps he should know have known better, but it was not intended maliciously.

Squeaky had physically touched the demonstrator cadet. This was wrong; he should have talked and guided the second demonstrator cadet to do the actions. Again, this was Squeaky's 'hands on' way to produce the best results, no ill intent was meant. The cadet demonstrator that Squeaky had touched stated that when he was showing the class how to turn a casualty over; he had placed his hand on her left breast. Squeaky said he didn't know breasts were on women's shoulder blades and collarbones. Other students supported Squeaky, so the complaint was ignored. The same cadet objected to Squeaky 'exploring her tonsils', as she put it, with his fingers and claimed his fingers tasted of tobacco.

Squeaky rather lamely said he didn't smoke. He should not have put his hand and arm through the casualty's legs, as he was training women the correct procedure would have been around the back of their legs. Squeaky's viewpoint was the victim was supposedly unconscious and wouldn't know anyway. Certainly, he was guilty of placing his fingers in the student's mouth. He would not even have stuck his fingers down a man's throat. What made him do that? Mac wondered.

The overall outcome was a formal warning to:

Avoid touching students at all times and avoid language that could distress.

No charges were filed, but Squeaky had been brought to the attention of 'The Almighty' and from now on his every move would be screened.

Squeaky tried hard to conform, but his previous long and successful service of training men kept coming to the forefront of his teaching style, predominantly when he was enthusiastic over a subject.

Mac felt Squeaky should have been posted back to a male teaching school, for the good of everybody, including his own protection. This turned out to be absolutely spot on, as in spite of his efforts to be correct and play by the rules, it didn't take long for Squeaky's second blunder to occur.

Squeaky was again teaching first aid, and the lesson was nerve and established shock. Imagine the female officer cadet's faces as they listened to Squeaky earnestly explaining how dog muck could cause nervous shock:

"It's easy to remember the differences between the two types of shock, ladies. Established shock is caused by a continuous loss of body

[31]

fluid, for example, severe hemorrhage or excessive sweating caused by fever, such as which occurs in the cases of malaria and cholera or with diarrhea in dysentery. Unless this condition is quickly treated, it can kill, and often kills very rapidly.

Nerve shock, on the other hand, is usually not fatal. It is caused by something very distressing to any one or more than one of the human senses. If this occurs, it activates a drop in blood pressure; the blood drains from the extremities of the body into the deep organs. Any questions?"

"Yes, Warrant Officer. Could you give us an example of the type of things that can make us have nervous shock?"

"Of course, Ma'am. You could receive a telegram containing very bad news, this is an emotional and a mental invasion of your body, causing faintness, cold, clammy, pale skin, because the blood has drained away, and many more symptoms we'll learn about later. Any more questions?"

"Yes, Warrant Officer. You said one or more senses could be affected. Could you give us an example of what could cause this, please?"

"Of course, my dear. Have you ever walked along a street and come across a great big, hot, steaming pile of shit? I can see by the looks on your faces that you have. The revulsion you feel is because you've seen it. Number one, the sense of sight. Now imagine that you trip over on a banana skin, your balance is upset and it can cause fear. Another cause, but not a human sense. Imagine that when you fall, you land with your hand in the shit and it had squeezed up between your fingers with a sickly horrible squelching sound. Our senses involved at this point are touch and sound. Your face was only two inches away from the flattened pile, the smell was colossal, and a squirt of the evil stuff had gone in your mouth and tasted revolting. Now we have involved the sense of smell and taste. Where does this leave us affected now? In one incident we have had a disgusting, mentally disturbing, shocking, sickening, and frightening experience, involving all our human senses and also some human emotions."

[32]

Mac could just see the smug look on Squeaky's face when he had finished. Squeaky thought it a brilliant answer; his point had been made. He could see it, the way they fidgeted about and looked uneasily at each other.

"Of course you know the answer, but I'll just confirm: we saw the offensive item; you touched it; it squelched when you touched it, so your hearing became involved; you smelt the horrible stuff; and finally, tasted the gooey, sticky muck. Are you all happy? If you were asked a question on your final exams to differentiate between 'Established' and 'Nerve' shock, could you give a correct answer? A show of hands, please, for an affirmative."

Every hand was raised.

"Good."

Mac knew there was no doubt Squeaky had taught them how to recognize nerve shock. Squeaky had actually induced nerve shock in some of them with his vivid, gory description. However, this was not accepted practice. His return trip to the three witches was initiated because a WRAF Sergeant overheard two cadets talking about Squeaky's lesson. Also, because of the fact he had said 'shit' a couple of times, without knowing the context of the lesson, she reported him. Mac knows, looking back, that it's true, Squeaky could have said dog manure or droppings; but his style was to go for an impact the student would remember.

A second, formal warning to conform to the school standing orders was issued. In particular, there was to be no swearing in front of students, or within earshot of students. Secondly, he had to teach exactly as per the formal term of reference stipulated for each lesson. For example, first aid must be word-for-word from the St. John's Ambulance Basic First Aid Book: no deviations, no inventiveness, no personal experiences to assist student understanding. All motivation for Instructors to prepare and give interesting retention assisting lessons were removed. No lesson planning was needed; one might as well just stand and read from the book.

Mac's reaction was to recall his instruction under Squeaky, and he knew the current method would be a dreary way to learn. Thinking back on his own stimulating training, Mac could not help but think the new style must be mind-numbingly boring.

Again, Squeaky tried to follow the school's dictates for teachers, but he was too experienced and proud of his work and results to perform under those unintelligent, amateur constraints for too long before falling foul of the system again, and this time with his favourite subject: Drill.

A wet, miserable day is always a good time to parade cadets for a good, hard drill session. It's a character test; a lot of concentration is needed to follow strict orders efficiently. A trainee must stay rock steady and still, without the slightest movement when called to 'Attention'. They are required to keep a set drill stance, chin in, chest out, stomach in, for long periods of time, also keeping their heads up and eyes straight ahead, with arms straight down at their sides, fingers curled, with the thumb forwards and in line with the seam of the trousers. Between drill movements of 'Stand at Ease' and 'Attention!' One has to make sure that the final feet position is with the heels touching and the feet splayed at forty-five degrees.

All this attention to detail with cold fingers, freezing cheeks and lips, and a nose running its contents down one's face, drags determination and discipline out of all and sundry on parade.

It was at this drill command that the problem arose. On 'Attention!' a female cadet didn't quite manage to get her heels together; in fact, there was a gap of about four inches between them. Once the drill move has been made, it is important that if a mistake has been made that it is not corrected, the reason being, people will notice an individual movement when one and all are standing completely still, however they would possibly not perceive a mistake.

For example, a Welsh Guardsman dropped his rifle during a 'Present Arms!' command during Trooping the Colour in the presence of Her Majesty the Queen. After his blunder he stood perfectly still and retrieved his rifle when movement recommenced on parade during a Right Dress Command. Instead of a punishment, he received a unit commendation for his initiative.

[34]

Our luckless Cadet did the correct thing after making her mistake. She stood perfectly still, and she should have been ignored, unless she made the same mistake again. Mac realised, upon hearing this story that Squeaky must have been in a bad mood. He wasn't enamoured with his female students anyway, especially after his previous run-ins because of 'women' rules, and he reacted in the usual man-trainer Squeaky style.

He stood menacingly tall and imposingly in front of the rigid girl (who was obviously aware of her wrong stance and foot position) and with his peaked cap hiding his eyes, he jabbed his pace stick toward her wide apart heels with his white-gloved hand, and finally he spoke:

"The position of 'Attention!' in Her Majesty's Services is with the heels together and the feet displayed at forty five-degrees. Get your bloody heels together and stop standing there as though in anticipation of a hot cock, Ma'am."

That was it. The official wheels turned rapidly. The same afternoon, Squeaky was in front of the three witches yet again. Squeaky was suspended of all teaching duties, whilst the powers-that-be decided his future. Within forty-eight hours he was posted to Watchet in Somerset as unit Warrant Officer to the ground-to-air Gunnery Range.

On hearing of the punishment, Mac shook his head and pondered on the absolute waste of a professional Instructor that had cost the military hundreds of thousands of pounds to train.

One would have thought that the senior command, on seeing the warning signs and being aware of his dislike for teaching women would have posted him to more suitable work, rather than allowing the situation to continue and finally ruin his career.

Even with this unfortunate ending, Mac reveled in the stories of dear old Squeaky Boots, and remembered him fondly, especially when he himself was no longer at the brunt of Squeaky's verbal onslaught.

Although at that time Mac didn't know it, is working relationship with Squeaky Boots would later continue, and they would meet up again on the humid terrains of Tanzania in East Africa.

CHAPTER 4

Civilian Squeaky

Some years down the line, fortunately for Squeaky, he was eventually able to retire from the service as a highly qualified and very experienced Warrant Officer. After Squeaky had completed his military service, Mac was to hire him as a Field Operations Advisor in the Tanzanian Ugandan war. He was selected to teach Tanzanian Army Instructor courses on a variety of subjects, and in line with this most important work, he carried out liaison visits to the local tribal chieftains.

The aim of these excursions was to gain information on anything that may act as a pointer to the war's progress, and supply Mac with continuously updated intelligence to help in the bid to outsmart and defeat Idi Amin in the Ugandan War, and promote goodwill with the local nationals.

Mac had sent Squeaky to the Northwest to pave the way for their logistics guided and deliberate slow advance toward Jinja, and what the men hoped would be the final battle. One week after Squeaky departed for his mission, Mac arrived at a kraal. A kraal is a village surrounded by circular thorn hedges and internal thorn compounds for holding cattle, goats, and other livestock with even denser thickets of thorns enclosing the rondavels, or mud houses, thus protecting the villagers and their livestock from the abundant wildlife predators.

Disease, in the local name of 'sleeping sickness' was rife in this area. Sleeping Sickness was a killer disease spread by a fly called the Tsetse, which fed on blood and waste from the cattle. The fly's digestive juices acted like a poison and people could catch the disease by the fly biting them, eating the maggots, or indirectly by drinking the contaminated cow's milk and cow's blood, which they mixed with goat's milk, making a mixture called 'chowder,' one of their preferred high protein meals. The unfortunate souls who caught this disease would develop a strong fever, severe vomiting and diarrhea, excessive sweating, and therefore general dehydration. Shock, coma, and death usually quickly followed. Strength, youth, and good health could delay the effects, but could not prevent death. No one had built up an artificial immunity against sleeping sickness over hundreds of years.

Armed with this knowledge, Mac was not surprised to see the villagers – men, women, and children – running around, completely naked, but covered in large, thick layers of cow manure and sludge to protect themselves from the close attentions of the fly. Mac thought that they looked like phantoms in camouflage, because some of the cow manure was dry, and a whitish gray in colour, and some of it was wet, giving it a dark brown shade.

A cow shit shade, Mac bemused.

When Mac walked into the compound, a cow started to urinate and a stampede of children rushed at the beast to interrupt its business with squeals of delight. Many of the children were clutching old rusty tins. The purpose of these classical containers was to catch the urine so they could use it to rub into the movable joints of their bodies: ankles, knees, hips, elbows, wrists, shoulders and necks. If they didn't carry out this ablution on a regular basis the manure dried rock hard, and they could not move. They had to keep their joints moist.

Water was at a premium, not for wasting on joint lubrication, so urine was the GX500 joint oil. To some, the practice might have seemed appalling, but for the villagers it was part of their daily routine - as natural as walking or sleeping.

As Mac noted, who was worried about piss anyway, when they were covered from head to toe in shit?

Fred Likili was the village headman, an acquaintance of Mac's during the past eighteen months. Previously, Mac and Fred had met in a small township, where Fred's elder brother and family lived, a short distance north of Entebbe. On that occasion, Fred had sworn to Mac his very sincere allegiance and help in any way possible to assist in ousting Idi Amin from power. Fred had lost two brothers and a sister to the tyrant.

Although this was a Mark Hudson's first visit to Fred's kraal, Mac had visited many other villages, so he was well aware of the customs and traditions that were necessary to follow in one's presentation.

First, a visitor stood in silence, looked straight ahead with a large grin on their face, ensuring they were showing as many teeth as can be sported and with arms crossed over the chest. This showed the people that one did not possess devil's eyes and that his mouth was human in shape, neither did it contain animal-type fangs, as did Baboons, which they feared as the spirits of long past ancestors. The crossing of the arms meant one came in peace and would hold the villagers to their bosom if they needed comfort or help. They could also see that the visitor did not carry any weapons. After a suitable delay for close scrutiny, the headman signaled that he wished the visitor to follow him and proceeded to the large Acacia tree that stood in the centre of all of the kraals. Indeed, the tree was selected as the centrepiece before the kraal was developed.

All decisions were made under this tree, hence its communal title, "the thinking tree". Beneath the tree was a homemade bench, facing the direction of the sunrise. Most of the thinking and decision-making took place just when the sun was beginning to show and the temperature was cooler. Also, that way any new orders dreamt up that morning beneath the tree could be passed on to the cattle herdsmen before they left to graze their beasts.

Mac and Fred headed for the tree. When they sat, the headman gave an almost imperceptible hand signal, seemingly to no one in particular. Instantly, two small but fat-bellied children ran out of a hut, carrying a folding flat table, which they rapidly erected in front of the Amasses, or big bosses. Following behind them, in a far more sedate and stately fashion, strode an older woman, whom Fred introduced as Kate, his first, or number one wife.

Kate placed on the table a rusty Peak Freen biscuit tin, half-full of what looked like sand, but turned out to be dust impregnated salt. Salt was the most important gift the villagers could present.

After this, was a period of silence, no speech at all, which was called the "contemplation time", and could last up to half an hour, depending on how much was to be said, the importance of what was to be said, and the severity of a wrong outcome of the meeting for either party. On this occasion, contemplation time lasted about ten minutes, but seemed a good deal longer to Mac.

On some unseen signal, fourteen children, aged between about four and ten, came out of the round mud and straw huts, each one carrying a bottle of White Cap beer. This offering was clutched tightly to their bodies with both hands, as though it was the most reverent article on Earth, which, of course, to them it was - next to the salt. They lined up in front of Fred, and as each child placed the beer on the table, he would pat them on the head and indicated to Mac that he should do the same.

"These are my children from my four wives. They are all male offspring, but one. The Lord has been good to me, and I have few dowries to pay for daughter's weddings. Come, let us drink and talk our minds clear of the morning mists and sun's haze that haunt inside us at the moment."

Talk about skits of Shakespeare, Mac thought.

The reader must understand that Mac's retelling of this story is not literal; but rather the nearest translation of mixed English, Swahili, and bushman tongue that Mac can give.

"Thank you for the talk time. My great joy must show at the chance of seeing your family again, and I see new sons from since our last meeting. All are well, and you have no great problems, I think?" Mac queried him.

Fred replied, "You are true in your joy, and I see happiness in your face at my family. You are indeed wise to see they are all well, but I would like for some help with the Kaki and fever medicine you bring, I think?"

Mac knew that the Kaki and fever medicine was a mixture of saline morphine to stop stomach problems and fever dehydration and dysentery. This drink is a United Nations developed drink in a sachet to feed the children, containing a mix of everything they need in the form of vitamins, calcium, and other nutrients. Later on, Mac was to discover that statistics proved this drink was a great lifesaver.

Mac said, "I have with me what you ask for in small quantity, but new tablets called Paladin Salts which you take by mouth, two, once per day in the morning cool. These will keep away the mosquito fever and salt dehydration. Is there more for me to know?"

The bushman paused for a moment, as though in contemplation, then quickly and quietly stated, very matter-of-factly, "I do not like your Squeaky Boots man".

Mac was not surprised, and in fact, he had almost expected something such as this where Squeaky was concerned.

"We speak when we have calmed and had much to drink in our happiness." Mac used a deliberate delaying tactic by that statement.

Fred's short 'Contemplation Time' before he came out with that potent statement meant that Mac had to be very shrewd about how he handled what was obviously going to be a problem.

Instead of continuing the conversation about Squeaky, the two men talked about the reports of 'swine fever' in domesticated animals spread by warthogs, the outbreak of bovine tuberculosis in cattle, and the import of dozens of European vets to carry out tests on wild animals and establish a cause for the fever.

Also on Fred and Mac's "general calm agenda" was the pregnancy rate of his wives, their "fruitfulness" in comparison with his cattle. Things such as what were Fred's chances of managing to acquire another wife this year, or should he buy more cattle and leave the new wife to next year?

After 30 minutes or so of general discussion, the contemplation and calm time was over, and Mac knew now was the moment to broach the subject of Squeaky Boots. This man would not speak so openly, so quickly, unless his wife and her family had been nagging at him, or something had distressed the whole group and caused fear for the well-being of the village. It must have something to do with the mental health of the village or the financial position of the village-type worries, and therefore, Mac knew he had to find out what Squeaky had done to cause this.

With this in mind, Mac let himself in for Fred's answers by asking a question.

[40]

"And what has Squeaky done to offend you, and how can I decide on his offense, if any?" Mac tentatively asked. Fred's gave a long drawn out sigh, before replying. His reply was not exactly what Mac had expected. "You know we have the problem with the Tsetse fly?"

"Yes, I know you have the problem with the Tsetse fly in these parts; it is a pity for your people." Mac answered.

"We protect against the Tsetse. Our people cover themselves with what they can protect with from the cow."

"Yes, I am aware of your practice, and I think it is a very sensible practice."

Fred continued, "When your Squeaky came to look at our kraal, we show him goodness and kindness and I gave him one of my young wives for his comfort and for his company during the cold of the night. You understand my thoughts and gift?"

"Of course, I understand. This is very kind of you and your people. You are very famous, and I hear much village talk during my travels about you for your kindness and generosity in this way." Mac was mildly amused by the man's relaying of the events, but he managed to remain as solemn as Fred's demeanor appeared.

"Squeaky-man, he takes my wife, and he desires to have comfort with his loins. He takes away the protection around her baby channel and around her baby feeding buttons. He then makes good comfort with great power. It is good for his comfort and for wife it is good; she enjoys making his comfort with her heart. She is very happy that they stay all night, making comfort."

At this point, it was difficult for Mac to maintain his composure, but being the officer and gentleman that he was, Mac managed to reply, "I am glad that he made good comfort with your wife, and I am glad that your wife was happy with this comfort. So if your wife was happy, what has he done to have made the problem with you and your village?"

"Because he takes away the fly protection to make his comfort with my wife, but he does not cover the exposures on the baby channel and the baby feeder buttons with the protection from the cow when he has finished his powerful comfort. So my wife, she was

[41]

bitten by the fly. He should have made protection for her by covering everything he had used for his comfort after he had made his comfort, do you agree?" Fred asked, with a look of sincerity and concern clearly written on his face.

Mac still managed to keep a straight face and solemnly nodded his head in agreement, but inside, Mac was hurting from restrained laughter at the thought of Squeaky plastering her "mound of Venus: and breasts up again with wet, sloppy, stinking, cow shit after he had screwed her all night. Mac knew he knew he would revel in the retelling of this story.

To this day, Mac still does not know how he managed to choke out his straight-faced reply, but manage he did, when he said, "This was a bad thing not to cover, but this did not come into his mind, I think. I think, the comfort with your wife is in his mind, and after he make good comfort with your wife all night, he was very deadly tired, so he went to sleep and he forgets to cover your wife with the protection from the cow as protection against the fly. I do not think that this was a bad thought, I think this was a bad forget. I think this... he was tired because he made good comfort for a long time with your wife".

Fred seemed to contemplate briefly on Mac's words, nodded solemnly, and then replied, "I know you are wise, I think this may be the same as you think, but we are not happy, and we would not like to see this Squeaky here again".

"I am sorry to hear this, because Squeaky likes you and your village very much. He is very proud to be your friend, and a friend to your wives, and to your children, and your cows, and your goat's friend." Mac again had to restrain his laughter, because, according to the headman, apparently Squeaky Boots indeed liked the people of Fred's village...all night long.

"You wait a while before I make the final decision. I will check with the stones and the shells to see what the Spirits and Masters see about the Squeaky man."

The family came out of the huts and gathered around Mac and Fred as though by magic when he took out a bag from under the "Thinking Tree." From it, he emptied stones and shells on the ground,

[42]

and then he knelt on his hands and knees in the sand by the side of the chair, and indicated for Mac to kneel, facing him. Mumbling and occasionally letting out a loud yell, he then started to move the pieces about.

After about five minutes of this demonstration, he looked up at Mac with glazed eyes and sweat pouring down his face.

This must be bad news on its way, Mac thought.

Fred then replied, "I talk with one of my favourite ancestors. I speak with Albert, Albert the Happy. He pretty well feels good when he looked at the shells and stones and he says there is no problem."

"Does he say that Squeaky can come to your village again?" Mac asked.

"Come, wait again. I speak with Albert."

With that, he picked up the shells and the stones, juggling them about in his hands, and then threw them about two feet in the air. They fell and settled on the ground, and then he studied them for a long time.

"I speak again with Albert. Your Squeaky can enter the village again. The village greatly needs these things after the spiritual delegation we make with the spirit of Albert and his spirit friends in their eternal place. You'll give this message, please to your Squeaky man?"

He handed Mac two A4 sheets of close print writing full of what Mac assumed were demands that must have taken Fred and his family the whole week since Squeaky left to put together and see what they could 'blackmail' the whites into parting with.

It was not good etiquette to read the list or show surprise at that time, Mac knew. Later, out of sight, Mac could scream, rip his hair out, and thump walls or his men if that would help with the knowledge that he had been taken for a sucker. This supposedly stupid village man had robbed Mac and Squeaky so cleverly that through his frustration, Mac had to laugh to himself.

Instead of laughing out loud, Mac responded, "My dear friend, of course I will. I am pleased to be of help to you, and will give these papers that your favourite Spirit Albert has prepared in his Spirit place

[43]

to my man Squeaky. It is good for Squeaky and for me and for all our friends to find that Albert, your spirit, lives happily and is still filled with wisdom and there is no more problem with Squeaky".

Mac managed to complete the 'transaction' without losing his composure and breaking into fits of laughter.

Later, Mac heard Squeaky's version of his visit to the kraal. Squeaky delighting in telling the men how he "cracked the black egg, and sucked its yolk".

The dirty, lucky bastard, Mac thought in the silence after Squeaky relayed his story.

However, Mac had to wonder if he would have "cracked the black egg" personally.

CHAPTER 5

Josie's Revenge

So far, it would seem that Squeaky Boots played a very large part in Mark Hudson's life. While this is true, Squeaky was a part of Mac's life in the career and professional sense. While Mac had a healthy respect for Squeaky and reveled in his amusing antics, Mac had a personal life, aside from his military career. In Mac's personal life, he had another person who was quite influential to him, also. Her name was Josie, or Jo, as she liked to be called. Jo stood at four feet eleven inches tall, and she was made from a conglomerate of explosive elements, meaning she had a volatile demeanor. It was well hidden by her size. Appearances were deceiving where she was concerned.

Once, in a pub and after a few pints, Mac was overheard saying that Jo contained within her the characteristics of Nobles 808 plastic explosive, Pentolite, RDX, TNT, Semptex, and Nitro Glycerine all mixed together and left sweating in a Middle Eastern sun, primed and ready to erupt and explode at any second. She was a virtual nuclear explosion, disguised as a short, well rounded, feminine, lovely, cuddlesome, adorable, sexy, sensual, no-nonsense, one hundred percent woman, with long blond hair and lips like those only previously seen on the lovely Bridget Bardot. Indeed, Jo was extremely kissable and made for a man to love, admire, and respect.

Jo was Mark 'Mac' Hudson's wife.

Mac never lost sight of Jo or stopped loving her, but while he became more and more involved with his regiment and amassed the increased responsibility that goes with promotion, they inevitably began to grow apart.

They had fallen in love and married at a very young age, he being nineteen years old and Jo a year younger at eighteen years – a disaster in military life. Jo should have had some understanding; her father was a soldier and had done his best to talk her out of the marriage, obviously seeing that Mac was not promising husband material. Yet one knows youth; they were in love, and not prepared to listen to anyone. They were blind to other's opinions and thought together they would conquer the world.

The forthcoming marital mess was compounded by the fact that Mac was absent while on jobs all over the world. He had very little time to share with Jo between excursions to Cyprus, Kenya, Malaya, Borneo, Oman, Sudan, and South Arabia; these tours had no accompanied tour facilities for wives and children. They unquestionably were not surroundings for a wife, and without doubt, no place for children, but it was Mac's job, his career, and so much a part of his life. Sadly, it eventually became more a part of his life than Jo was.

Before Branch Commission, Mac was an exceptional military officer, and he quickly received high decorations for his work and reached the unassailable heights of W.O.1 (Warrant Officer One Regimental Sergeant Major). It was at this time in Mac's life when Jo planned a small revenge.

Jo wanted revenge on the Military because Mac, the man she had loved and acclaimed for years, had consistently put his first wife – the uniform – before anything else. The Army was always placed before her when it came to claiming Mac's time, attention and affection.

The truth was, like many people, Mac should never have married. He was far happier in a bar swilling beer with his army comrades than spending time with his wife and children. Women were never very high on his list of priorities either during his marriage or after it ended. He was definitely a man's man, with little interest beyond the military, beer and sports; brief sexual interactions with the opposite sex were enough to satisfy him as far as women were concerned.

Of course, if one asked Mac if this were the case, he would most certainly not agree, and he never agreed when Jo broached the

[46]

subject with him either. Jo could play his responses back in her mind like an overplayed song.

Mac would say, "You have a good home, plenty of housekeeping money, spare cash to spend on yourself, position and respect from other soldiers and their wives. The kids are doing well, and have respect at school. What more do you want for God's sake?"

How many hundreds of times had Jo heard the same weak excuse? She had lost count.

So she would ask, "When did you last speak to the C.O. about giving you a break to spend some time with us? He owes you one."

To which Mac would reply, "You know the rules we have to live by; nothing and nobody can alter what the MoD dictates, not even a Commanding Officer. He can only make recommendations and if that doesn't suit the overall picture, they just ignore him."

However, both Mac and Jo knew they had already been given a break. Mac had been made the RAF liaison officer at Coltishall Flying Station, near Norwich, a single position for his Regiment, the Royal Anglians, and his last posting before taking a Quartermaster commission to Captain, with the chance of Major, before he would retire with a very good pension. Their future was mapped out and secure, but Jo's hatred for the military and feelings of neglect blinded her.

As the senior military man in the camp, Mac accepted the ceremonial parade duties when they arose. These were few and far between, but on this occasion, a big one had cropped up – a Royal Guard of Honour for Her Royal Highness, the Princess Margaret – and it was to be held in front of the town hall in Norwich.

On the night before the parade, Mac had to act as host to French Foreign Legion Paratroopers who were dropping the next day over Norwich Airport as part of a further demonstration for the Princess. This signified Mac's presence was required at the Sergeant's Mess before the Mess Steward could open the bar at seven o'clock. This was a nightly task that Jo hated. It was just one extra factor that took her husband away from her, and as Mac was always happy to partake in a few beers plus some, he was often away for hours.

[47]

Mac had prepared his kit for the coming parade, with the exception of his collar, and his trousers still needed a press. Everything else was in pristine condition. The Sam Brown belt and sword were gleaming, as were his boots, Royal mounted medals, brasses, white gloves, and blue sash in honour of the RAF instead of the red of the Anglians.

"Jo, darling, do me a favour and press my trousers and starch one of my collars. There's an angel, or I'll be late opening the mess bar." Mac requested.

"Be late for the bar. Do them yourself. I'm not your lackey." Jo snapped back.

"Oh, come on, Jo. Don't be a spoilsport. It's not as if I ask you every day, and anyway, it's for your benefit. You and the kids will want me to look smart on the TV parade report."

"Mark, just go and open the bar, and then come back and finish your kit. I'm not having any part of it. I don't give a damn if you look scruffy. It's you that has to put up with it, not me."

"Okay, but I am Chairman of the Mess Committee and the official host, so it's important to stay long enough to see our guests served a complimentary round of drinks and we toast The Queen and President De Gaul. It's a duty." Mac responded indignantly.

"There you go again, duty this, duty that. You'll get the correct act together when the kids and I are considered a duty." Jo spat out the words and turned on her heel, leaving Mac alone.

Mac stared after her for a moment, and then he too left. Jo annoyed him, and he was hardly in the correct frame of mind to play host to a load of Frenchies, but he was determined to do so. Mac figured he'd also have a few bevvies himself to remove the bad taste Jo had left in his mouth.

Perhaps it would have been better for Mac to have laid off the booze, but still wounded from Jo's snubbing, he proceeded to drink with a vengeance.

Military uniform collars were Chinese laundered, and held to the shirt with front and rear collar studs. They were heavily starched, shiny, stiff and a nightmare to put on. This was Jo's first point of attack, as by the time ten o'clock came and went, she knew Mac would not be home before midnight. Mac would be the worse for drink, his kit would be ignored, and he would go straight to bed and sleep like death until his automatic mental clock awoke him at seven o'clock in the morning.

Knowing all this, Jo collected Mac's six collars, sized fifteen and a half, and took them to a neighbour, asking her to put them in for cleaning and borrowing one of her husband's seventeen inch collars for Mac to wear in the parade. Next, she pressed his trousers, and proceeded to sew the bottoms up on her sewing machine. Finally, knowing from Mac's previous conversations that Princess Margaret was the strictest of all the Royal Family for dress and discipline on parades and visits, Jo turned his hat badge upside down. This act has always been classed as an insult to the Crown, as the Royal Crown of the badge is then shown at the bottom and is displayed the wrong way, under other emblems on the badge.

Jo was an astute woman, because true to form, her calculations were right on target. Everything happened as she had planned. Mac, getting up late and hungover, struggled like a crazy man, cursing, going ballistic about the oversized collar, looking for his others to no avail, and ended up with his tie coming out of his collar from just underneath his chin rather than his neck. Mac nearly broke his toes putting on his trousers and sat down, almost howling, unpicking the stitching from the bottom of the legs.

Very late now, he stuck his hat on, not checking himself in the mirror, and ran to the parade ground, buckling on his sword as he went.

Jo was satisfied, very pleased with herself. Mac was the brunt of her revenge, but it was the Army and all it stood for that she was kicking. Mac carried out his parade duties in an immaculate fashion. It was rumoured by the hundred man Guard of Honour that the large collar and the upside down hat badge were deliberate tests for the Princess, set by their RSM to see if Her Royal Highness knew what she was looking for when on parade. It was considered a prime example of the RSM's courage. Jo had her revenge, but Mac didn't do too badly either.

Married life can be dull, and although their marriage lasted less than 15 years, it rarely was for Mac and Jo.

BOOK TWO – FIGHTING THE EOKA

CHAPTER 1

An Overview of the Politics

The beautiful, glorious Island of Cyprus, now one of the most visited of the Mediterranean holiday resorts, has come through some grizzly, gruesome, and terribly traumatic post war periods.

The island's ancient history covers many volumes, and includes the histories of such matters as Richard the Lionheart's castle at Kolossi; the famous Curium Amphitheatre from Roman times, and Aphrodite's Rock; where the most beautiful woman in the world walked out of the sea.

Most have ignored the terrible past that has still not been completely resolved, probably at the request of the Cypriot Government, who wants to sweep the past under the carpet so not to detract from the island's lucrative tourism trade.

The problems began with the call of the Cypriot Church for Enosis (the Union with Greece).

The problems escalated due to the activities of EOKA (The National Organization of Cypriot Fighters). There was civil war between the Greek and Turkish Cypriot communities and also a Turkish Invasion of the Island, which resulted in partition.

Partition is still a fact in Cyprus. Many more political barriers still have to be overcome for the place to earn the title it deserves – "A little chunk of Paradise on Earth".

Mark "Mac" Hudson, a Special Operations Group Officer and his fellow British soldiers who were posted to Cyprus had many trials to overcome during the emergency periods. The first emergency period was from the 1st April 1955 until the truce by EOKA in February 1959.

During 1952, Archbishop Makarios, the head of the Cypriot church, started the Churches' call for Enosis in Athens on the Greek mainland, and received tremendous support; with tens of thousands of the populace parading in sympathy and agreement for the churches' wishes for the Island people. Events taking place in Egypt slowed the progress of Enosis when Abdul Gamal Nasser and a group of Egyptian Army Officers decided to expel the British Garrison troops from the Canal Zone bases.

The British Middle East Command HQ moved to Cyprus, and because it was sovereignty, no political body could legally throw Mac or his fellow soldiers out. As HQ, the Middle East became more important to them.

A major political blunder occurred by Henry Hopkinson MP, (Minister of State for the Colonies 1952 to 1955) who, when replying to a question by the Labour party in the House, used the word "never" in relation to Cyprus Independence and Enosis. Serious rioting followed in Greece and across Cyprus, not to mention other countries with large Greek communities.

Thus EOKA was born - the dream child of Makarios, to fight the British for his people's wishes. Makarios, a man of God who refused to denounce violence, baffled the British. They didn't realize he was the movement's founder, along with Andreas Azinas, and he was also the movement's Commander in Chief. Makarios recruited a Greek ex-Army Officer, Georgios Grivas, who had also led a right wing partisan group in the Greek Mountains to head the military wing of EOKA. Every priest in Cyprus was a nationalist leader, recruiting officer and teacher of Enosis from the pulpit. The British banned the teaching of Enosis in schools, churches and anywhere else - but it still continued underground.

Recruits selected by the church for service with EOKA were religious young men who went to church and communion on a regular basis. Barflies, womanisers, or criminals were not welcome. They trained hard in weapons and explosives purchased by the church and gave an Oath of Allegiance, which went as follows:

"I swear in the name of the Holy Trinity, that I shall work with all my power for the liberation of Cyprus from the British yoke, sacrificing for this even my life."

On the 1st of April 1955, in the early hours of the morning, battle commenced. Bombs went off at pre-selected targets all over Cyprus. Mixed with incidents of criminal activity, most people thought these actions were taken by only a misguided few under the influence of the church.

There were many very good Criminal Investigation Department men in the police force. They looked upon these incidents as criminal actions by youths, and they were very effective at catching the culprits. Grivas, who had kept his name secret and used the title Digenis, a legendary Greek hero, ordered the killing of all informers and police who went after the bombers. He also sent them a letter:

TO THE POLICE

Do not try to block our path or you will stain it with your blood. He who tries to arrest or search Cypriot patriots will be shot.

This is where Mac and his men found themselves on arriving in Cyprus. A difficult situation, to say the least.

CHAPTER 2

EOKA- The Leader Dighenis

The assassinations of police officers, both on and off duty, was so intense that after only six months the skeptics about the movement were saying, "We are EOKA, too." By the summer of 1955, the EOKA campaign was attracting worldwide attention.

Britain turned to another country with a stake in Cyprus – Turkey. Approximately twenty percent of the Cypriot populace was Turkish. This minority's safety worried Turkey, as well as seeing the situation slipping out of British hands. The Greek police were giving EOKA the anti-terrorist plans devised by the British. The Greek customs officers were allowing arms to be smuggled in for EOKA. Turkey became the British ally with a special Turkish police force to combat EOKA.

Britain brought in their top soldier, Field Marshall Sir John Harding, Chief of the General Staff, and made him the Governor of Cyprus. Makarious liked Harding at first, and after a number of amicable meetings he made an offer to drop his claims for Enosis if Harding managed to achieve assurances from the Government to grant Cyprus self-determination in the near future.

Harding flew back to meet the cabinet and returned with a carefully worded document, which became known as 'the double negative'. This was presented to Makarious on the 21st November 1955.

" Her Majesty's Government adhere to the principles embodied in the Charter of the United 1716 Nations, the Potomac Charter and the Pacific Charter, to which they have subscribed. It is not, therefore, their position that the principle of self-determination can never be applicable to Cyprus. It is their position that it is not now a practical proposition on account of the present situation in the Eastern Mediterranean." In other words, it claimed self-determination may one day be a possibility, but not at that point in time.

Makarios rejected the document. Nicos Kranidiotis, his political secretary at the time, said to Makarios, "Your worship, I am confused, you have managed to make the British give you the assurances you wanted for future self-determination, which will let us all embrace Enosis, and you reject the document. Why?"

"Nicos, we have what we wanted, this we keep in our pocket and make it better."

EOKA stepped up its campaign of violence, and Harding prepared to go to war against the movement for the first time, deciding politics had run their course.

After eight weeks, at Makarios's request, the two parties met yet again. John Reddaway, Political Advisor to the Governor, said of this meeting that Harding made an impassioned plea to the Archbishop to lead his people away from violence.

Makarios replied, "Field Marshall, I cannot lead my people where they do not want to go."

"A bloody funny kind of leadership, to my way of thinking." Harding snapped.

Reddaway had to agree.

Makarios asked for time to meet his council, and he also met Grivas at Kykko Monastery. Grivas didn't trust the British, but agreed to a ceasefire if Makarios called for it. He also demanded the British give amnesty to his men, security against future arrest for them, and compensation for any of their properties lost or destroyed during the campaign.

Makarious met Harding again and said he would denounce violence if Harding would give him more concessions, including the points made by Grivas. Harding was tired and worn out with these futile, never-ending bargaining sessions with Makarios, and decided talks were at a deadlock. Therefore, he asked Alan Lennox-Boyd, Colonial Secretary, to talk to the archbishop. Lennox-Boyd however, thought the offers made by Harding were enough to impress the world and the House of Commons.

A report at the time from Makarios' political advisor said the Colonial Secretary told Makarios, "I have not come to negotiate. This

[55]

you have done by the Governor, and you can take or leave the proposals already made by the Field Marshall."

Makarios wanted to talk about the extra points and said he could not accept what was already on the table as final.

Lennox-Boyd stood up, closed his files, and said, "Archbishop, God save your people."

Then he left.

Makarios had held out too long. All British offers relating to Enosis and self-determination were withdrawn, and Harding decided to inflict a military defeat on EOKA. To do this, he told Lennox-Boyd he needed Makarios out of the way. Makarios went to Nicosia airport to fly to Athens to discuss his next moves. The British had other ideas. Instead of Athens, he was flown 3,500 miles to the Seychelles Islands, into indefinite exile, with no chance of external communication. He had screwed himself completely.

Mac still thinks that Makarios being forced into exile is one of, if not the most amusing, dim-witted examples of British idiocy he has ever witnessed. Mac can still recall the images of Makarios' aircraft taxiing down the runway. Six Land Rovers bristling with machine guns and camouflaged soldiers drove down the runway alongside the plane. When these 'shock' troops arrived back at the terminal, Mac asked the Royal West Kent Lieutenant in charge about what had been the purpose of this dynamic show of arms.

The lieutenant told Mac, "To prevent any sick person ambushing him as he took off."

"But nobody knew he was going, including himself." Mac replied, astonished.

"Ah, there you go, nudge, nudge, wink, wink," was the Lieutenant's brainless reply, as he tapped the side of his nose.

From this moment on, Harding went all out to defeat EOKA and play them at their own game. It had to have been difficult for EOKA; the British had better resources, more manpower, and very experienced anti-terrorist operatives. The British had the choice of target and could hit first without warning. There was no doubt about the outcome in the mountains. In the streets and towns, however, it would be more difficult for the British, because the local populace was with EOKA. Mac knew that whether it was through fear or loyalty, it did not matter; they were still on the other side. Casualties were unavoidable on both sides. The mountain gangs were effectively destroyed, but the Greeks had shown the will and determination to continue the fight.

Harding's forces were now in command of the situation, but no new leaders came forward to speak for the Greek community at any conference or negotiating table. By early 1957, events in the Middle East again influenced the British attitude towards Cyprus. British, French, and Israeli attacks on Egypt to retake the Suez Canal in November 1956 had ended in disaster, with American and world intervention and condemnation, forcing Sir Anthony Eden, the then British Prime Minister, to resign.

Mark Hudson recalled that some said Eden's resignation was due to ill health, but everybody with even the smallest amount of insider knowledge knew the real reason. Eden's successor, McMillan, thought the British would save a tremendous amount of money in maintenance and administrative costs if Cyprus was given independence or self-determination, while keeping the Sovereign Bases for Britain in the form of secure airfields and Army garrisons, in order to keep British commitments in the region secure. Without having a Greek executive with whom to negotiate, McMillan released Makarious from exile, but forbade him to set foot in Cyprus.

Makarious arrived to rapturous acclaim and support in Athens on the 17th of April 1957. This release infuriated the Turkish, who believed Britain was going soft and was considering a withdrawal from the island, leaving the Turkish minority to their fate. After all the support they had given Britain during the troubles with EOKA, their fury was reasonable.

Lennox-Boyd again visited Ankara and suggested there was a way to protect Turkish interests – partition the island. Orhan Eralp, the Turkish Foreign Ministry official, agreed wholeheartedly. "Partition or Death" became the Turkish slogan seen on posters and sheets hanging from almost every house and street corner. Looking back, Mac recalls that many of these people later themselves died fighting.

Makarious refused to negotiate with McMillan if Turkey and partition was on the agenda. As a solution, McMillan, attempting to break the frustrating deadlock, appointed a new Governor – not a military man, but a conciliator, known to be a friend of the Greeks. Sir Hugh Foot was the man selected, later to become Lord Caradon.

Mac remembers Sir Hugh riding around the island on horseback with his highly polished black riding boots, white riding trousers, black riding jacket, and cravat, visiting the villages in the hills. He talked to the people in the villages and town squares, drunk locally produced wine with them in the taverns, and generally tried hard to do a good job in a bid to solve the problems. Unfortunately, with the Greeks having such a large majority of the populace, four times greater than the Turks, it seemed to some Turkish diehards that the Greeks were being given favorable treatment. Trouble was brewing up in a terrible fashion. Civil War was about to break out.

On the fateful day of the 7th June 1958, this disturbed, but relatively peaceful period erupted into violence. An explosion at the information bureau in the Turkish Consulate was the trigger, and all that the volatile situation needed to set off the resulting chaos. Large crowds of Turkish youths were already protesting outside the Consulate when the explosion occurred. This outrage was blamed on the Greeks and the Turkish swore vengeance.

This incident started a night of riots in Nicosia with Turks looting Greek shops and houses, and beating up, sometimes killing, any Greeks they came across. Soon EOKA retaliated with a counter attack. The fighting rapidly spread all around the island, even to the small villages where Greeks and Turks had always been friendly neighbours; working together to bring in each harvest, building together communal houses and barns. Now they were bitter enemies killing each other.

The British soldiers hurriedly built barricades to try to keep the warring factors apart. Some terrible atrocities took place. One such case was at a small, predominantly Turkish village called Guenyeli, and

[58]

here the small Turkish community hung the eight Greek inhabitants of the village from trees, lining the road into the Kyrenia area.

Mac's troops approached the village in a Land Rover and trailer draped with Union Jacks and loaded to the brim with ten man compo food packs, jerricans of paraffin, water, and first aid kits to help out anyone they found in need. A huge barricade completely blocked the road, but there was not a soul in sight to confront Mark Hudson and his men.

In this particular case, it eventually cost two boxes of food, and one can each of paraffin and water for the Turks to allow passage beyond the barricade so they could cut the bodies down. After radioing 23 Para Field Ambulance to come and collect the bodies, Mac and his men moved on to try to help others under siege.

Lo and behold, on their return, just twenty-four hours later, the bodies were hanging from the trees again; and the ambulance crew was being held at bay. The Turks were demanding one box of food for each body. The food Mac arrived with had already been given out to others in need. At this point one had no choice but to threaten and, if necessary, use force to achieve the aim. Such was the soldier's thankless task at this terrible time. Against this background, McMillan and Foot tried to launch a new initiative to establish some peace and calm to stop the bloodshed. McMillan offered to share the Government of Cyprus with Greece and Turkey. The Greeks rejected this idea. No way could they share a piece of their land, as they saw Cyprus being, with the Turks.

Makarious also called the church out to preach to the public against the plan. McMillan told the Greeks that the plan would be imposed in two months time unless they compromised. Foot backed this up with a very strong speech, telling the Greeks the plan would go ahead and the Greeks had better accommodate themselves or they would be left out of everything in the future.

Desperation forced Makarious to call for help from his friends. Barbara Castle and the Labour party had promised Enosis help if they ever were to come to power. Nonetheless when they met in Athens, she brought Makarious bad news, saying Labour would not back

Enosis unless he compromised. He did and offered to accept the status of 'Independence for Cyprus', if Cyprus should not be linked with either Greece or Turkey. In other words, rule out partition, and rule out Enosis. Cyprus should become an Independent State, whose position was protected and guaranteed by the United Nations. This offered an acceptable way out of the deadlock.

Greece was astonished when they heard of these proposals, and Evangelos Averoff, the Greek Foreign Minister, expressed disbelief that Makarious could make these statements to Castle without informing or discussing them with Greece. Grievous was also amazed and angered by this turn of events and tried to force an untenable situation on the British by ordering his execution squads to "strike at will against all British targets, service and civilian alike".

It was in Famagusta, Mac remembers, where what was called "the most brutal outrage of all outrages" took place. The wives of two British servicemen were shot in the back and killed. One of them, the mother of five children.

This terrible, senseless, uncalled for murder sparked a wave of revenge attacks on the Greeks by British troops all over the island, not just in the Famagusta area. Royal Ulster Rifles in the Famagusta region put dozens of Greeks into hospitals with severe head injuries on the same day the women were shot. Also, there were numerous cars and properties destroyed whilst conducting the search for the killers. It was truly an awful time.

World opinion was so outraged at these murders that 'Iron Man' Grivas denied responsibility, but continued the killing of British servicemen at an increased rate. The situation seemed to be rapidly deteriorating, until November 1958, when a development at the United Nations took the matter out of British hands.

Greek Foreign Minister, Evangelos Averoff proposed independence for Cyprus, his purpose being to defeat the McMillan plan. Turkish Foreign Minister Fatin Rüstü Zorlu proposed to back the McMillan plan. As usual, the two sides disagreed. The Greeks lost the debate, and then Mac recalls that a strange thing happened. Outside the debating chamber, Zorlu told Averoff that the Turks would support

Cyprus Independence, if guarantees could be given to protect the Turkish minority on the Island.

Over the next few weeks, they worked out their plans, a deal was struck, and two months later, their respective Prime Ministers signed the agreement in Zurich.

Averoff and Zorlu flew to Britain for talks on their joint proposals with the British Foreign Secretary Selwyn Lloyd. He was delighted with their initiative and the outcome, and, as Mac remarked at the time, who could blame him?

The plan meant Britain could escape from the debacle and political traumas of Cyprus yet retain two large military bases in Sovereign Base Areas. It meant security for Britain and saving face, along with a tremendous reduction in costs, both in finance and loss of life.

Greek and Turkish Cypriot leaders were invited to London to meet all the parties involved at Lancaster House, and sign the agreements made in the meetings in Zurich. These agreements could not be changed, so the signing in London, situated close to Buckingham Palace, was basically a ceremony put on for the world to see.

Makarious attempted to make amendments to the document, much to the annoyance and chagrin of the other members involved. This caused Konstantinos Karamanlis, the Greek Prime Minster, to fly to London and order Makarious to sign. After a one-day delay, Makarious signed, because war or peace in Cyprus depended on his signature; he wasn't sure, nor did he have time to find out, if the people on the island would support him if he didn't sign.

Grivas, under an independent Cyprus, dared not clash with Makarious as the new President. Grivas ordered his men to lay down their arms, and he returned to Greece, although he did return later to plague Makarious.

[61]

Makarious moved into Government House in Nicosia, and as the new President, endeavoured to repair the damaged relationship with the Turkish Cypriot leader, Rauf Denktash. Rauf made many demands, as per the Zurich agreement, on which the President promised to take action, but delayed time-and-time again, in the typical Makarious fashion.

One day, Rauf said to Mac, "I can see well now why John Harding deported the bastard. He's the most infuriating, insincere, two-faced, backstabbing liar I've ever had the misfortune to meet."

To which Mac whole-heartedly agreed.

The deportation of Makarios in March 1956 pushed EOKA into its most audacious attack to date – the attempted assassinations of Sir John and Lady Harding.

A young waiter at Government House smuggled a bomb past the house security by holding it next to his body within a woman's corset. The young man, Neophytes Sophocleos, worked at the House during 1955-1956, so he was well aware of guard changes and procedures. He was very well known himself around the house, and he knew the building's layout in detail.

Going straight to the Governor's bedroom, he placed the bomb under the mattress of the Governor's bed, which was next to Lady Harding's bed - about one foot away. The idea was to kill them both.

Mac had stayed in Governement House that night, to attend a meeting early the following morning in Nicosia. Mac always rose from bed later than most, but as he was rising, he noticed nobody seemed to have performed the typical chores that were usually well underway by the time he got out of bed. Then suddenly a soldier opened the door of the room, and informed Mac there was a bomb in his Excellency's bed.

Mac went across to investigate, and found an unidentifiable object near the bed. Mac had never seen such a bomb before, and he reached out and nearly touched the entity with his fingers.

Mac spoke aloud, but to no one in particular, "It must be a dud. It's been here all night, right?"

Mac watched while a young Officer, whom Mac reflects back on being very brave, placed the bomb on a shovel and walked right through the House, which was quite extensive, and put the bomb in a sandbag pit. When the clock struck twelve o'clock, about three minutes after this brave, young man had laid the bomb in the pit and walked away, there was the most sickening explosion that blew all the windows out of the near side of the house.

The feeling Mac had upon the unfolding of these events, was quite indescribable, especially after he realized had they arrived a few minutes later, he himself, several soldiers, and other members of the household would all be dead.

After this attempted murder, the young waiter Sophocleos became a most wanted man, escaping to the Troodos Mountains and working with a mountain gang under the command of Colonel Grivas. He later organised executions of informers, and later was to tell Mac that at an execution, nobody spoke to the victim, just shot him in the head, no explanation, no signs, nothing. "If you are an informer, you die."

This man was unfortunately correct in his attitude; war was not a pleasant occupation. If one had to be in it, Mac knew you must always win.

After the bomb attack had been made on the life of the Hardings, Harding immediately implemented plans to limit the freedom of movement of EOKA. There was the introduction of strict curfews, no-go killing areas, fines for entire villages, internment without trial, protection packages for informers, as well as the death penalty introduced for carrying arms, thus giving an interrogator the power to barter life for information. In addition to this, there were severe jail sentences for harbouring or shielding partisans, covert watch, report and kill OPS (Observation Posts), overt military watch towers and garrisons to isolate whole villages, and many more measures, some of which worked to a large degree.

One of the biggest factors that did eventually lead to the military defeat of EOKA was the undercover intelligence gathering and "eliminations" by the Special Forces.

CHAPTER 3

Operations

After the house bomb, the anti-terrorist campaign took on a new pattern. Large areas became no-go killing areas. At one stage, the Gordon Highlanders, some Cameronians, and the Parachute Regiment combed four hundred square miles of mountain shrub and forest in the Southwest of the Island, acting on information sent back by an undercover covert OP, who had observed strong mountain gang presence in that area.

Unfortunately, because this was a sealed off killing area, large mortar barrages were fired into the valleys at the same time as the slopes were raked by machine gun fire. One of these barrages started a fire in the valley floor, when a curie, a type of whirlwind, picked up the fire and carried it like an express train across the treetops on one side of the valley. These flash fires move so fast, if caught in its path, it cannot be outrun.

This is the horrible fate that was dealt to the Highlanders. The flash fire raced across the treetops, which sent a deluge of leaves, twigs and branches falling like blistering, burning ash on the men below. A total of 13 men were to die. Mac and his men could not penetrate the area for a long time, because charcoal type burning ash ten to twelve inches deep covered the ground and burnt the boots off their feet, while the heat scorched the air from their lungs.

When Mac's group did finally manage to enter the area, they found very little identifiable remains.

Mark Hudson distinctly recalls an example of the type of heat involved. On what was once a mountain track, Mac and his troops found a Land Rover, but all that was left looked something like a molten gearbox and engine - there was nothing else left.

Covert OPs were also caught in the path of this flash fire and the four-man crew all perished. Upon reaching the OPs after the fire, all Mac found of the two off-duty men in the lay up point were molten metal parts of their weapons and equipment.

Mac was told afterward that their death was due to hot air damaging the lung tissue, making it secrete fluid, and eventually the victims drowned with hot water in their lungs. After this incident, the mountain OPs carried respirators with oxygen fittings, fireproof oxygen bottles, and asbestos fireproof suits.

Mac remembers that they also ensured future Lay Up Positions had cover from flash fire direct heat and ash fall. Sadly, Mac reminisces that if they had only calculated the problem of flash fire before, these men might have survived.

The purpose of these area tactics was to kill Grivas and his men. On this operation, one patrol stumbled across Grivas bathing in a mountain stream. The soldier who came across him was so shocked, he allowed Grivas to escape. But seven of his men were captured, some with £5000 on their heads. However, a few days later the Operations men who achieved this were killed by "friendly fire" but their information paid off in the end.

Grivas managed to escape to a cellar under the kitchen sink in a house on the outskirts of Limassol in the south part of the island. Not even his area commander knew where he was hiding out. Incredibly, Grivas conducted operations and sent out orders to his execution squads from this cellar for two and a half years. One of these executions killed two and seriously injured a third RAF man in Metaxas Square in Nicosia. The executors were in civilian clothes and shot from behind. An undercover OP team saw the shooting by one man, and on the follow-up, arrested a young terrorist called Nicos Kochs, still in possession of a .38 revolver.

During interrogation, Mac reported that Kochs said, "I have fulfilled my oath, and now I'm not afraid to die."

To which Mac replied, "Would your mind be any easier if you had not shot the victims in the back?"

"We cannot win our struggle if we fight you face-to-face. You have more men and guns. For us to fight you from the front, gives you victory, to fight you from behind, means I kill and you live in fear. I am like the camouflaged snake in the grass; you do not know I am there. You cannot see me until I bite you. If I bite you quickly and slide away to hide, I can bite someone else another day. I have bit seven. My poison is the bullet, and they are all dead. This way, we, EOKA, will win."

Such was the mental attitude of the terrorist. One had to respect their belief in themselves and their cause. This same terrorist fought a discrediting war against the British, even whilst in captivity. He claimed to Barbara Castle, the infamous Labour MP on a fact-finding visit to the Island for her Party, that he had been badly beaten during interrogation, had sticks pushed up his backside, had almost been suffocated with wet rags wrapped around his face, endured electric shocks to his genitals, and so on.

Mac was extremely disappointed, though not entirely surprised that 'Nosy Parker Castle' believed Kochs. Castle then proceeded to make such a song and dance about the bad treatment the terrorist had supposedly suffered in interviews on radio and in press reports, she became as good as fifty terrorists to the cause of Enosis and EOKA. British troops, Mac and his men included, considered that for her to have spoken out this way against her own country's military, she surely had to have something going with a Greek somewhere.

Nicos Samson, the editor of the Cyprus Times, reported many such cases of cruelty by the British soldiers toward the Greeks at the time. These reports received world press coverage. Mac knew that Samson was a terrorist leader himself, even standing for the Presidency after independence on the grounds that he was a leading freedom fighter with EOKA.

After Independence, thorough investigations were carried out to confirm or deny the claims against the British troops (with the exception of the actions of a few overzealous individuals after the killing of the two servicemen's wives in Famagusta) no orchestrated policy of cruelty was found, never mind proven.

[67]

Mac smirked at knowing that dartboards with photographs of Barbara Castle, as the prime aiming mark, existed (and still exist to this day) in Sergeant's Mess bars in Cyprus - a constant reminder of what "a misinformed, do-gooding, meddling, ignorant politician can cause the uniformed services engaged in war."

Calm followed independence, from 1959 until 1961, when things again began to rumble and bubble up over the Greek's leaders failing to honour the Zurich agreements, especially the protection of the Turkish minority issue.

All this discontent exploded into violence once again on Christmas Eve in 1963.

CHAPTER 4

The Escapades of Mark 'Mac" Hudson's Special Ops Group

Military commitments in the Middle East and Near East Commands, including Africa, meant that Airborne, Commando, and other Special Forces units were continuously engaged in some conflict somewhere; always on the move either to or from some area of combat. It could be months before members of a unit saw each other, due to their working in different places.

Mac's unit was like little Orphan Annie at the time. A new, large airfield was under construction in Southern Cyprus on a promontory called Kolossi, halfway between the town of Limmassol and the large sprawling village of Episkopi. Called Akrotiri, one could see the airfield construction was going to be a very large project simply by the size of the groundwork taking place. Thousands of British engineer type forces were involved, such as the REME Royal Signals, Royal Engineers, Pioneer Corps, and many more - plus hundreds of Greek Cypriots.

One giant runway seemed to be completed for daylight landings and take off. Canberra bombers, Meteor, Vampire, and Venom fighters often dropped in, but never stayed long. Mac assumed they had come from the Cyprus Northern airport of Nicosia or the Canal Zone in Egypt; British bases were there until November 1955. There were also bases in Iraq, Jordan, and Libya plus Malta and Şardinia; therefore the bombers could have come from any one of these locations.

Two large corrugated iron buildings along with two smaller ones were the only structures to be seen completed for the troops. One was the Officer's Mess, shared by the Sergeants. The other was the NAAFI, which was open 24 hours to meet the needs of the shift workers involved in the camp construction. Another one of the huts had been designated as the cook-house and dining room. It ran on the same basis as the NAAFI and served food to all ranks. No cooking took place in the Officer and Sergeant's mess.

Finally, there was a cinema, with seating for about 250 individuals on wooden folding chairs, which managed to show a continuous flow of films around the clock. Every third day there was a film change supplied by the Army Kinema Corporation. These were shown on a rotating basis, two hours of films, followed by two hours off.

Other large corrugated metal and asbestos covered buildings were in different stages of completion, some of them huge in size. One assumed they were aircraft hangars. These facilities were not for the soldier's use, hence Mac's Orphan Annie comparison.

Away from the messes, cinema, and hustle and bustle of the main station, about two miles across the other side of the main runway, the soldiers had their little camp.

The camp contained eight one hundred and sixty pound tents, which normally slept eight men, but at the time the men were lucky and there were only around four to a tent. There were also two EPIPs, which were large, twenty by forty foot tents, that made up another cook-house, a dining room, a briefing room, an armory, an equipment store and a recreation room in use after the men had cleaned away the debris from a meal.

Two five-foot high sandbag walls served as the weapons load and unload pit and a petrol/paraffin dump. Twenty metres away, down a small slope, running toward a very large Salt Flat Lake, the soldiers had constructed a deep latrine. This was a fifteen-foot deep trench, two-feet wide and twenty-feet long. Over the top of this, mounted on three-foot high sandbags, was a wooden plank with four holes in it, large enough to sit over and do one's business, but without partitions between the holes. A trip to the 'bogs' was normally a chatty thing. A roll of Hessian cloth completed the structure, wrapped around tent poles at each corner of the pit to give a little privacy from the outside.

These deep latrines were marvelous in hot climates, disinfectant was poured down them to sterilize and reduce the smell, but bacteria did most of the work. Heavier-than-air Methane gas generated from the decaying components of the trench and kept the smell and other gases in the bottom two feet of the trench, giving the hundreds of flies, plus other insects nothing to eat, nor any material on which to lay eggs.

An Army Catering Corps corporal attached to troops managed all the base camp cooking. According to Mac, it was very good, too. The food consisted of a mixture of composite rations and fresh food collected three times per week from the main camp. Composite rations, or compo, were special boxes of chemically treated food that could last for years if unopened, and up to four days in Middle Eastern temperatures when opened. Packs of compo to last ten men twenty-four hours were the standard issue for base camps, and a one-man pack to last the same period when on patrol. They were great. Mac loved them. Tins of rolled bacon, separated between each layer with grease-proof paper, and sausages without skins, compressed in the tin so that they came out square... these were, and still are Mac's favorite foods. Unfortunately for Mac, they cannot be found in civvy street.

Spam, corned beef, hardtack biscuits, steam pudding, tins of custard and rice, curried mixed vegetable soups, tins of fruit, cheese, onion flake dehydrated, chocolate, matches, toilet paper, boiled sweets, and much more, came in a ten-man pack, including ten very thick rubber condoms, no gossamer lubricated stuff here. Thick and thick again, an STD would need an electric drill to get through one of that issue. The men actually used them over their rifle barrels to keep the dust out of the guns. They reminded Mac of an oversized baby's dummy.

Orphan Annie? Not really. They had it a lot rougher in most locations they served than this one.

The nearest neighbours in Mac's little paradise were a tremendously humorous bunch of anti-aircraft gunners from number 3 LAA Wing, Numbers 27 and 37 Squadrons, RAF Regiment. When the large runway was built at this new Air Force Base, all the excavated earth was piled up on the north side of the runway, between the camp and the Salt Flats. The high mounds of earth, trees and shrubs stretched the whole length of the runway, in places as far as a mile wide and varying between thirty and fifty feet in height.

These anti-aircraft gunners and their Bofors Guns thrived amongst these large, earth hills, buried underground. They had their living quarters, eating and rest rooms, and their own toilets. All that could be seen was the barrel of a gun, draped in cam nets, poking out of the side or top of the earth in the direction in which it was supposed to fire. They were so well camouflaged into their positions that Mac did not even know they were there until they made themselves known to his troops.

They seemed to have a servicing force of Royal Air Force Armourers that moved about from gun to gun, stripping them down into little pieces, gauging them, servicing them, greasing them, and then putting them back together again. Apparently, they fired the guns twice a year off the cliffs surrounding the base near a large radar station called 280 Radar/Signals Unit. Most of the time, Mac would see these Regiment guys, armed to the teeth and camouflaged, walking out across the salt flats toward the mountains. About eight, nine, or ten days later, they would be seen coming in again from wherever, stinking, covered in muck and obviously exhausted.

When Mac tried to find out what they were up to, he used to get the standard reply, 'Going somewhere, doing something.' That's as much as Mac ever found out, but it doesn't take much guessing to realise that the EOKA terrorist organisation was forming in the mountains, and in the urban townships, and Mac felt that these men 'Going somewhere, doing something' were not in favour with the interests of the mountain EOKA terrorists.

One day, Mac nearly killed Corporal Galloway down the deep latrine. Galloway had received one of the very latest Ronson

[72]

Varaflame gas cigarette lighters from a girl back in England. Sitting on the toilet, having a smoke, he accidentally dropped this piece of latest technology down the deep abyss, a long way down to a dirty, sticky end.

"Never mind," would have been Mac's last thought on the matter. Not so for the Corporal. No one knew this had taken place for a while, because Cpl Galloway did not want to make himself look a fool, and he tried everything he could think of to retrieve the item himself, but he could not even see the bottom of the trench shining the most powerful torch he had down the hole.

Enter Mac- dropping his trousers, he nonchalantly sat on the toilet and let out a tremendously long, drawn out fart, going red in the face to keep it going, then a bubbling sound when he started what he came for.

"I won a farting competition once. A village fair laid it on. Ten bob was the first prize. My two mates and me had about three Mansfield Bitters, then some pig's trotters, followed up with two plates of vinegary cow tripe. All that crap mixed with popcorn and ice-cream produced the longest, loudest fart I've ever made." Mac exclaimed rather proudly.

He proceeded to wipe his backside with pages of the Beano comic, and then, he noticed Cpl Galloway looked perturbed.

"What ho, Cpl, me old mate. What's with the torch, then? Looking for Greek spies down the bog are we? You'll never find them down a hole unless you go looking for them in a brothel. Then they won't be down it, but up it."

His laugh at this stage of his own joke was high pitched, rasping, and wheezy, not at all in keeping with his fitness, but an imitation of some well-known cartoon character. Cpl Galloway caught with the torch decided to confess.

"What do you think I should do, Mac? I really must get it back. This Maisy who sent it to me wants to engrave it when I get back to Blighty." The embarrassed Cpl finally admitted.

"Buy another one. She won't know the difference. Where's the problem?" Mac asked.

[73]

"She'd know. I'm certain she would. It's easy to upset her. She's awfully sensitive. It's my first real girlfriend. Help me get the lighter back?"

Mac mumbled something about hoping we never had to fight a real war with poofters who worried about girlfriends, who on top of it couldn't hold a fucking lighter properly.

"Okay, here's what you do. Go to the equipment bay and collect a forty foot, one inch diameter rope, and I'll lower you, head first, down the hole...

"No, never mind that. You're about five foot ten tall, with your arms stretched over the head, we'll call that eight feet. Give me your toggle rope. I'll tie that to one foot and my toggle to the other, and we are home to the bank." Mac spouted off without much more thought.

Toggle ropes were approx a ½ inch in diameter, eight feet long, and were carried as an individual piece of equipment by most British units. They are very strong, made out of sisal, with a Rogue Yarn running through them, which ensures they are made to British safety standards. Each toggle had a safe working load of ten hundred weight. The soldiers joined them together for temporary bridge building, and many other purposes.

Mac was very safe with one toggle on each of the Cpl's feet.

"Right, mate." Mac said. "Let's get on with it."

Mac rather roughly pushed the Cpl into a headfirst exit position on the edge of the pit, having previously moved the top plank of wood aside.

The Cpl, with a torch in one hand and a large soup ladle borrowed from the cook in the other, gradually started to disappear over the edge into the dark. Mac was braced with his feet against the sandbags of the parapet, and one toggle rope in each hand, double secured around his wrists.

"Just a little bit more to your right. That's it. That's it. Stay there." shouted Galloway.

This sounded promising. It seemed the Cpl's conscience and love life had been saved. Now silence. A rather long silence. Followed by even more silence.

[74]

"How's it going down there?" Mac yelled down the hole.

Silence.

Mac started to look uncomfortable, but wisecracked, "He's stopped for a dinner break."

Silence.

"You're coming up." Mac finally yelled.

Mac, with that shout, started to heave on the toggles and brought the sloppy, unconscious body of the Cpl over the edge of the trench. Cpl Galloway was bright red, breathing profoundly, drenched with sweat, and he had peculiar blue streaks on his cheeks, lips, nose, and ears.

Methane gas poisoning.

The medic attached from the Army Medical Corps treated the casualty, wrapped him up in blankets, put him face down on his bed, and gave him oxygen. After a while, he came round, with a tremendous headache, and severe vomiting, but after several days he fully recovered.

According to a medical officer Mac spoke to later, the Cpl was very lucky to be alive. He ought to have suffered severe brain damage, at least, caused by the oxygen deficiency to the brain for a long period of time.

Mac's quick decision to pull him out of the latrine made the difference between life and death. However, Mac still thought the Cpl was extremely odd. The strange, unexplained result of this Ronson rescue, Mac still finds hard to believe. When the Cpl was pulled back over the edge of the trench, he was still clutching the soup ladle. Even though unconscious, his brain or sensory motor nervous system made his hand clasp tight on to the spoon handle. Piled high in the ladle was a fairly solid, steaming heap of the trench contents, with lo and behold, the lighter, covered in shit, slime, and muck, yet still glinting in the sunlight.

Cpl Galloway left Cyprus shortly after this affair for a post at the jungle warfare training school at Kota Tinggi in Malaya. Did he ever manage to have that Varaflame engraved? Did Maisy ever know of his near death because of his labour of love for her? Mac wonders...if the Ronson is still working, has he ever dared to admit his idiocy?

Salt Flats, endless miles of them, stretched between the bivouac and the town of Limassol. White, shimmering, salt encrusted sand strips run through the flats like crooked fingers covered in large warts. These warts were pre and postnuptial mating nests for the hundreds of flamingos that lived in the moonscape, spaced about four feet apart in each direction. They managed to break up the pulsating, shivering, distorted mirage effect reflections of the powerful sun shining on sand and salt. Apparently, these flamingos bred in Africa, made mating bonds for life, and then flew back to the Akrotiri salt lakes to rest and recuperate, building the nest, a one foot diameter by one foot high bowl of sand and salt, to rest in and maintain their bonding.

To Mac, it seemed folly of the highest order to allow large flocks of birds, however beautiful to look at, to live and fly in their hundreds so close to an airfield. Nevertheless, they did, and what's more, the RAF encouraged them. Eventually, the RAF Station, Akrotiri, honoured the flamingo by using it as the Station Mascot and mounted a picture of a flamingo on the Station Regimental Crest, or Shield, as the RAF called it.

EOKA, the military terrorist element, intent on forcing the British to accept the political movement toward ENOSIS, began misbehaving somewhat in 1955. They began with a few bombs at outlying British facilities, such as the Radio Relay Station at Ayios Nikolaos near Famagusta, and the telephone link exchange, connecting the North and South of the island.

This last target was miles from habitation and placed on top of the highest mountain in Cyprus, Mount Olympus. Night watchmen were supposed to be on duty at these targets and were conveniently absent

[76]

when these attacks took place. Intelligence information began to filter into British Ground Defense Operations Centre that informed them that the Greeks employed in these watchmen type duties were in danger of their lives if they hindered EOKA activity in any way. Who could blame them for being conveniently absent, during any of these life-threatening attacks? The guards were low paid, unarmed, and very vulnerable. Mac and his men had to act quickly.

Only a few British troops acted as Cyprus Garrison forces in the mid fifties. Most were to be found in the Canal Zone and North Africa. A solution to the problem Mac's men faced was for the military to bring in more troops and to put British forces on protection duties on all outlying, easy to attack and vulnerable points and areas. Not as easily accomplished as said.

An interim measure adopted was to covertly position small units of men into strategic positions to watch and report on any suspicious activity. Back up to this intelligence was an immediate reaction force, helicopter mobile, ready to instantly act on any information and take pre-emptive action to avoid damage to British property. Mac's tasks followed this latest doctrine.

Working in small, completely self-contained groups, the men took on the mantle of covert watch and report operations. After being injected into the area of observation by unconcealed methods, their job began. They would remain as an individual unit, until they were under command of 45 Marine Commando or another prime military unit with regular logistic command.

An example of how this works is shown by Situation Reports, what Mac called Sit Reps. On this patrol, the call sign was Alpha 2. Alpha 2 left Mac's base by helicopter just when dusk was falling for a short, fifty-minute flight to 45 Marine Commando base at Platres Camp on Mount Olympus in the Troodos mountain range. Mac's unit would be part of a Commando patrol on the way out to the objective, acting in an overt manner and letting any intelligence watchers know that they were about. Mac's troops would then covertly drop off, while the Commando continued; this manoeuvre would hopefully pass off unnoticed.

To help with this subterfuge, Police dogs were taken and teased to make a lot of noise; the dog presence keeping the watchers at a distance, far enough away to prevent observation, yet detailed enough to notice men 'disappear'. These tactics, plus many variations, worked very well and could have defeated EOKA's attempt at countryside sabotage completely if Mac's men could have used support weapons and employed Combat Air Patrol to take them out at extra long range. Again, due to politics again, this was not permitted.

Mac was commanding this detail. No set timings were given for the duration of these ops; he would be informed when the urgent situation unfolded and developed. Therefore, more equipment than normal was taken, because once in position, Mac knew one stayed until job completion. To move before the task end for equipment, or really for any reason at all, would give the game away and compromise the patrol.

"Looks like we're at it again, mates" Mac mused, whilst checking the helicopter loading plan. "Bet you a tenner I pull myself a bird, the woman type."

"Not if she's a Greek you won't, Mac boy. They don't like being called birds."

"By the time I've used my charm, style, personality, culture, and character, and they've had a whiff of my Old Spice up their nostrils, they'll be ripping their bras off. A few more words by my deep, sexy voice, explaining what a bird means to me, and they'll be slinging their knickers at me. You mark my words. That's it. Mount up my little Golly Hunters. Let's go and do and think things evil and ugly."

That was typical Mac-type of behaviour, rambles on about everything and nothing while thinking, writing, watching others, planning, and the call to action all at the same time.

"When I've laid on all the trimmings, come up and see me sometime." The last bit said with his hands on hips and a poor imitation of Betty Grable with his eye flutter and mincing step, he pushed the last man into the chopper and climbed on board himself.

"Good luck and hunting." With that, he slid the aircraft's door closed. He was going to need a little luck where he was going;

[78]

Amiandos, a terrorist hot spot in the Troodos Mountains, and a very strong threat to the asbestos supply that was mined near the village, not to mention the North South telephone relay hut.

Crickets, the Cyprus Locust, were not friends of the soldier. Crickets gave off a crescendo of unadulterated sex. That was what their noise was all about: mating, calling for, and finding mates. 'Come and screw me' type messages they sent, mainly at after dark. These creatures were definitely creatures of the night. 'I'm ready to be implanted with your genes', or, 'Who wants the full Monty?' was the paramount message of their call. The moon and stars seemed to get bigger as the night went on, and this acted on the breeding patterns of the insects. The noise got louder, seeming to come from everywhere all at once. When this happened, a new World opened; a panorama of sound started to unfold. The orchestra of the different ages and sexes of the crickets, some soprano, mezzo-soprano, base, tenor, baritone, all began to take shape in the evening cacophony of sound. This made movement at night easier for the men, taking away much of the need for stealth and not having to worry about footsteps being heard above the crickets. In fact, one could be quite bold in an approach to a target.

However, the soldiers had to remember the same advantage was available to the enemy; therefore manning observation posts at night could be nerve wracking. Minds could begin to wander and imagine things and see things and movement that is not there. Training came in use there. The more one forgot his family and other distractions and kept thinking about soldiering, forcing himself to keep his mind on the job in hand, the more he was going to win this mental battle against the hellish noise distraction created by our little friends the crickets. Strict training helps in more ways than blanking out unwanted noise.

[79]

Many more decisions have to be made to avoid becoming that inanimate lump of stinking dead meat that losing to an enemy means. The screaming of the crickets was one hazard to overcome.

There were several little friends who were believed to be in the employ of EOKA. Ants and other insects crawling into every orifice of the body, up the nose, in the ears, mouth, old wounds, arse, penis and any other entrance available to the little monsters were the men's biggest problem if they were in a scrape OP. A scrape being an underground place of hiding, normally easy and quick to construct, but nearly impossible in the mountains, because of the very shallow topsoil. The men tended to have to build up, and were therefore easier to spot.

When the military man began to reminisce and think about women, family, and all the other things that meant both nothing and everything in a soldier's world, he was vulnerable. Discomfort caused by the pestering of insects could bring this about; it acted like a mental anesthetic, an endorphin induced block against the insect attack discomfort. These abstract thoughts could take over decision-making powers. They demoralized. They became more important. They niggled and nagged at will power, suggesting to anyone with the slightest modicum of a brain, "Now's the time to go, I don't have to put up with this, what am I doing here? Now is the time to become a sloppy civilian".

Overcoming such sickeners really came down to training and experience; some people, even trying very hard, could not overcome them. A case for a mental rejection of these outlandish ideas no longer existed for them. It was time to go for these few people. The military normally weeded them out in training. The little, itsy bitsy, tiny weenie insect had beaten them, added to their strong feelings of inadequacy, and made their life unbearable.

Because the men were big, unbeatable, strong men, in their own opinion, in a man's world, full of oneself, answerable only to one's own determination and other professional abilities, they had a tendency to think they were infallible against all the many problems that fell in their path. This was soldier imagination: nothing could beat

[80]

him. An even better thought: nobody had ever dreamt up the scenario that could beat him.

Yet insects and bugs could beat them, hands down, if they started to compare to them. Their insect world was only full of positive things: food, sex, breed, and survival. Hardly any sleeping existed in their world, and the same again and again until infinity. To be as good as they were, the soldiers had to follow these basics, as well as know his weapons, tactics, and the hundreds of other skills he holds in his own personal armoury.

Insertion for Alpha 2 went off without a hitch, an observation base was established, overlooking Amiandos, about eight hundred metres higher than the village, but giving clear observation of the track that wound its way up the hill, away from the village toward the telephone relay hut. A scrape was managed with an unimpeded view of the potential target. It lay about one hundred and fifty metres from the hut itself, well inside small arms range and with very easy access and well-camouflaged route into and out of the lay up point.

The LUP was a cut back into a rock formation around the side of a cave complex, overgrown and inaccessible for years. The two men, off duty from the scrape observation, could rest and relax here as much as it was possible to relax in this close proximity to someone who will try to kill you if given the chance. Mac's observation team in the scrape had to be fully aware of everything that happened around them during their tour of duty. They mostly managed to rest a little when it was their turn in the LUP.

Communications to Ground Defence Operations Centre were also in the lying up position and a series of night vortex torch signals (black beams of light, which cannot be seen by anyone unless the beam points directly at them). These were arranged for every hour on the hour from the scrape to the LUP, letting both parties know all was well. This meant a two-hour sleep opportunity at a time for the LUP men.

Changeover between scrape and LUP took place around three o'clock in the morning, before the night dew settled to show up footprints or wildlife activity started at first light. An unusually late or early dawn chorus from the birds was a giveaway. Goats and dogs were the greatest compromise hazard on these types of jobs anywhere in the world, not just Cyprus.

Mac and the men limited the chance of any compromise as much as was humanly possible, but these fall downs existed and one needed a bit of luck, as well as professionalism. Disposal of waste had to be well thought out and planned. Once the disposal programme was established, it had to be scrupulously enforced. Life depended on carrying out the agreed plan to the letter, comma and full stop.

Large quantities of heavy-duty plastic bags are always part of an OPs inventory for all waste - human and otherwise. Even when placed inside a plastic bag, it was not always possible to bury waste. It really depended on where the man was and what the problems were. Concrete or rock does not lend itself to burial, for instance. On many occasions, the waste had to be carried out of the area, sometimes by the men and sometimes by another friendly covert patrol. Men on such a patrol moved out of their camp to the OP area with empty backpacks and returned with full ones... a very hard tactic for an enemy to spot at night. Emptying the backpacks was not a very pleasant job.

The simplest calculations one made in waste disposal was 'Will this give my position away?'

Even if buried, a bag can leak, or in hot climates, it can also sweat, showing a dark stain of damp earth. A giveaway.

Insects and animals will be attracted to poorly disposed waste. A giveaway.

Smell, apart from human detection, attracts small airborne insects, gnats, carob mosquitoes, and even heavier than normal concentrations of tree born dwellers, if it happens to be buried or dumped below a tree. Another giveaway.

Defragging was essential to work successfully on covert ops. Not the defrag that computer buffs talk about nowadays, but similar in concept. Defragging a computer means to straighten everything out and make sure it's working to maximum capability. A pre-op defrag served virtually the same purpose. In this instance, we defragged the human being, plus the equipment he was going to carry or use.

Later, when posted to Aden, Mac was to discover working in Arab clothes and living among Arabs was quite different to watch and report on a mountain in Cyprus. Politics and doctrine were different, as well as the individual's job, so different standards of defrag were called for. Sweat, the passing of wind, or a human belch carry a smell of a previous meal, garlic for instance, and if this wafts downwind it could easily give a soldier's position away.

Toothpaste, aftershave, deodorants, soap, mint sweets, all were personal giveaways that have to be avoided.

Rifle or gun oil, blanco, starch, boot polish, noisy equipment, slack weapon slings, rattles from items carried in packs, and poor camouflage are all giveaways that could cost a soldier his life from his equipment.

Mental defrag refreshed the 'Slist'. The Slist was a memory jogger for the S list, as follows: Shape, Shine, Shadow, Silhouette, Size, Spacing, Signals, Sound, Speed, Subterfuge, Slinky, Sly, Savage, Senses, See all. SSTs, or the S directory, were lists of actions to avoid compromise for close proximity to the enemy operations. Combinations of the Slist helped one to stay unobserved, helped to observe others, and helped move to a kill point, or the intended position of killing the enemy.

At a kill point exploit, surprise, aggression, and speed were known as 'The Ideal Three', with the necessary type and volume of firepower to achieve the aim: win.

If any two of the kill point three were employed, one could still win. For instance, if the soldiers had speed and aggression, he could compensate for the loss of surprise. The speed and aggression used could create further surprise and add confusion. He could still win.

It may sound far fetched, but smell was the single greatest giveaway, apart from sighting the target. All hunters approach from downwind of a victim. The soldier's requirements for pre-task defrag when working in South Arabia was to enter Fort Morbit Arab jail at Sheikh Othman for five days before going out to work. During these five days, they never washed, cleaned their teeth, used toilets, or ate anything other than Arab food, the same issued to the Arab inmates. They chewed Qat, an Arabian leaf-type drug similar to cannabis. This drug produced illusions of false well-being. The soldiers became sloppily relaxed, without a worry or an enemy in the world. Eighty percent of the Arabs used it. It oozed out of their skin, clung to their breath. Without using qat, a soldier would easily be detected with possible capture to follow.

The men went into indoor ranges everyday to fire their Browning high power weapons through the drug haze, aiming for the larger "centre of the main target mass," to learn to compensate for the drug's debilitating effect, instead of the top of chest and head shot double tap, two shots together, that they had been trained to do. In this way, they lived like Arabs among the Arabs. At the task end, however long it took, they went back to prison to debug, delouse, debrief, and humanise again... before the next time.

Withdrawal symptoms from the qat were the worst part.

CHAPTER 5

In The Field

Command HQ decided the op, plus fast back up with the immediate reaction force was very successful and should stay in force. Services and units then started infighting to see who should do which task. This inter-service, inter-unit sparring was quite normal. The main difference on this occasion was the small number of men available for the ever-increasing workload. For Mac, it meant even longer duration than normal in the field. Unless the existing doctrine changed, Mac could expect up to three months in an operational area without relief.

After four days in the field on compo rations, it became important to make sure the troops had fresh rations. All team leaders were well educated on local plants and their nutrient value, especially the many kinds of fungi. Large, edible snails were in abundance in the early morning mist, which blanketed the mountain every day. Trapping meat sources became second nature. The only problem when involved in this survival activity was to avoid giving away the defrag.

For example, one unit made a fast exit when they inadvertently compromised their position. They went around the area at night, sticking long twigs coated in glue into the bushes and olive trees to trap birds that settled on them. It worked well, but the unusual terror screams and noise made by the victims invited a response from the Greeks. These gentlemen would be easy to take out, but politics said, 'Get out'. Mac thought it was very frustrating, because sometimes an open fire was unavoidable. On the few occasions that this happened over the full operational time scale, a total of seven terrorists were killed and two injured, and their weapons and explosives captured. A high kill to injury ratio admittedly, but Mac's men gave no chances or quarter. As Mac recalled, "It was them that decided they wanted to kill us in the first place, so screw them."

Chemical preservatives in the standard compo deliberately caused severe constipation in the squaddie eating the stuff. Policy being, they would win any battle in three days, but not if the men were behind bushes with their trousers around their ankles.

One operational procedure actually considered by the men was to utilise the compo bung as a weapon to demoralise the enemy and to hell with defrag. This method had been written about for many years, even before the 2nd World War. Compo bound troops were to be positioned up wind, and then turn their backs on the enemy positions, and then allowed to fart as often as possible after the three day compo incubation period had set in. This was easily done. The stop excreta chemical embodied in the compo had an 'allow farting' safety device, in order to avoid men suffering from severe gas stomach cramps. Resultant smells enshrouding the enemy positions could not have been classified as chemical or biological warfare, but the next best thing, and without NATO or the UNO having to deal with any backlash on the political arena.

However, re-supply was now going to cause a slight problem. Initial equipment carried in to an OP would have to suffice, so a "live off the land policy" was invoked.

In Amiandos village square, markets for different goods were held on different days. Mondays were the booze-up day, Tuesday the livestock day...both of these functions caught Mac's interest and set the wheels for grand theft in motion, especially the livestock, considering the men's newly increased time in the field of operations. A rope tied to a back leg, and then to a stake driven into the ground always secured animals for sale. These ropes were normally about fifteen feet in length and allowed the animal to go on circular walkabouts.

Mac noticed that the villages brought their animals to the sale on Mondays, and then took part in the booze up, a monumental affair. Local grape growers set up large barrels of their homemade wine for tasting and selling. A customer bought a wine glass at a barrel for one Cyprus pound. He or she then drank as much wine as they wanted from that barrel without more money, and then could move on to try the next barrel; same procedure and again, as many times as they wanted. Needless to say, by the end of the night, a lot of people were crashed out in the square, pissed out of their brains, and sleeping it off.

Their animals were still doing the circular walkabouts. What a target for Mac and his need for fresh food supply! Mac's only problem was choice: pork, lamb, goat, veal, rabbit, duck, geese, pigeon or chicken, snails and crayfish by the thousand, and cages full of mixed migratory birds trapped on their routes south or north. He settled for pork as the primary target, because, even though it "went off" fast, once salted, it made a good, long lasting pemmican. Veal was the second choice. Goats and sheep roamed the hills in large numbers, so he could acquire them more or less as needed.

Mac made his plans in such a way that someone else would get the blame for the theft, namely 45 Marine Commando. Some time previously, during a major piss up at Platres camp, an 'unarmed combat' competition, for fun, took place. Each contestant had to defeat certain attacks against him. A simple competition really, because the defender knew what attack was coming. Attacks followed this sequence: under arm knife thrust – where commandos used real bayonets, over arm knife attack, punch from the front, kick from the front, bear hug from the front with arms clasped to the side, then same with the arms free, strangulation from the rear with a rope, then strangulation with bare hands. For each successfully attempted defence, the attacker gave the defender a piece of his uniform. These items started with insignificant things like a Patrol Aid Memoir, a puttee, a bootlace and so on. Eventually, the more alcohol a person downed, the more careless he became, and thus, more precious items became prizes. Our hero Mac had a fair variety of Commando

Equipment to plant at the scene of a crime, the main one being a Commando Green Beret.

LUP duty was the time period for 'Operation Pork'. A simple plan was defined. Whilst Mac and his stint buddy Dave Butt were on the early, two o'clock LUP shift, things would happen. They would take a circular route to approach the village from the direction of the Marine camp. During this directional approach, a Green Beret would attach itself to a bush in such a position that it must be found, even by a bunch of wine-addled Greeks with crippling hangovers.

On the outskirts of the village, the approach would change, so they came into the target area with the mountain behind them, reducing the chance of being seen, because they would melt into the black bulk of the hill. This would also keep them downwind of the animals, in case they spooked them. It was very doubtful that the Greeks would hear with all they had drunk the night before, unless, by chance someone was awake, while throwing up or something.

Target in sight, on hands and knees, remembering the Slist, keeping themselves at approximately the same height as the animals, they stealthily advanced into the square. Kill technique was easy. At the time of finality and on Mac's signal, Dave had to cut the rope securing the pig to the stake. At the same time, Mac would muzzle the pig with a prepared toggle in his left hand and down-throat-heart stab with his knife. Completion of the task meant dragging the pig southward out of the village toward the Platres camp, confirming the Commandos involvement. When safely outside the village, it was necessary to disembowel and behead the animal to reduce the weight to carry and leave more markers to the marines being responsible. This done, they would skirt the village again, with the pig in a plastic bag to avoid blood spilling, and then head into the mountain, away from the OP, 'a double bluff to any followers,' skirt around, and then enter their own area from higher up the mountain.

A good plan, easy to carry out and it would achieve the aim, and procure fresh meat. However, the pig didn't know the plan. Mac had failed to let the animal have a copy of the operations order, and it did not play ball. When Mac went for the muzzle-heart-stab sequence,

Dave slashed the ankle rope, and the pig took off at a fast rate of knots with Mac spread-eagled across it's back, hanging on to its ears with his left hand and tail with right hand. The muzzle had not been properly secured, allowing our very frightened beast, full of the adrenaline of fear, to screech and scream like the proverbial stuck pig...forgive the pun. The pig careened in an erratic fashion through the other animals and cages of chickens, geese, and ducks. Just imagine the noise, enough to awaken the dead, never mind our drunken Greeks.

Chaotic is a mild way to describe the scene. Even in the best of situations, the Greeks are highly volatile and demonstrative, so imagine the poor bastards being aroused from a drunken slumber with some sort of dragon on the loose trying to get at their livestock. Was it a dragon or a mountain lion? That would be the trend of thought hurtling around in their booze-befuddled heads.

The women would be joining in by now with what is commonly known as the 'Arab Trill,' a very high pitched warbling made by vibrating the tongue against the top of the mouth and kept going with long deep breaths. Those people who have heard this sound will never forget the fear that can it can invoke in ones breast or brain or wherever fear implants itself in the human frame. Mac had managed to create a certain kind of Mediterranean madness with a catalyst of its own generating power. One didn't want to adopt any special type or kind of attitude toward them, but their behavior left no doubt in one's mind that the average villager was really a crazy type of nutcase. Hopefully, these lunatics would not manage, by some fluke, to cause the capture or even death by accidental drunken shooting of Mac's looting team; such were Mac's thoughts.

CHAPTER 6

Rivalry and the Drink

Follow this madness up with rudely awakened Greeks, grabbing their twelve bore shotguns and blasting away all over the place at imaginary targets they could not see in the dark or through their alcoholic haze. Eventually, Mac rolled off the pig and lay face down in the village until the shooting died down. Even though our Greek friends did not know what they were shooting at, a stray bullet was a distinct possibility and could do the same damage.

Mac and Dave met up at the Lost Rendezvous Point about one hour later and folded up with hysterical, maniacal laughter at the recollections of the debacle they had been involved in and left behind. Dave delved inside his Dennison smock and pulled out two very dead chickens he had 'rescued' on the way out of the village. Mac's tally was two ferrets to use to catch rabbits. Not bad for a night's work.

The Marines faced the resultant political and diplomatic flack, and eventually paid three hundred pounds Sterling compensation of the two thousand pounds Cypriot claim the Greeks made against them. We had the most expensive ferrets in the world, and the chickens were tough, even in a stew. They had been robbed.

Anyone visiting Cyprus can now read about this OP and some of its results in the telephone hut that is still standing. The day and night watchmen maintained a "daily occurrence book". They are still maintained as yearbooks. One report was as follows:

"Claim twenty five pounds of British Government for my donkey called Andréas. Andréas, he on mountain. It is nighttime. My Andréas, he moving eat food. Bad Englishman hear my Andréas walking. He shout, Halt! Who is there? My Andréas, he no a speaker de English. Bang. He dead two times. Two shots make Andréas big mess. No good for the eating. Claim de twenty-five pounds. Government make bad Englishmen pay."

Mac never paid; 45 Marine Commando did, out of unit funds.

During the period from November 1955 and February 1959 when the ceasefire was implemented, the Covert OP system led to a confirmed twenty-seven kills of known terrorists and sixty-four arrests. The mountain gangs were defeated, hence they called for a truce. Urban terrorists still stayed operational, but the mountain men never recovered and never formed a threat again. The British have used the OP watch and report with a firefight on many brush fire skirmishes, in different countries since, and won. If the firefight is unavoidable, start it and make your kills first. Such is the way to win.

At one stage, certain mountain terrorists were deemed essential targets, because they were beginning to be legendary figures to the local populace and had to be removed from the scene, efficiently, cleverly, and without them gaining 'martyr' status. Two of these men, code named Troy and Pellagrous, operated in the Kyrenia Mountain Range and were selected as targets for Mac and his three men. Simple, general outline orders were given, 'Remove them from operational theatre. Eliminate.' Then it was up to Mac.

It took six weeks of long ops and hard patrolling to finally put the finger on the men, but hard work paid off and Mac arrested Pellagrous on a narrow mountain track above Templos village. Mac had the drop on his man, because, when they came face-to-face on a bend in the mountain track, Mac had his SLR rifle at the low port and ready for fast action. Pellagrous had his weapon slung over his shoulder and across his chest.

[91]

Mac stated during debriefing, that the look on Pella's face at this meeting was one of complete shock and disbelief, which faded finally to resignation and acceptance of his situation. After disarming his man and a further thorough body search for concealed weapons, Mac invited Pella to sit down with him on the narrow path and have some food and a drink, whilst Mac explained his situation to him now that he was captured.

Mac carried with him on these long mountain forays: four water bottles, two containing water, and two containing the local Greek brewed Ouzo, a rotgut drink. Ouzo was one of the Seven Wonders of the World for soldiers who worked away from the safe confines of a base camp. Its properties were amazing. Having an extremely high alcohol content, one could cook with it. All a soldier had to do was simply put one's compo in a mess tin, pour some ouzo on it, and drop in a match. Voilá, one cooked hot meal in seconds.

Ouzo was also a painkiller. Mac once had a man under his command who had a severe toothache. His face had swollen up like a small football, but because of their situation at that time, there was no way to extricate the tooth. Had it not been for the severe swelling, the extraction could have been carried out in situ, but the swelling meant it was abscessed, making this choice invalid. So they gave him Ouzo. The man never appeared to be drunk, but his pain went away, and he stayed at his post for a further three days.

On return to Nicosia and a visit to the dentist, the swelling had disappeared and the pain no longer existed. The dentist said his teeth were fine. The only treatment needed was a scrape and clean by a dental hygienist. Such was the power of Ouzo.

Ouzo also acted as an insect repellent. If a soldier took a mug of the elixir before a night operation and it sweats out of the skin, it does not smell and give away defrag, but no insect will come near, especially mosquitoes. Ouzo's only pitfall was that if one drank too much, he became badly pissed, suffered major, crippling, nervous hangovers, and if he took a drink of water or swallowed water when cleaning teeth, the next day he'd be pissed again. Very dangerous when in 'bandit country' as one needed to keep his wits about him at times.

So Mac and Pella shared one tin of compo bacon and sausages made into thick doorstep sandwiches with a mug of Ouzo each to wash them down, and then the talking began. Pella spoke reasonable English, Mac spoke a fair amount of colloquial Northern Cyprus Dialectal Cypriot, so communicating was not a problem. This is how one of Mac's Debriefing Officers remembered the story as it was told:

"You knew I was after you?" Mac asked.

Mac's idea was to see what background knowledge Pella had, if any.

"Yes. We were told by most of the villages that Special Commando teams wanted to kill us. Where are your other men?"

"They are on those three hill tops with rifles and telescopic sights aiming at you now as we speak. They have orders to kill any of your men who try to intervene in my arrest of you."

Mac slowly and deliberately pointed out the three hills, varying from two hundred to four hundred metres range, making sure that Pella realised that he couldn't make a move in any direction without getting himself shot.

"That will not be necessary. I am now alone in this area. My men have either died or gave up the fight and gone back to their families."

"Where is Troy?"

"Troy is dead."

"Bullshit! Troy is my second target with you. There has been no abort signal to me about Troy, so he must be alive."

"He is dead as far as Cyprus is concerned. He has gone back to Greece, to Piraeus. You get your intelligence to check. I would not lie to save him. He is a traitor to Enosis and to EOKA."

Mac believed him. The venom in his voice when he spat out 'traitor' said it all; it was soldier language.

"If you say so, I believe you. When did you see him last? When did he leave Cyprus? How did he leave Cyprus? Did any men go with him? Did he stockpile arms and ammunition? If so, where?"

Mac continued interrogation in this way for a good three hours, and all the time the pair of military 'buddies,' because that was what they had become, were drinking Mac's Ouzo and water, and Brandy and water from Pella's goat skin containers. Obviously, when the booze went in, their tongues became looser. Combine this with the stifling heat of the day and sitting on a mountain track in the sun with no shade, and these men were becoming very drunk indeed.

Mac's training in resistance to interrogation kept his mind a couple of plateau's above Pellas, who was demoralised in defeat anyway. This gave Mac the upper hand in the conduct of the interrogation and memory banking the material for the obvious follow up intelligence debriefing in front of a board of officers.

"You must realise why the British sent me to find you, and why you are a special case?" Mac asked Pella.

"I am a good partisan and cause you much trouble I think?" was his reply.

"You are so right, my friend. You've been a thorn in the Brit's backside so long and it's starting to go septic and hurt the bastards. They want it pulled out. I'm the doctor, understand?"

"Yes, it pleases me that I am special." Pella muttered.

"It shouldn't."

"Why?" he asked.

"Because now I have to kill you and make it look like an accident, so your people cannot make you a martyr for the cause. If you have an accident, you become an unintelligent man, not a hero, savvy?" Pella started to throw up, whether from fear or booze, who knows.

"The British have given me the power to make you certain promises and guarantees if you die in a preplanned accident, do you understand?" Mac waited until Pella finished spewing, and then repeated the statement.

"It's important to me and you that you are clear about what I'm saying. I have an offer from the British Government. Do you understand?"

"Yes. I have to die. What do you offer me: bullet, hanging, poison, long drop from aircraft with no parachute, Hari Kari? Do I really have a choice on how I die?" he asked.

"You can die with grace and by the method of your own choosing. You simply have to kill yourself, and the British will pay the rest of the mortgage on your house, look after your wife with an allowance, which will be very generous, and see to it that your children are awarded a fine education. What do you say?"

A long, long, silence followed.

"Do I have this in writing?"

"No. You just have to trust me."

"Do I look stupid man or something?"

"Far from it, but what choice have you? You've shit out, mate. You haven't anywhere to go. You are finished, finito, kaput." Mac replied.

"You know all about my family?"

"I've read up on you for weeks before I even came after you."

"Tell me one thing about my family that only I should know."

"Nicos had to be circumcised at Nicosia General Hospital last March, because he hit himself on the knob end with a hammer while trying to crush flowers for Marulla's Church covenant and acceptance into the Holy Order."

"How did you find this information?"

"I know everything about you. You are my mark. The British are very thorough when it comes to removing someone from the scene who is alien to British interests."

"Let us have another drink."

"A very good idea, and now, I will shut up and await your decision."

"Let's make this a special one, Ouzo and brandy, to the top of the mug, and no water."

"Sounds good to me."

"Enosis and the cause." Pella raised his glass and drank deeply.

"And up yours." Mac followed suit.

[95]

A long silence followed, Mac knew for him to speak now would break Pella's concentration and deliberation about the facts and his hopeless situation.

Suddenly, Pella stood up, stood to attention, saluted Mac, and said, "Let my family down, and I will haunt you for the rest of your life."

Then, to Mac's complete and utter amazement, he jumped off the cliff.

"I've received no promises from the Government Pella, nor have I men positioned on the hills to shoot you. They are in an OP ambush five miles away. I was on my way back from a reconnaissance when I bumped into you. I've been duping you, you sucker. I bet you never won at poker!" Mac was raving and shouting down into the valley, as though Pella could hear him, and the numerous echoes ricocheting around the cliff faces.

Mac was elated at doing a good job, but would have preferred to kill his mark in a firefight, rather than with the 'snake in the grass' method he had employed.

After sitting for about thirty minutes, kicking around the recent happenings in his drunken skull, logging them, putting them in sequence, orientating himself and his position so as to be able to find the body, he collected Pella's goods into a stockpile and covered them with rocks to show the jump point and keep mountain dogs from getting at them and destroying evidence. He selected a route down the cliff, climbed down it, confirmed Pella had died, leaving the body in exactly the same position it had landed.

Mac, again, made a cairn of rocks to keep the scavengers at bay and evidence intact. Free climbing back up the cliff was fairly easy. Back at the top, he put his own kit in order and began to walk down the track toward the main Kyrenia road, knowing he should soon be arrested by some unintelligent bloody Military Police patrol for being drunk and in charge of a weapon, and out of bounds or any other inane charge of which they could think.

"The shit heads," Mac muttered under his breath.

He continued thinking, "What sort of bastard volunteers for a job like that? The posing red top bastards.

Such was his frame of mind on his return to civilisation after six weeks in hell.

Mac was right in his estimation of arrest, fortunately the MP patrol had a Sergeant in charge with some experience, not the normal acting Lance Corporal Protection Stripe fool, which was the standard dummy one meets. Mac told the Sgt to take him to Ledra Palace Hotel in Nicosia and to radio Brigade HQ and tell them he had picked up 'Starlight', his code name for this operation. He also used the police radio to contact 'Starlight two,' his men on ambush OP, giving the recall abort code for them to come in from the field.

The police Sgt went along with all his requests, and obviously realised his passenger was no normal squaddie. Mac wore no badges of rank or emblems of any kind, so this added to the policeman's confusion as to what to say or do. It was quite obvious to him the entity he had picked up was drunk. Mac made it easy for him.

"Sgt, thank you for your help. I am drunk. Now do your duty and proffer your charges, but I will advise you that you will be writing charge sheets and charge reports and attending the charge to give evidence for nothing. My name is 'Starlight' of 27 Special Operations Group, and we don't give a fuck about charges unless they are made against us by our own people, so my mate, save yourself some work, and shut your fucking lance jack up before he starts to speak or I'll shoot the bastard." The Sgt dropped Mac at the Ledra Palace Hotel, after telling his lance jack, "Don't look at him, for your own good. The man's crazy."

They listened. No charges were ever filed.

----

[97]

The Ledra Palace Hotel was the top class hotel in Nicosia at that time. Only a few people realised the existence of the 27th Special Operations Groups HQ that covered the whole of the top floor. This floor was not accessible by lift, nor was it shown as being there at all. Elsewhere in the hotel, it simply did not exist.

The personnel of this combined services unit had a number of varying specialist skills, but the one thing they all had in common was the ability to speak Greek and Greek Cypriot. The Turkish desk also, in addition, spoke Turkish and Turkish Cypriot.

Many of the operatives filled in appointments with false names and service documents. Even Commanding Unit Officers did not know of their presence until they had pulled off an intelligence coup against the locals by using their linguistic ability, eavesdropping on conversations, and gathering information about any activity that could be used to defeat the terrorists.

One Sgt of 45 Marine Commando worked in the airman's mess kitchens as a trade assistant general. An RAF Leading Aircraftman, he washed plates, pots and pans for two years, but the information he gained from Greek kitchen staff and passed on to RAF Regiment security, foiled seven bomb plots. Only one explosion with a bomb placed in an easy chair in the airman's NAAFI went off. Thanks to him, the others were defused in time and saved many lives and damage to expensive equipment.

The field operations group, of which Mac was a member, consisted of sixteen four-man teams, each one a completely independent entity, capable of sustained long field operations without support, but which could be reinforced rapidly by helicopter born troops if they called for such. At that time, helicopters were rarely seen.

The SOG had six Sycamores for use, and all of them were fully occupied with work schedules. Most of the operative's movements were by helicopter from a specially constructed heliport in the centre of the Ledra Palace roof. No surrounding buildings near the hotel overlooked the roof, and a helicopter in the centre of the roof could not be seen from ground level, hence the movements went unobserved.

Mac's debriefing began the following morning when he had cleaned up, sobered up and slept. His men had arrived back the same night on a helicopter lift, so individual debrief Officers took notes from the four men in the group on a rota basis, each one doing statement verification with the others. The only thing that could not be cross verified in this manner was Mac's activity with Pella, because Mac had been on his own. True, there was Pella's equipment stockpiled stone cairn, and Pella's body cairn, but there was nobody to confirm Mac's promises of financial rewards for Pella's family.

Mac had a bad hangover during this question period and lost his cool.

"Look you miserable sods, the mark is dead. That's what you wanted, and it was done my way. That's also what you wanted, so stop fucking about and honour my promises. I know you've given his accident theory to the Cyprus Times and shown them his weapons and kit, now do the decent thing and look after his wife and kids."

Mac had rarely been seen so angry, and it was obvious that other Officers, who didn't know him well, were visibly shocked at his outburst. One even started to pull rank, until Mac shut him up, in no uncertain manner. It always happens in terrorist situations where some British Officers who treat a soldier who has done a good job and killed a terrorist as though he were guilty of murder or manslaughter, instead of just taking the facts as the soldier reported and let an investigation team check out the story.

Mac always abhorred those officers, as did any other professional field operator. The fact was that they had done nothing themselves and were covetous of those who did good soldier work and tried to give themselves importance and ego boosts by trying to screw other people around. They all dressed the same yet were supposed to be covert. White shoes, white calf-length socks, white shorts, and white shirts with a brown belt. One could pick them out a mile away.

Some people called the British 'brutal torturers' and many other derogatory names during the EOKA campaign, but many times, they

[99]

also came up on top of the 'good guys' list. They did so over Pella, too. From somewhere, Mac knew not where, finances were found to honour Mac's pledge of support for Pella's family. The Chief Pay Accounts Officer gave Mac the unofficial news that, "Mrs. Pella will never want again on the financial front. Neither will her sons have any problem with a top class education."

To maintain pressure on the mountain groups, the British conceived the 'starvation plan.' A good idea, following the success of isolating the terrorists from the local population in Malaya, combined with anti-terrorist experience and operations used against the Mau Mau in Kenya, and Adou in South Arabia. Whole mountain villages were put under overt surveillance, with prominent, well-protected watchtowers, and employing the latest technology in night surveillance equipment to observe movements at night. These towers were manned twenty-four hours per day and were supported by platoon strength infantry, who rotated on a six-week basis. All this was high profile. Villagers were invited in the OP towers at night to look through the night vision equipment, so as to understand that any night activity was seen as clear as during daylight. This information obviously was meant to reach the terrorist's ears, and did.

This defense strategy was in place all around both the Troodos and Kyrenia mountain ranges, in a very short time to prevent the terrorists realising what the overall plan was and escaping off to the mountains or stockpiling food before Mac's group was in place. This was a good tactic. It meant that the terrorists, to be able to survive the winter of 1956, had to come off the mountain below the snowline to stay alive.

Mac and the covert SOG Ops were waiting for them when they did. Every time there was a movement off the mountains, they were observed, and helicopter borne troops arrived to capture them. Even innocent people were picked up, because of the simple policy; if you were coming off the hills you were a terrorist until proved otherwise.

Certain high-ranking terrorists, if recognised by SOG, were allowed to continue under constant surveillance, with the hope that they would lead soldiers to their safe houses, other terrorists, arms dumps, or hopefully, Grivas himself. They were given freedom of movement all winter. The plan was to arrest them when they went back to the mountain in the spring, after leading Mac's men to their hideout.

Such was the situation for two top men, Grigoris Afxentiou, second in operational mountain command to Grivas, and his aid, Avgoustis Efstathiou, code named 'Matrosos.' Matrosos was wanted for a number of killings in the Nicosia district. These two charmers were Mac's team's pick up, so they were his babies all winter.

Afsent, as Mac called Afxentiou, made his base upstairs in the village coffee shop in Athalasa village. Matros, as Mac called Matrosos, stayed in the village church at Kolossi near RAF Akrotiri. Was it a coincidence; two top terrorist leaders, wintering near the major Army base and the RAF operational fighter and bomber base? That gave Mac's intelligence and strategy planners something to think about, remembering of course that Mac had troops returning to these bases after the invasion of Suez in November 1956.

Not much happened during the winter. Matros had a few meetings with two individuals in Erimi village. In the spring, when Matros left, these men were picked up and were found to be the 'wall bombers' at Akrotiri and Erimi villages. They had planted remote controlled bombs in the Derbyshire stone walls, at the roadside of both villages and set them off when a military vehicle came by. The Akrotiri bomb blew the leg of a young airman called Jack Lemon. The one at Erimi killed three soldiers in a Land Rover.

Spring came early in Cyprus. Mac and his team noticed that Afsent and Matros met up in Athalasa more frequently. On the 26th of February, one of the team saw four full goatskin water carriers on a table on the coffee shop veranda and six Greek bread loaves. These had not been placed there previously during the winter, so Mac guessed that his babies were on the move. All OPs were alerted for

[101]

'Golly Hunt' activity: everybody on full alert on every covert OP right into the Troodos Mountain range.

The babies moved that night. They left, cross-country, on foot, following the partially dried up river bed that led to Platres. They were under surveillance all the way. They stopped and camouflaged up the following day, obviously to avoid detection by helicopters, and moved off after dark the next night. Everything worked to perfection. By first light, the two men went into a cave. The nearest OP watched Matros lay out a thin radio aerial across the top of the bushes and around the cave, and then threw matching shrub over it to hide its presence.

Mac reasoned that they would not establish communications unless they were staying for some length of time. They had not been carrying a radio, so it must have been there all winter. This was surely their base camp. Another twenty-four hours of surveillance saw both men briefly repairing camouflage over a corrugated, iron balcony-type roof. It also revealed men in the shadow cast by the roof, unrecognizable, but with easily observed binoculars used for scanning the countryside.

Mac made the decision. This was their hideout, from which they set off on attacks. Mac radioed "Catch Golly" grid, and read out the map reference. The SOG call sign came on the net and said, "wait." To Mac's surprise, Brigade came on the net and told him to stay, watch and report: But no kill.

He said to his signaler, "Something strange going off here. What the hell are Brigade doing jumping an SOG net?"

"It happened to me before when Brigade took over an SOG operation in Kenya."

"Where did that leave you in the job stakes?"

"We were out of it, relieved of responsibility, and helicoptered back to HQ without any explanation."

"If Brigade takes my mark away after I played fucking babysitter to them all winter, I'll go ape shit."

"They won't do that to you. They've given you too many medals."

That is just what happened, though. The British decided to make a public spectacle of the arrests, or killings, to show we were on top and

[102]

in charge. Newsreel cameras and all the press were invited to watch and talk freely with the Officers involved; Officers, not Squaddies. These news parasites were even flown in by helicopter, which were practically impossible to get for troop operations unless you were SOG. Soldiers have feet to walk with, is the Officer's cry.

In all Mac's service, or so he said, he had never been so embarrassed to be a British serviceman.

Two tired men in a cage, which he now called his ex-marks.

Hundreds of onlookers and cameras, airborne cameras, and a brainless, out of proportion use of firepower from a platoon of troops tasked to clear the cave.

Why hadn't the powers that be left it to him? It was his own fault, he had decided. He could have killed them both, four times over, and should have done so. Fuck radioing back – take action, and tell them when it was finished.

This molded Mac's future behavior in a number of situations and dropped him in trouble more than once.

The spectacle of capturing the marks lasted six hours. It was a wickedly one-sided battle, so how did it last six hours? Mac was sure the troops had been told to miss their targets to drag the propaganda spectacular out, for the change round of reporters who were flying in all the time. The finale was a disgrace. Dozens of gerry cans of petrol were poured in the cave. If soldiers can get close enough to a target and stand there pouring out five gallons of petrol, he can throw a grenade in the fucking place. What an immoral bastard decided to burn them to death? Mac tried to discover who was responsible, but never did find out. The officer in charge at the scene said he had received orders from 'higher up.' Mac wished he knew from whom.

They fired the cave. Afxentiou shouted to Matrosos while he burned, "Do not be afraid. God is with us."

Avgoustis Efstathiou (Matrosos) put his hands up to protect his eyes and face, and with his hands badly burning, jumped out of the cave.

"I did not want to live." He said afterward. "I jumped out, wanting someone to shoot me. I wanted to die, but not by flames. I must have

[103]

been unconscious, because the next thing I remember was being surrounded by soldiers."

Matrosos was unconscious when he jumped out of the cave, and he fell down the slope. He was flown for burn treatment to Akrotiri Hospital. His fighting days were over. It was February 1959, the start of the truce. He was declared a Cypriot National Hero – and he was.

Grigoris Afxentiou was made a church Martyr, and a Cypriot National Hero. Mac saluted two very brave men. If asked, Mac would say, "It's a pity we have to kill people like that."

Mac was not an EOKA sympathizer, far from it. He did, however, respect good soldiers and brave men doing a hard, dangerous job whatever their nationality or cause, and most professional military men feel the same.

Apart from a few more little skirmishes, this just about finishes the EOKA campaign; not much more action took place in the mountains. The urban groups still operated, but in a much more limited fashion, due to increased British covert intelligence gathering and many more soldiers on the streets in the towns. A few rather dynamic bombs went off, one of these blowing up a large aircraft hanger with Canberra Bombers inside at the RAF Base at Akrotiri. Another one blew up the newly built Officers Mess on the same camp, plus a few temporary 'Caywood' houses and barracks.

Because of these explosions and outrages, or what Mac considered to be 'successful terrorism', a RAF Regiment Squadron (194 Rifle) was moved in to take over the search for local nationals from the RAF Police in an attempt to stop this movement of explosive materials. They apparently did too good a job of it and were a bit too rough, because the local nationals went on strike. One of the terms for them to return to work and finish off at the building of the camp was the removal of the RAF Regiment Squadron, and that the Royal Air Force police replace them. This was done, and all returned to work. Shortly after this, 194 Squadron, who were living in a tented camp within easy call out range, were used as scapegoats by the top brass. The Squadron's method of operation was not supported by their CO. Ridiculous petty charges were raised against the Squadron NCOs, and this situation led to near mutiny. Grenades were thrown at the Officer's mess tent, or so the police claimed. Police dogs were used to try to calm the situation. The men and dogs were well known to each other, because they worked together on night patrols, so therefore, the dogs just ended up gorged with NAAFI meat pies.

Three Wing Squadrons were told to intervene with fixed bayonets. This order was promptly refused with a polite 'Fuck Off.' A Regiment Squadron will not support any action against another Squadron. Eventually, the situation came under control when the CO was relieved of his command. Shortly after, 194 Squadron was disbanded. A pity, because they were obviously top-notch at the job.

After the removal of 194, the explosions started again. This was further proof of the unit's efficiency. These explosions happened because of the thousands of Greek construction workers employed in building the base in a hurry. If a very thorough search had been carried out as was with 194 Squadron, on these large numbers coming through the camp gates, the time taken would have prevented much work. After all, mused Mac, 'Why did we have the work done when the bastards blow up the finished product?'

CHAPTER 7

Cyprus, The Peaceful Years

As he took up office in Government House, Nicosia, Makarios, the New Greek Cypriot President said:

"Now we have before us a time of peace and prosperity for all the people of Cyprus."

This was the beginning of what can only be described as Heaven on Earth. The 'Peace Agreement' recently signed at Lancaster House by the British, Greeks, Turks, and leaders of the Greek and Turkish Cypriots promised well for the future of the island.

For the soldiers and airmen left in the Sovereign Base Area Camps at Akrotiri, Episkopi, and Dekalia near Larnaca, the peace agreement meant they could begin to lead a normal life. Places that had been "out of bounds" for their safety during EOKA now became very much "in bounds".

Movement restrictions into the mountains were lifted, opening up huge areas of fantastic scenery. Duty free civilian cars could be purchased once again, and the whole island was accessible for touring. The Pine Trees Holiday Centre opened up in the Troodos Mountains for servicemen and their families. Many more wives and girlfriends came out to live on the island, and because of the shortage of married quarters, nearly all were accommodated in a "hiring", which were houses rented unfurnished from Cypriots and furnished for the families by the military.

Living in these accommodations meant living with the local nationals in their own areas. Indeed, some of the landlords lived in a small, one-roomed shack at the back of the lovely house they let out. This lead to a better understanding between the locals and servicemen, and many intermarriages took place. Because of these

[106]

factors and the slow increase in tourism, a building boom started that lasted until 1963.

Work for the military was to maintain efficiency and a requirement to be ready if called upon to partake in any emergency that may arise in the Middle East. This meant training and more training, but because of this skills became honed to a fine degree, and therefore, plenty of time off was available. Otherwise, the keen edge of efficiency would blunt. Because the men now had more free time, beaches and bathing became a favourite pastime.

Service clubs were starting up: sailing, water skiing, archery, rally driving, and sea diving were popular themes. There was also, of course, the servicemen's favorite pastime whenever the chance arose - deep sea fishing.

Because of the troubles, normal service pastimes that had been temporarily forgotten, such as inter-service football, cricket, boxing, hockey, athletics and other contact sports, restarted.

Mac's Special Operations Group found a rather unusual pastime: falconry. Whilst carrying out cliff climbing training on the island, a soldier who went by the name of Fred Rolph came across a falcon nest with three chicks in it. Fred brought one back to base, describing his previous falconry experiences, and educated the interested men to the fact that this luckless chick, being the smallest of the three in the nest, would more than likely be eaten by the other two as is Mother Nature's way of selection.

Over the next few weeks, the servicemen got involved in hand feeding this little chick with all sorts of concoctions. The bird grew and grew and was soon stretching and flapping its wings. Thus Fred began its flying education. He forbade the men to feed it and tied strong, thick leather thongs to the poor birds' legs and proceeded to call it with a special whistle. Fred waved a service bed leg base post around his head with a big juicy lump of meat tied to it, tempting the bird to fly after the meat. After some wing-flapping, feather-ruffling, and raucous screeching accompanied attempts at flying, and when hunger took over, the falcon would jump off the perch and amble in a rolling gait to catch the meat being lured, a giant leap before it flew. When the soldiers saw this success, they decided to make a squadron of falcons to terrorise the Station Commander's pet pigeon flock.

Cliff climbing became the order of the day, and any falcon nest with three chicks in it soon only had two. Training was carried out in secret on our 'Kamikaze' flock of birds of various ages, nine in total, and in no time, the men had a squad of evil dive-bomber 'Stuka' falcon raiders.

After a few months they took the squadron of trained birds, who were now killing and bringing prey to the ground, onto the cliff tops overlooking the Station Commander's house. Just before dusk, the twenty pigeons or so started their evening pirouettes around the CO's house and loft. Taking off our killer's screening hoods, we let them see the juicy meal over their heads, and then with a whistle, threw them up at the prey. It was beautiful to watch. In seconds, they had climbed high and dived with wings fully folded straight into the flock of the fantails. Mac and his men had barbecued pigeon that night, and the CO never found out who had orchestrated his flock's destruction without a shot being heard.

The Islanders themselves became more optimistic about their future, and dozens of additional small businesses sprouted up to supply the service industry. While the budding economy began to thrive and incentives for self-employment became available, a state of good will and well being had begun to rise out of the embers of fear, hate, and distrust that had been prevalent for the past six or seven years.

Local entrepreneurs developed the beaches and put up facilities, bars and restaurants. Indeed, a large number of servicemen invested in local businesses, mainly bar-type enterprises. The many small bars and cafes were clean, cheap and friendly, and stayed open until at least three o'clock in the morning. They were a Mecca of fun for the troops, who, with extra overseas allowances, could afford to partake of the fare in these delightful houses of entertainment.

Houses of ill repute, or brothels, were disguised as cabaret bars. They were cleverly crowded together in one square or street so that any gangs of drunken squaddies were all contained in a set small area.

This had the advantage of making them easily confinable if trouble started, which didn't happen often, and the servicemen could enjoy a rip-roaring hangover breeding night without upsetting people in the "nicer" areas of the towns.

The beauty of the island itself, the gorgeous weather, the fantastic scenery, the extra money to spend on the dozens of pastimes, and the feeling of well being caused by being on top of one's job because of the training time available, made this a glorious time for all. RAF servicemen who spent a standard two years, six month tour on the island were permitted to volunteer for extended tours. These favours, especially for the married men, were in great demand and quickly taken. Very rarely did one hear of any wives complaining about this trend. Mac knew many men who served a five-year tour, and then asked to serve another.

These were good and rewarding times, but they were not to last as fighting broke out on Christmas Eve 1963. The subsequent battles left a lot of men in the unforeseen and unenviable position of having to complete their extended tour alone, without their wives and children, who were forcefully evacuated from their hiring back to the UK during the fighting.

On top of this shock, and because men were confined to camp and families were no longer at their local homes, many suffered looting and burning of their property still in situ in the hiring during the conflict from both sides of the populace. Men lost their savings, stereos, televisions, bedding, as well as furniture that they had purchased themselves, and then had to pay the RAF back for the hiring losses that the RAF had provided. The RAF Nicosia Commanding Officer changed this last rule, but the Air Commodore in charge of RAF Akrotiri forced them to pay. Maybe it was this callous, uncaring action that won him a Knighthood.

When the new outbreak of hostilities began, the Mac's SOG moved straight back to Nicosia and into the bloody battle that was taking place. Some of the heaviest and most merciless actions had yet to take place in Cyprus.

CHAPTER 8

Christmas 1963, The Greek Reprisals

The most undocumented series of atrocities took place in Cyprus, on Christmas Eve of 1963, during a pre-planned assault by the Greek Cypriots against the minority Turkish Cypriots. This was a severe breach of the Zurich agreement, prompting the Turkish military to fly over the island with Jets, closely followed by British Javelin fighters.

A Turkish invasion fleet was putting to sea. Things looked very bad and it was only frantic British Diplomacy and military intervention that prevented the invasion taking place. (The British could not stop a later invasion in 1974; as the Greek Junta had gone too far).

The 1963 attacks took place mainly in Ormorfita, Trachoni, Neapolis and Gonyeli, but the Kyrenia Mountain villages of Templos, Thermia, and Xeros were also badly hit. Nicosia and the old walled city itself were virtually flattened during the fighting.

British Garrison forces were involved from twelve o'clock Christmas Eve, trying to stop the fighting and push the warring factors apart, while using themselves as a buffer zone to prevent further battles with attempts to mediate between the two ethnic groups.

The only garrison forces available for such a major task were the Royal Green Jackets, based at Dekalia Barracks Larnaca, and Number Three and Five Wings of the RAF Regiment, based at Akrotiri and Nicosia respectively. It was noticeable that nearly all the Senior Non-Commissioned Officer Patrol Commanders during this flare up were the same seen on the 'Salt Flat' base in the late fifties, and in other theatres of special operations. Whether by design or accident, the same select few men were always in the thick of the action.

The Royal Green Jackets crowd of 'Freddie' Edwards, 'Bunny' Caldwell, 'Aussie' Read and Dick Brookes, who had just completed a SAS tour, covered the Ormorfita area and encountered very heavy fighting. Whole window frame edges had been blasted out, leaving huge round gaping holes rather than squares, where the intense machine gun fire had tried to hit the men behind the frames through the walls. This seemed to be without the use of support weapons. Bodies littered the streets by the early hours of Christmas Day, and the local dogs were having a feast on the corpses, but the troops were simply too stretched to have time to remove the dead.

The fact that they managed to stop the firing and push the two factors two streets apart from each other is, to this day, one of the most amazing feats of daring bravery and soldiering skills one can imagine, because they were carrying rifles with no bullets. The powers-that-be didn't want anybody shot by the British, so the troops went in the middle of the firefights, hitting people with rifle butts and pickaxe helves to stop the shooting and then dragging the warring individuals away. Not one man was killed on the Green's side, although many were injured. The two street separations between the two sides became known internationally as the 'Green Line'.

This is the story of one field operations team consisting of four men from 27th Special Operations Group, which was commanded by Mark "Mac" Hudson, now a Warrant Officer. Mac's men were Fred Rolph, John Kennedy and Scouse Poynton, all seasoned veterans, acting as an independent tactical headquarters unit with a free license to go anywhere in any district if trouble was announced over the military airwaves. Mac, with the overall boss JR Marshall, controlled 16 four-man field operations teams. Once again, the top floor of the Ledra Palace Hotel became Ground Defence Operations Centre (GDOC).

During the Christmas Eve fighting, numerous stray rounds of ammunition hit the hirings properties mentioned earlier, where the wives and children of the servicemen lived. By Christmas day morning, it was decided to evacuate these unlucky souls to a safe haven inside RAF Nicosia camp. All they could take with them was a small carrier of some sort with a washing kit and change of clothes. All other personal items had to be left in the houses until they could return when the fighting ceased.

[111]

The evacuation meant loading the families and their pets into a service three-ton vehicle and escorting them to RAF Nicosia through some areas that were still battle grounds. The risk of someone being shot was very real, so the RAF lined the vehicle sides and floor with sandbags to offer some sort of protection to the occupants. This action did save lives, because one vehicle, on arrival at Nicosia, had three bullet holes through the metal side, just above the seat. The rounds had stopped in the sandbags. Had someone been sitting on the seats, the bullets would have hit in the middle of the back and through into the victim's stomach; a kill shot. The fact these bullets were all at the same height, and equally spaced suggested that the vehicle occupants were deliberately being targeted, and killing them was the intent, despite large Union Jacks covering the vehicle and being flown as convoy flags, letting everybody know who the occupants were.

The SOG were tasked to get these snipers, whatever side they belonged to, and deal with them in a manner befitting bastards who had tried to shoot British women and children.

Mac checked the vehicle and found all the shots were on the near side. He checked with the driver and detailed his route, and then broke the route down into Greek and Turkish areas. If the shots had been fired from any area, it didn't necessarily mean they had been fired by that nationality. It could mean that one side, for example a Greek, had fired from a Turkish area to lay the blame for the attack on the Turks. Ballistic reports on the bullets found in the sandbags may shed a little more light on the weapon type, penetration power, and range. Mac was guessing that the weapon would be low-muzzle velocity, therefore, a close range gun, but it had to be rapid firing to put three shots in the side of a moving target. At least this little pre-investigation helped the SOG in area selection when they went covert to find the culprits.

Kennedy came up with a course of action that every team member agreed to during a 'think evil session', which was a communal discussion on what action to take in a situation. The results:

"Let's use different team members with WRAF Police Women acting as our wives, and ride on the evacuation vehicles, paying particular attention to suspicious activity in our pre-selected 'possible' areas, from which an attack can take place. If we see a sniper aiming, take him out, from inside the vehicle, no questions asked. If somebody finds a dead man, he will assume the other side has shot him. We stay low profile so as not to bring revenge attacks against our transport." John shared his thoughts.

"Good idea, John. Anyone want to add or cut out?" Mac passed it on.

"This will only work if the mark is at close range. We cannot be seen carrying rifles or SMGs (Submachine Guns) in plain clothes. People would be suspicious." Fred contributed.

"Agreed, but we can hide required weaponry in the back before the truck leaves Nicosia, and if it is a close range, we Browning High Powers are ideal for the job." Mac replied.

"What do you think then, boss?"

"I like it, but we will arrange other teams to be in covert ops at our pre-selected areas for follow up. That would be normal procedure anyway. We've only two days to do this before the evacuations are completed. Let's do it. Move now." Mac decided.

With that, the teams went into top gear and inside of two hours were acting as evacuees, with the backup units in place in the required areas.

Kennedy, because it was his brainchild, was given the previous attack route from Trachonas via Neapolis Bridge; the only single track crossing over a wide, dried-up river bed that separated the Greek and Turkish regular armies. Kennedy's hiring property was only fifty metres from the British Embassy and the residence of a Corporal McAllen, who was conveniently on duty for twenty-four hours, and whose family was to be moved from another friend's hiring on an adjacent street. It would be easy for Kennedy to get back into the city area of conflict from the camp, because RAF Regiment Patrols covered this area and also guarded the British Embassy. These patrols were changing over from RAF Nicosia.

There was also a SOG team at the Embassy, because conferences were taking place there between Greek and Turkish Leaders, as well as

[113]

Duncan Sands, who had flown in without delay from the UK to mediate between the warring factors. Kennedy sat in the back of the truck in civilian clothes, with his back to the driver, and his partner, Corporal Joan Whitely, RAF Police, also in civilian clothes, sat on the opposite side, with her back to the passenger seat. Both were in full view of any potential sniper, but neither of them showed any weaponry. An uneventful round-trip of two hours followed, which was useful, because Kennedy was eyeballing what he had only previously seen on a map.

At the end of the round-trip, the vehicle pulled into the Embassy compound, which was surrounded by a high wall to keep out prying eyes. The changeover took place with Rolph and Corporal Jean Summers also RAF Police, to make the next trip. Kennedy gave Rolph a briefing on his observations, two of which he emphasized: the Regular Greek Army, and the Greek Cypriot Central Police Station were both on the near side of the vehicle, the side hit by bullets.

Why this observation? Memory and experience. Both the Greek Army and Greek Cypriot Police had worked on the side of EOKA against the British and the Turks. They could do it again to discredit the Turks, and take people's minds off the crimes they were committing.

Mac radioed SOG units to pay particular attention to these two establishments, using a scrambler code in case they were picking up the airwaves. Mac also asked the Special Branch to speed up the Ballistic reports on the bullets retrieved from the sandbags.

A second trip went by with no incident, but more eyeball information was gained to pass down the line.

Then, Bingo.

Just when Poynten was taking over from Rolph, the Ballistic Report was wired to Mac's attention at the Embassy.

The ammunition was standard 9mm, fired from three different weapons, indicating a three-man team ambush, because no one man could fire three weapons at a time. The separation line, which is the line where the projectile seals into the cartridge case, had been treated with a graphite grease type chemical to prevent rusting and corrosion in hot and humid climates. Special Branch also confirmed this ammunition was manufactured for NATO forces, and both the Greek and Turkish Governments had received issues of the type. It was possible that the irregular Greek units that were supposed to be doing the fighting had a supply of this type of ammunition, supplied by the Greek regular Army.

Mac asked HQ for increased surveillance again with a top priority, and for HQ to include all the latest high-tech equipment available at that time. Every movement in these establishment's perimeters was to be photographed.

Poynton's round-trip was uneventful, but the increased surveillance paid off that same night. From the Greek Army Camp, bodies of armed men in a mixture of clothing, some civilian, some military, were seen moving from the camp's perimeter into an adjacent street, and then going into three separate two-story houses. From the map, followed up with ground observations, it was seen that these positions overlooked the two streets of single-story Turkish houses, facing the riverbed and the Turkish Army, and had an uninterrupted view of the road upon which the evacuees had traveled.

Surveillance continued all night but the men stayed in the houses. Back at HQ the photographs taken with the then very new night surveillance equipment were developed. They came out hazy and unclear, but they did give a body count of a total of thirty-nine men who had moved into the properties. They also showed a mix of weapons, including rifles, submachine guns, two medium machine guns, and American 45mm pistols. The submachine guns were Schmeiser and fired the standard 9mm round.

The following morning, Kennedy and his partner rode the evacuee vehicle, and as expected, when they passed the suspect street two holes cracked through the side of the vehicle. Instantly, Kennedy yelled 'smoke' into his radio, alerting all OPs he had been fired on and for everyone to look for smoke emitted from a weapon after it had been fired. Seconds later 'have seen' came over the radio, meaning someone had seen the smoke. "RV now" came over the radio, dictating Kennedy and the "have seen" to return to the Embassy immediately, but every other unit stayed in place.

At the Embassy, the rounds were quickly recovered from the vehicle sandbags. A helicopter was called in and sped them away to SB forensic. OP 3 "have seen" positioned the smoke on the map; it was from the end house of the three occupied by the men from the Greek Army camp, spied on the previous night. The British mandate was to disarm irregulars and arrest people committing a crime, but Mac decided to wait for forensic before taking further action.

Information arrived back very quickly this time. The rounds were Standard 9mm, with separation line chemical, and one was fired from the same gun as the previous attack. Solid, irrevocable evidence as to who were the culprits. Action was now needed to clear out the three houses, disarm the occupants, and detain everyone in the end house until it was certain who shot at the evacuees. This would mean test firing any 9mm guns in the house.

Orders were issued, and the RAF Regiment began the house clearing operation. It was cleverly done. The Squadron concerned called in the 14th 20th Hussars to position two of their Ferret armoured cars, one at each end of the street containing the houses. They were to point their Browning Heavy machine guns at the two end houses. All the corresponding properties were surrounded. A four-man squad of the Regiment's paratroopers banged on the door of the end house. No one answered this persistent hammering, so they just knocked the door down and rushed in, hitting everything and everyone in sight. No questions. Payback time.

There were eight men in the house, all were swiftly tied, gagged, and the weapons they were in charge of tied to their backs with the rope around their necks. Pre-observation had shown a field telephone line between the three houses. One prisoner was told to ring the other two houses, explain to the occupants what had happened, and tell them to leave their positions and be disarmed or suffer the same fate. They had fifteen minutes or the Browning Machine Guns would knock the occupied house down brick by brick, with them inside.

It worked. The occupiers came out just when a Greek Regular Army vehicle pulled up outside with a Major in command. He tried to insist the men could not be disarmed, and demanded the release of the eight prisoners. The RAF Regiment told him to fuck off and disarmed the remaining suspects with minimal force. The eight prisoners were then taken to the Special Branch for interrogation.

Mac and his crew were not surprised at the eventual outcome. Ballistic tests uncovered one of the snipers who squealed and named the other three. All the thirty-nine people evicted from the houses were Greek Regular Army posing as irregulars. After this, it was proven that the Greek Regular Army committed the majority of the attacks against the Turks.

This information was made instantly available to Duncan Sands, much to the severe embarrassment of the Greek Government. The Commander of the Greek Regular Army and his Senior Officers were relieved of command. The Greek forces were confined to their barracks and if seen on the streets, without direct permission from the British Sector Commander, they could be disarmed and arrested. Part of the barter used by Sands to end hostilities was the promise to release the sniper prisoners for trial in Greece by the Greeks. For this, he received many concessions the Greeks were previously refusing. In many cases, these included the withdrawal of forces from strategically threatening positions.

Rauf Denktash told Mac that Duncan Sands was, "Like a child with a new toy" when during discussions, he received the information about proven Greek Regular Army involvement in the fighting. He wouldn't let it go, and wouldn't put it down until he had bled the Greek delegation dry. It was a fair outcome from one SOG operation, with many more to come.

The fighting, apart from the odd round being shot was over in four days. This was largely due to the chain of events following Sand's intermediary discussions and agreements. Nevertheless, the armed camps and suspicions remained. The SOG had a lot of work ahead of them to try to sort things out.

[117]

One of the main jobs was to demolish the Greek landline communication system. The system was incredible. Sands had demanded, at SOG request, that the plans of the system be handed over, and a Greek Army Liaison Officer to be attached to SOG to assist when moving into people's property to dismantle lines and anything else that needed to be done.

The system covered the whole of the island. In every street in the Greek sectors there were at least two command post links. Every public building was operating under a ten-line switchboard link that was active in that building. All the lines had been cleverly disguised, some of them underground, but most taped to the normal telephone line routes; this made them almost impossible to spot unless one was deliberately looking for them, and that meant advance information. Intelligence knew the Greeks were planning something, but for when and where was not known. The sheer size of this system meant they must have been working on it clandestinely since the British first picked up the hint of trouble brewing in 1961.

After the SOG and Special Branch had taken the intelligence information they thought they might need out of the system, the dismantling job was given to the Royal Signals and Royal Engineers. A Signal's Warrant Officer, who Mac met about three months later, told him that they had been working on the demolition for a good three weeks when the Danish Army, part of the United Nations Peacekeeping Force, asked them what they were doing. On finding out, they took over the Greek System in their sector and used the two houses per street on the command line as their own, also evicting the Greeks living there.

The Warrant Officer went on to tell Mac that the Danes caused a bit of a sensation when they arrived. It was six o'clock in the morning when the Danes came into their sector to relieve the RAF Regiment, who had worked around the clock and kept the peace for four weeks and four days. The Danes were on bicycles with huge packs on their backs and rifles, plus machine guns at the ready over the handlebars. Apparently, when asked by a curious RAF Regiment Sergeant how far they had come, the Dane nonchalantly replied, "Only Dhekhelia." This was a distance of sixty miles.

When Mac heard this, he made sure each SOG team spent one cross-training day with the Danes, as part of their development. One never knew if one day, somewhere, the British might have to defeat Danish trained terrorists, as had occurred in the Congo years before. The men hated it as all the patrolling was done in full kit on bicycles. The Danish Commander assured Mac that this 'Crazy' image made the locals behave themselves, because they didn't want to fall foul of these madmen on bikes. Mac wasn't sure if he was right, but who knows?

CHAPTER 9

Cigarettes, Vodka, and Turks

Never, ever mention the 'Ice Factory' if you should meet Mark "Mac" Hudson. He'll go ballistic. During this time in Cyprus, ice was a premium commodity. Few people had fridges, other than service married quarters and hiring standard issue. Everywhere one went, one saw iceboxes. Large metal-lined, insulated boxes, in which beer and soft drinks could be kept cool and food chilled while the ice slowly melted. These boxes came in a variety of sizes. Some supplied to the camp bars and cafes were the size of a chest freezer, supplied by Coca-Cola.

This ice was delivered on a daily basis in four feet long by one-foot square blocks. During the fighting, the ice factory was taken over by a contingent of Turkish irregulars, giving them control of all the ice for the Nicosia district. They also gained the large stock of butchered meat, rows and rows of lambs and goats, wrapped in hessian and housed in the cold-store facility in the factory. This stranglehold on the ice became a bit of a pain to the British, because no ice meant warm beer at the camp when off duty. A troublemaker can do a lot of things to a British soldier, but take away his cold beer and he can become pretty angry.

JR sent for Mac. "Do you think you could nip down to the ice factory, Mac? The Turks down there are behaving rather naughtily. The Green Jackets have asked them to leave, but they opened fire with shotguns in reply. You know, most of the Mukhtars. I'm sure they'll listen to you, don't you think?"

I haven't got much bloody choice whether they do or not, thought Mac.

However, he replied, "Okay, Boss."

"Poynten, mount 'em up. We're going Turk bashing for a change."

[120]

"Oh, goody, goody. Save some for me," was Scouse's sarcastic reply.

Approaching the factory-loading yard, Mac spotted a young Green Jacket lieutenant, introduced himself, and received a briefing on the state of play so far. The Turks, frightened of being deprived of their meat and ice supply, had taken over the buildings in the early hours of Christmas morning. Regrettably, the factory staff, consisting of the duty engineer, stock control foreman loading bay supervisor, plus three labourers, all Greeks, were presumed killed.

The Turks were refusing to answer any questions about the alleged deaths. Whichever of the Turkish leaders had thought this one up had obviously not thought it out very well. The Turks were completely surrounded by hostile Greeks; they couldn't deliver their stolen produce to any of their enclaves or villages, even if they had transport. On top of that, the British troops were waiting to arrest them.

Their obvious dilemma gave Mac his bartering points. Tongue-in-cheek, he approached the building's main entrance with Kennedy, who was the most apt Turkish linguist. His hands in the air and flying a Union Jack as an indication to the Turks that he wanted to negotiate. If the Turks opened fire now, there was no way out. The only thing to do was put on a brave face.

Mac said as much to Kennedy out of the corner of his mouth.

"John, I think they will fire over our heads to make us shit ourselves, all of them know they're going nowhere fast and will want to talk. If they fire, just stand still and turn and talk to me. Call me a twat or something, and then start laughing. Okay?"

"Right Boss. I'll never have trouble calling you a twat with some of the scrapes you manage to conjure up for me."

"They fired one shot at the Green Jackets, according to that young Lieutenant, and missed. That must have been deliberate. You can't miss with a shotgun at thirty metres."

When they arrived at the side of the loading bay, a shot was fired and instantly a voice shouted from a skylight in the roof. "Come no further. State your business."

"We have come to arrange transport and a military escort for you to help you get food and ice to your villages. It's doing no good where it is. Let us in. We need to talk and arrange things to all our satisfaction. Let us in. We are unarmed. I am a personal friend of Rauf Denktash, your senior leader." Mac was flying this problem with the seat of his pants.

"Proceed to the side of the building on your right. We'll open the side door. Have you brought any cigarettes?"

"No, sorry. But I can arrange you some. How many do you need?" Mac asked the voice.

"Fifty Packets of Camel."

Mac radioed on his scrambler to Rolph at the Land Rover to fetch the cigarettes by confiscating them from the nearest shop, signing an IOU on behalf of Rauf Denktash.

"Fuck buying their cigs for them", Mac thought. They are causing enough trouble as it is.

Also, Mac was to inform HQ that there was an estimated fifty men in the building, which equated to one packet of cigarettes per man.

"The cigarettes are coming. I'll enter when I have them." Mac wanted their minds occupied by collecting and handing out the booty when he walked through that door, into a 'God knows what' situation with this bunch of crazy bastards inside the building.

Twenty minutes later, armed with the cigarettes and a thoughtfully provided twelve boxes of matches, Mac shouted, "I'm coming in."

He made his way down to the side door. It was wide open. Through the door was a reception type area, with large plastic strips acting as another door into what Mac assumed was the factory. Two men armed with shotguns, and one also sporting a revolver in his belt, came through the plastic screen and signaled with their weapons for Mac and John to go through, one of the men leading the way and the other taking up position behind. A tremendous shrill of voices and screams greeted them when they appeared in the hall. Just like Mac had hoped, the cigarettes were snatched from him and thrown about to the smokers who all immediately lit up and started smoking with

[122]

long drawn out breaths of obvious relief. That was just the effect for which Mac had hoped. Now they should be nice to him.

It didn't work. Once the smell of Turkish Camel tobacco was stinking the place up, the leaders turned their attention to Mac and John. They were ordered to strip naked. Mac's protesting of this caused John to receive a thump on the back of the head with a rifle butt, and then a tremendous bang in the kidneys with the same weapon when he hit the floor. Then, two men started laying in with their boots. Very quickly, Mac leapt into the fray and received blows from every direction.

Mac was aware that approximately three of his assailants were lying on the floor, out of the game, before another flurry of blows with boots put him to sleep. Slowly, he started to come back to the present and realised he was bound at the wrists from behind and completely naked. A glance around through his now swollen eyes and he saw John was in the same restricted position. Three Turks sat opposite him, and he was very surprised to see that one was a young woman.

The room was cold, freezing in temperature. All men know what happens if they swim in cold water. The balls seem to retreat back into the body, and the cold shrinks the cock into the size of a babies thumb. Classical interrogation technique, with hands behind the back and unable to hide the shameful excuse for manhood, the embarrassment is complete. A young woman looking at you will finish off any pride one has left.

"You and your friend are dim-witted to try to fight us. What did you expect to gain from coming to talk to us here?" The oldest looking was doing the talking so Mac calculated he must be the overall leader and, much to his disappointment, he did not know the man.

"We are trying to end this stalemate, for all people concerned. Everybody needs meat in the city. The only people with fresh meat are the mountain villages, and they are killing their livestock. It's wintertime, with insufficient sun to dry the meat and make biltong so, without ice, it will rot." Mac managed to explain through his swollen and cut lip.

Mac continued, "We also have a mandate signed by all leaders, including your Rauf Denktash. They have agreed that we, the British, should stabilise the situation to the benefit of all sides... disarm both the Greek and Turkish elements, hand over to the respective sides anyone we prove or find committing an offence against the law of the land, which is the same for both Greek and Turks." Mac paused here to let the words linger so they would be sure to understand him. Then he continued, "Also, it is our duty to ensure no one, anywhere, is short of food, water, or medical aid."

Mac paused one more time, hoping that his words meant something to the man, before he finally asked, "By what authority do you use or assume this abstract power against the wishes of your own leaders?"

John was having a terrible job translating all this through his badly split lips. It was just at this point, with his faculties slowly returning, that Mac noticed, over the men's shoulders in the distance, in line with all the bodies of lambs hanging up, seven human bodies with meat hooks through the back of their necks, obviously the Greek staff-plus one unknown. Now Mac knew these people would not give in. Different tactics needed to be thought up, and quickly, before he and John joined the meat hook dance.

Mac quickly added, "We are in sympathy with the Turks. They helped us during the EOKA troubles, and are subject to planned genocide by the Greeks. We want to help. This is why our HQ has sent us to talk instead of the large regular Army outside. We can transport you away from this with food and ice for your villages. Let us free and let's talk and organise."

Mac would be happy just to get John and himself out of the building alive at this point. Any arrests or retribution to these Turks would have to come later. Escape was the priority.

To his amazement, Mac's little speech worked. A young Turk, about seventeen years of age, came out of the shadows and started shouting and gesticulating, continually pointing at Mac.

"You lucky bastard" stuttered Kennedy. "This youth remembers you helping his village and delivering food, water, and oil during the

[124]

fighting in 1958. He's told old Attaturk that you are a friend of his father. He calls you burnt face - your birthmark I think."

"Thank you, Lord. I thought you'd deserted me," was Mac's only reply.

They were cut free and given back their clothes; two young women washed and treated all the cuts and bruises with liberal quantities of iodine. It was a major test of endurance not to scream. Eventually, they all sat down and everybody was fortified with large tin mugs full to the brim with vodka. These mugs were so large that four mugs filled, emptied one full bottle of vodka. This vodka was sent from Heaven for John and Mac. Their pain began to melt away, the young women started to look beautiful and desirable, the balls came back into this world and their cocks grew big enough for them to hold and piss out of. Another mug of vodka and they were all mates and long lost brothers; with Mac's four-man Army going to lead them all through the Greeks and back to their mountain fortresses, and God help any Greek who tried to stop them!

At the end of two more mugs of vodka, Mac suggested they all leave for a local bar under his protection, to drink some ouzo and Keo beer, because he felt thirsty with all that Vodka. They all agreed. Imagine the look on young Green Jacket's faces when they carried out their duties, surrounding the buildings when this motley crew of dirty drunken apparitions staggered out of the place, led by two British blood covered pied pipers.

The young Green Jacket Lieutenant started to approach, but Mac shouted, "Fuck off, unless you want to start a riot and shed some blood, count how many of us there are and order one Keo beer each from the nearest bar. Pronto, while we are in the mood."

Up until this time, Mac had no idea how many men were in the building. This was as good a way as any to discover it. When Mac passed Rolph he muttered under his breath, "Walk with me Freddie...tell the boss we've managed to clear the place, but I'm not sure, there may still be some inside. Seven bodies are hanging up in there. Watch the skylights for snipers. Enter by the side door. It's still open. Tell the boss to contact Denktash, and his senior police officer.

Arrests have to be made, and I'm not making them. It's their baby now. John and I are in the local bar drinking. Warn everybody, no arrests until we leave, or we may not see daylight again. Got it?"

"Got it. Done."

"And tell the boss, he owes me for this one."

"Right." he nodded.

"Come on then, my merry men, let's go and have a party and cement our foreign relations, you horrible Turkish bastards. First beers on the British, the rest are out of your limited Turkish pockets. I'm really going to enjoy them."

Mac and John had a strong advantage over the Turks on the drinking stage. The Turks were nearly all pissed on vodka when they left the factory. Now they were drinking in a bar that had been forced to open by the Green Jackets and therefore were mixing their drinks. In other words, the Turks continued drinking, but the British men merely appeared to be drinking. Mac left most of the talking to John, and concentrated on pretending to be drunker than he really was, but eyeballing the Turks so as to remember faces from mug shots. Mac was also determining which ones seemed to have a leadership role, or, if not a leader, a dominating character. Thirty-two people occupied the room. When he counted, he noticed how many were smoking, approximately twenty-five. The leader had ordered two packets per man.

You greedy son of a bitch, thought Mac.

After about one hour, one RAF three-ton RL truck pulled up with an RAF Regiment Land Rover escort. A sergeant from the escort shouted Mac's name, so he excused himself and tried to go outside. However, the Turks insisted he had a two-man bodyguard to go with him, so it still wasn't safe to try any new tactics yet. They were still suspicious, even though they were well out of their minds with drink by now.

Slowly... slowly... thought Mac, the time will come when it is right to leave their company and let the police handle what's left.

The sergeant asked for instructions, so Mac called out to the leader and said the vehicle was there to load food from the factory to be sent to their villages.

"Have you any men left in the factory?" Mac asked.

"No, they are all here." Was the reply.

One question answered, thought Mac.

"How many villages do you need food for?"

"Templos, Thermia, Xeros, and Gonyeli." Now I know where you come from, mused Mac.

"Send six of your sober men to load food on the truck now." The psychological effect of taking orders would unbalance the leader and leave him open to more suggestions, or so Mac assumed.

"Right. Sergeant, take these Turks and let them load the vehicle with whatever food they want out of the factory, food only, no machinery or anything else, just food. If they try anything, restrain with minimum force. You shouldn't need the Green Jackets, but use them if necessary. If you do have to restrain them, leave the RL at the factory, tell my staff at the SOG Land Rover in the yard near the loading bay. He'll scramble me, and we'll have to get out of here in a bloody hurry. Brief the Green Jacket Lieutenant before you go in. Got it?"

"Got it, Sir. No problem."

Everything went like clockwork; the Turkish leading party behaved and loaded meat, cheese and butter in amounts ordered by the leader. Once loaded, the Green Jackets and RAF Regiment provided escorts to take the food and men to their respective villages. Various Turkish leaders representing their own villages called for a rather long, drawn-out series of toasts, made with a mixture of Ouzo and vodka. They left, all wanting to shake hands with Mac and John, and offering invites as a guest of honour to their particular villages, something Mac was to call on many times before the troubles were over.

The final results of this fiasco did not come to light for at least six months. Even then, it was only when the United Nations became well established and in control of the mountain villages, as well as the major cities and towns. It was proven that three Turks committed the

[127]

murders at the ice factory; all three came from Gunyeli, in the Kyrenia Mountains. The unknown body, which was also from Gunyeli, was a Turk who protested too strongly against the killings of the Greeks and was himself shot for his trouble. All the other offences were dropped or forgotten, including the beating up of Mac and John.

In order to prevent riots, strikes, and further bloodshed, it was decided not to put the men on trial in Cyprus but to send them for trial in Turkey. The Greeks played up hell about this decision, thinking that the men would receive preferential treatment, and therefore should be tried in Greece. Obviously, the Turks would not agree to this, saying in the minds of the Greeks the men were already guilty before trial.

This state of affairs went back and forth until the United Nations finally put their foot down and ordered the men should be tried in Canada. The Canadians had a very strong contingent as part of the United Nations Force, and covered an area of North Nicosia, plus a number of both Greek and Turkish villages in the Kyrenias. These villages were mixed before the fighting, and now the minorities in a village had fled to a village where their nationality was in a majority, or they had been killed. Most of the Kyrenia Mountain villages had become Turkish and the Troodos Mountain villages were now all Greek. They effectively partitioned themselves.

CHAPTER 10

Guiding the United Nations

One operation for the SOG was to act as guides and interpreters for the United Nations Forces while they tried to establish their authority around the island. This seemingly easy task brought hours of hilarity to the battle-hardened veterans, because they were trying to educate a mostly green, young, and inexperienced force. Mac had the task of leading the Canadian Van Doos Regiment (French Canadians) into by this time Turkish-held Kyrenia villages.

The Canadians patrolled in Panhard armoured cars. This was a very light and fast, well-armoured, heavy-gunned vehicle. Each vehicle had United Nation's flags over the front and rear, flying from at least four radio masts and on poles sticking out of the turrets. Mac assumed that this display of 'Look who we are' indicated that the Canadians thought the Turks were as blind as bloody bats. Before the patrol left, Mac gave a detailed briefing, and because this was the Canadian troop's first time in the mountains, he briefed the whole patrol, not just the officers. This way, if anyone had a problem, became separated, or anything else that may happen, every single man knew what to expect and what to do.

"The aim of this patrol is for you to learn your future patrol area. The sector for your activity, gentlemen, will be the Kyrenia Mountain Region. Your specific task today is to familiarise yourselves with village patrol operations. Secondly, you should meet anyone of importance in your area, such as the Mukhdars, who are the village headmen. You will remove any roadblocks. This shouldn't be necessary, because we moved them all weeks ago, but the Turks, knowing you are taking over from the British, may test your resolve and try to cause you trouble. Again, that shouldn't bother you. That's why I'm here. I know every man jack of them in every village and they all owe me one.

"You will be fired on at a village called Templos. When you approach the village, which is situated on top of a large rock pinnacle overlooking the whole valley road, you will come to an S shaped bend. I will stand up in my Land Rover and give you a raised hand signal when we arrive at this bend. This signal is not just for your benefit; it is also a signal to the Turks that we are friendly. This is where they will start firing. They fire, because the Greeks have raided them twice with Union Jacks flying on their vehicles. I signal and they will fire over our heads. If we were Greeks, we'd run.

"I will be in radio communication with your command vehicle. The command vehicle will relay to the rest. You will carry equipment and food for yourselves to last twenty-four hours. Medical supplies and medical corpsman are necessary for you, and also to help villages in need. Extra food, water, and paraffin should be carried for the villages. This is a good hearts and mind policy, gentleman. It works. Weapons and ammunition are to conform to your United Nations Instructions, as are your orders for engagement.

"I am in overall command and control, unless we take casualties from an engagement against us. At that time, command goes to your patrol commander. At the S bend, when the Turks open fire, keep going into the village and park in front of the village church. At that time, the Officers should join me at my vehicle, and then will be introduced to the village headman, Mustafa Heckmen. Are there any questions?"

No one spoke.

"Last chance. By your silence, I assume you understand my orders perfectly and are completely sure what to do. Am I correct?"

Nothing was said.

Mac was quite happy with their reactions. The questions didn't matter.

"Good. Synchronise watches at 9 a.m. on my mark. 5...4...3...2...1... mark. Mount up, and good luck."

Mac's Land Rover, open-topped, no windscreen, and sporting a triangular barbed wiring stake welded to the front, pulled out of the

Van Doos HQ first. The wiring stake was in place to cut any neck snapping wires that may be stretched across the road.

At exactly 09.15, he scrambled SOG HQ his signal identity S1, which meant he was moving. As it turned out, he was heading for what was to be one of his greatest laughs and most often told story of the whole encounter.

The Van Doos, so far unproven in the internal security duties in Cyprus, had managed to earn themselves a dubious reputation as bar brawlers. A few stories about their easy attitude to using knives in a bar fight had also circulated. SOG were not impressed with these reports, but neither did they care. If the unit could do its job on the ground without starting international incidents, that's all that mattered. Nicosia was still unsettled. Shots could still be heard coming from outlying districts at night. The United Nation's road blocks manned by one Greek and one Turkish policeman each were in profusion everywhere one went.

As the patrol left the outskirts of Nicosia and entered the winding road heading up into the southern foothills of the Kyrenia range, John felt something was different in the countryside and surroundings. He pondered, but he couldn't put his finger on it.

He enquired of Mac, "Can you see anything different in the scenery today, Boss?"

"Why? What do you think is different?" Mac asked.

"I don't know. Something is niggling at me, and I can't see what."

"Keep looking. You never know. It might be the amusing bastards setting something up for our flag flying friends behind us. You drive when we debuss at The Seven Sisters mountain peaks and I'll be able to concentrate and have a better look."

"Okay. There's definitely something wrong, though."

Mac knew from experience to never to take anything John said about work lightly. Too many times in the past, his intuition had been proven correct. Uncannily correct, in fact.

"John, I wouldn't put it past our friends to try and fuck these new troops up, you know? It doesn't matter what nationality they are.

[131]

They'll try to better them in any way they can. Don't you think?" Mac asked him.

"I agree. Mainly to be able to dictate how much food and other assistance they can swindle out of them. Look what the bastards tried on with us. In a way, I bet they're looking forward to today and are glad to be seeing the back of us. Do they know we're coming along with the new boys?" John queried.

"You can bet the Tom Toms have been going like the clappers since we drove into the Van Doos HQ. The Turks still have a very effective intelligence network. The Duncan Sands employment plan for the British military bases ensured that, with 25% of the local workforce we employ having to be Turkish." Mac answered.

He continued, "Don't you worry, mate. They know nearly every move we make by road, and what they don't know; it's not hard for them to make an educated guess. The only secure way for us to move and cause surprise is by chopper from the Ledra Palace roof. We are important babies don't forget. If they can tab us, they have a shrewd idea of events."

"You're right." John agreed, "Though quite honestly, I don't mind the Turks knowing. It's the Greeks sneaking about that pisses me off. They must gain more information about us because we have to employ 75% of our workforce from the Greeks."

"Let's face it, we need to employ the WOGs (Worthy Oriental Gentlemen) to do all the construction work and so on. Our REME and Engineers have far too much on their shoulders dealing with the soldiering side of things, such as bomb disposal. They haven't the time to be building barrack blocks and toilets. Just look at the amount of time the Greek telephone system took to destroy. Imagine the hellish job that would have been, if the bastards had booby-trapped everything."

Preoccupied with conversation or not, Mac still noticed the Panhards were too close together and starting to push up his back end. "S1 for V2, three vehicle lengths between vehicles, now! Out." The vehicles instantly moved apart.

"That was short and sweet, Boss."

"Yes. I briefed the patrol commander on our signals procedures. He was a bit surprised it wasn't the accepted international NATO. I made him see that small units don't need all this 'Wilko' (I understand and will comply) and 'Over' shit, unless we are on a command net with other units involved. He's also very aware that our minimum use of radio gives people who are in the shit a chance to come in straight away with 'Contact' instead of having to wait for others to stop rabbiting."

When he finished speaking and started to round one of the switch back bends on the upward climb, a seemingly unmanned roadblock confronted them. The obstruction was at least five feet high and up against the limestone hill face on one side and a very steep drop into the valley on the other.

Impassable.

"STOP! Now, prepare ambush, out."

'Prepare ambush' ensured the Panard crews closed hatches in case of being fired on from an enemy above them on a hillside. Mac could have used a 'Contact' signal and would have done, had he been with a SOG team. That would have meant an immediate, direct assault up the hill to eliminate any target, attack being the best form of defence in these situations. Had he used "Contact" now he may have panicked the Van Doos. Mac gave a fire order, ensuring the Panhard weapons were trained up the hillside, and then called the patrol commander forwards to accompany John and himself to the roadblock.

It was an unusual structure, made out of sacks that the locals collected and stored Carobs in. They were filled with rocks.

"Rocks, John. Rocks and carobs- That's it! That's what's wrong with the bloody scenery. They've been collecting the rocks out of the crop fields, and since when have you ever seen grass growing, or anything else for that matter, underneath a carob tree?"

The roadblock was the trigger that set the Mac's mind onto the changes in the countryside. Like in all the Mediterranean countries, the topsoil over the mainly limestone rock is very shallow. Every year, when farmers plough a field, large rocks come to the surface and are

[133]

normally collected and placed as a boundary wall for that field. Most of the smaller stones are left in the field since the crops grow around them without any problems. Sewing of seeds was still carried out by hand on over 90% of the island because of the small awkward shaped fields, and their location on hillsides and terraces making them inaccessible to tractors and other large agricultural machinery. Ploughing was done by powerful, hand-held rotavators, the only machines for the job, and harvesting wheat and other grain crops was still cut by sickle and scythe.

They walked about fifty metres across the side of the hill to look at a Carob tree with long twitch grass beneath it, dead grass resembling dried hay that was often used as stock feed in the winter. Nothing can grow beneath a Carob tree. Nature has provided the tree with a marvelous defence mechanism against other plants trying to use its water, which, in hotter climates where the tree grows is always in short supply. While the fruit ripens from green to brown to black, a very strong acetic acid drips onto the ground under the tree and prevents any other plant growth.

"I thought so. They're preparing for a bloody invasion." Mac didn't seem surprised.

The base of the tree had been turned into a weapon sangar, and it was facing toward the Greeks in the South. A five-foot deep trench had been excavated. The earth from this hole was evenly spread around the base of the tree. Rocks from the trench had been used to provide a one-foot high rampart on three sides of the hole. Two and three-foot long clumps of twitch grass weave were interwoven between stones to hide the position. The carob tree itself gave protection against aerial observation.

"Leave one man with each weapon on the vehicles. Tell them to cover us from fire from the high ground above us and fetch the rest of the patrol up here now. If other traffic comes up the road, turn them back, but make a note of their license plates. We may need to know that information later."

The Patrol Commander complied. Within ten minutes, the eight men and patrol commander were ready for Mac's briefing.

[134]

"We seemed to have found something of great importance, gentlemen, and if I'm right, with far reaching implications. Quite a feather in your cap for being on your first patrol."

Butter the bastards up, thought Mac. I want some hard work now, and it's all on shank's pony.

"I need you to spread out approximately fifty metres between each man and walk across the south facing slope, and make notes for us to later draw into a location map of every weapon position, like this one, that you find. After one hour, climb higher up the hill and spread out again. Do the same on the way back here. Are there any questions?" Mac paused and looked around at their faces. They appeared very keen.

"No questions? Good. Continue on your patrol commander's orders."

No one interfered with their labours, and three hours later, they all leaned over the Land Rover bonnet to collate and orientate the information to a map. After a short while, it was clear they had uncovered a master defence, and a launch pad for offence, tactical, and a strategic plan - a plan far too elaborate to be masterminded by a small Turkish Irregular force.

A plan for the invasion of Cyprus by the Turkish combined forces.

"We will have to have patrols cover a far greater area. It wouldn't surprise me if this preparation doesn't stretch the whole of the 1958 proposed 'Partition Line' the Turks were so keen on. Any other observations?"

"Yes, Sir. Just as we stopped and started to go higher for the return, we found what seemed to be a very large area, completely cleared of rocks and bushes. It's as if they were building a football pitch, but it couldn't be, because it's on the forward slope of the hill, and you could fit ten football pitches in it. The clearing was square as well, not oblong. At the bottom end of the square were the heaps of rocks that had obviously been cleaned off the square, the funny thing was that they seemed to be in heaps by their size, you know, all the large ones together, then medium, then small. Does it mean anything?"

[135]

"We'll go back, all of us, and see. Maybe measure it out. John, go to the Rover and scramble HQ. Fly me a chopper over and photograph it in half an hour. If not available, then, soonest. Clear?"

"Clear, Boss."

"Patrol commander, ten minutes, feed, water, piss, shit, fart, move out. Okay?"

"Okay."

Ten minutes later, they moved out. Mac noticed that the Patrol Commander had changed over his gun crews during the short break, obviously to reduce their boredom and rest others, so he seemed to be thinking.

Give him a little red star in my book, Mac chuckled at his own schoolboy thoughts.

One hour later, they had arrived at the spot.

"One man on each corner please, PC."

"Wilko."

Quickly the men ran out to the four corners. When one saw it marked out like this it was huge. It couldn't be helicopter-landing pads, the hill slope was too great, nor a vehicle park, unless they intended to build access roads.

Parachute drop zone? No, too small.

Helicopter borne resupply depot? Could be, but surely not in full view of the Greeks.

Casualty helicopter evacuation area? A possibility, but again, in full view of Greeks and in range of gunfire it was unlikely.

John came up with the idea, as usual.

"Why have they put the stones of different sizes in separate heaps? That has to give us some idea. They want to use them to build something, or paint different colours to mark the boundary or some other crazy idea...

Wait a minute! Maybe not such a crazy idea after all. Centuries ago in the Middle Ages they cut big pictures of horses and giants and things in the chalk of the Downs. Maybe these people are going to make a picture or write something for the Greeks to see. Why else would it be in such a prominent place?"

[136]

Another one of John's uncanny predictions, as was proven later when the Turkish Red Crescent Flag was recreated in stone in the very same clearing for all the Greeks, right up to and on top of the Troodos Mountains, to see. The flag is still there today.

Mac's requested helicopter photographs showed the faint outline of the crescent and star and a revisit found them marked out in very small brownstones, hardly visible at ground level. It was quite obvious by these revelations that the Turks knew a major fight was brewing, initiating preparation for a Turkish invasion to protect their people. They did not know when the fight would happen, but they must have worked clandestinely for years on their defences.

Of course, the British kept all this information close to the chest. Why rock the boat? On British advice, remember a lot of the United Nations soldiers on the ground in Cyprus were British. The United Nations HQ kept the information under wraps also.

Of course, the Canadian Van Doos were recognized for their tremendous initiative and observational awareness, but ordered not to disclose any of this information to anyone. Within one week of the patrol completion, the news spread around the island that they had found rockets trained on the Greek hospital: nuclear, biological and chemical weapons. Rumours spread wildly - trained man-eating tigers that could tell the difference between Greek and Turk and God knows what other shit was thrown about.

After the groundwork discoveries, Mac had the patrol dismantle the roadblock, throwing the bags of stones over the cliff into the valley below, and then continued the journey. At the Seven Sisters Peaks, which is now a favourite tourist attraction, the whole panoramic view and the villages in the patrol sector were shown and map oriented to the Patrol Commander. Down the twisting switch back roads of the Kyrenia pass, the Panhards were swaying about a lot, giving the soldiers a rough ride and creating early fatigue amongst them, bordering on travel sickness.

Mac sent the Patrol Commander up and down again to find the speed that gave the troops the best ride, without reducing their patrol efficiency by travel fatigue. It was important to do this now, while the

[137]

climate was cool, because in another three to four weeks there would be a sharp increase in temperature that would make the going even harder for the men. Passing through Xeros, Mac debussed the whole patrol, except the vehicle guards, and led them down a path that lead to a large outcrop of rock overlooking the sea.

From this vantage point, he indicated certain areas of the coastline where the small Turkish smuggler boats pulled in after their forty-mile journey from mainland Turkey. Guns and explosives were the main cargo, and the patrol had the job of stopping this trade. What came over, as food and fuel, meant that discretion was needed. There was no sense in supplying food to the villages, and then stop them fetching their own.

The sea had a one-mile wide slick of copper silt stretching down the coastline as far as the eye could see. This residue flooded out of the copper bearing hills in the winter rains, killing all inshore fish, and putting an end to all the inshore fishing for the winter months. Consequently, the local fishermen turned to smuggling to earn some cash. A boat travelling through this silt became copper in colour when in contact with the water, so it was easy to pick out who had been out to sea by checking the name on the boat registration number. The owner couldn't say he'd been fishing. If there had been any fish in the copper silt, it would be contaminated and banned from sale. Mac pointed all this out to the PC because he had to, it was his job, but he and the rest of SOG never bothered these local Turks doing what they had been doing since the days of the Ottoman Empire.

Continuing the patrol meant a courtesy visit to Xeros and an introduction to the village Mukhdar, who was famous for his tremendous sense of humour. He knew Mac would have told the PC about the copper slick and smuggling. When the Mukhdar, Mac, John, and the PC sat down in the village square for the traditional Turkish coffee, which was just a tiny cup of ground sweet black coffee and a glass of water, he offered the PC grilled fish, saying it had been caught by rod and line from the cliff top. It was, therefore, obvious that the culinary delight had been fished out of the contaminated copper silt.

The poor man turned a whitish shade of puke green, and looked at Mac with a helpless expression.

"What do I do, Sir?"

"You have to be polite and eat it if you're ever going to have these people respect you." Mac replied matter-of-factly.

"But the fish is poisoned..."

"I know that. You know that. They know that. They even know that you and I know that. It's just a test of courage."

With that statement, Mac and John took a large fork full of fish, spread it on a chunk of Turkish loaf, and ate it with relish.

"Come on PC, eat up. When we leave, we'll pull in somewhere and stick our fingers down our throats before the poison manages to circulate and establish itself in our systems."

Gingerly and with trepidation our poor PC started to eat the fish. It looked good. It smelt good. It was good. It was fresh from the smuggler boats just back from Turkey. Our humorous head man was winking at Mac, while the luckless PC nibbled gingerly at his food. What a prankster and piss-taker the Mukhdar was. Mac liked him. After one hour, the customary staying time, Mac made his farewells, and mounted everybody up to continue the patrol. John said a strong farewell speech to the Mukhdar on his and Mac's behalf and asked him to cooperate with the United Nations for the good of his village. The Mukhdar agreed to comply with this request and on that encouraging end of the visit, they moved out for the next destination: Templos village, Mustafa Heckman, and the test of fire. A steady drive followed with Mac advising the PC by radio if they passed anything he should know about.

The approach to Templos was now in sight. Mac radioed, "S bend coming up. Out."

Near the first bend, he stood up and punched his right arm in the air three times. When he finished this manoeuvre, the Land Rover turned through the first bend. The Panhards were now out of sight. True to form, the Turks in the village above opened fire, but today, they did so with a difference. Normally, they fired a few rounds from shotguns. Today, it was long, sustained bursts of automatic fire from a

Bren gun. Mac knew they kept one hidden in the village, but had closed his eyes to the knowledge.

This new firepower demonstration was an obvious display of intimidation toward their new protectors and law enforcers. When Mac's Rover pulled into the village square, they were greeted with a hilarious sight. The village occupants were falling about all over the place, clutching at each other, bent over, holding their stomachs, tears streaming from their eyes, faces red and contorted from the exertion caused by the screaming fits of maniacal laughter in which they were indulged. Mustafa Heckman walked, or rather staggered, toward the Land Rover, arms outstretched in welcome with tears streaming down his face. Mustafa had always had a strong respect and affection for Mac and John ever since the Ice factory saga.

"Welcome my friends. Welcome to our village, but what have you brought me today? Eh! I know. Don't tell me. You have brought me the chickens. Eh?"

With that, he strutted around with his hands on his chest flapping his elbows and clucking in a fairly good demonstration of a chicken.

"But what have you done with my chickens, my friends?" He continued.

More strutting and clucking.

"I know. You make them lay down in trench to rest. Yes? Come, I show you your chickens."

With that, he took hold of their arms and walked them to the village embankment that overlooked the valley. They couldn't believe their eyes. The Panhards were abandoned in the middle of the track. No men in the turrets at the weapon posts, all hatches open. Not a sign of a soldier.

Instead, from inside the irrigation ditch at the side of the track, waving backward and forwards, and side-to-side, were six United Nations flags. It just was not conceivable after the briefing and the detailed information they had received about coming under fire, at this village in particular, and that the fire would be over their heads as a warning in case of a Greek attack. How and why did they go to ground? On top of this, if you are under fire, one doesn't leave an

[140]

armour plated car and the protection it affords against small arms fire for a ditch. Armoured car tactics state that if one comes under fire, go straight for the aggressor.

Mustafa, still laughing his head off, offered Mac and John a ringside table for the event, and signaled for a bottle of brandy and a Turkish Mesas food tray laden with small plates of varied dishes to be brought to the table.

"A toast to my good soldier friends." Mustafa raised his glass full of brandy. "Bottoms up, as you say in English."

With that, the drinks went down in one gulp, and then were instantly refilled. "Cheers to the chickens below."

Mustafa was having fun, but Mac could not bring himself to share this toast without adding his disrespect to the Van Doos, so instead made an excuse.

"Maybe they have something in their rules of engagement you and I don't know about Mustafa. I'll go and talk to them now."

"No! If they do this in trouble, how do they protect us, eh? No. I think maybe we protect them, eh? No. You tell United Nations you and your men stay in the mountains. You good soldiers. You good men. We like. We respect. No. You stay. Tell chickens go home. We no want chickens. What good chicken to my people, eh?"

Have we got a bloody problem to sort out now, mused Mac.

"Mustafa, my dear friend, you cannot think or talk like this until you understand their position. We cannot stay in the mountains. The United Nations soldiers have relieved us. They are new to this business, and we have been at the game many years. You must speak with them and learn to understand each other and work together for the good of your village. I'll go to fetch their leader now. You must agree. Okay?"

"I agree, but no like."

"Good. John, see to it that Mustafa's men unload the compo rations off the trailer before the Van Doos get here. What the eyes don't see and all that."

With that, Mac left to walk down the hill to see his luckless friends. Mac was actually standing on the rim of the irrigation ditch before

[141]

anybody noticed he was there. Then, as if by some communal signal, everyone looked up, saw him, and forced out sickly grins. The PC climbed out the ditch to stand near Mac.

"Patrol Commander, walk with me." Mac wanted to move him outside the earshot of his men before he let fly any verbal barrage. He was having difficulty controlling himself.

"Well, tell me why you left the cars and dived into a ditch. Tell me if you understood my briefing. Were you aware that the Turks would open fire over your heads at the start of the S bend? Is there something in your 'Rules of Engagement' that means you couldn't obey my instructions? If there is, why didn't you say so at the briefing? Is it normal procedure for the Van Doos to vacate their armoured cars when under small arms fire? Are you trying to take the piss?" Mac spat out in rapid fire succession.

Barely taking the time to draw a breath, he continued, "Don't speak now. Think of some fucking good answers to my questions and give them to me when we arrive back at base. I don't wish to go ballistic or threaten you. You still have work to do yet. Carry on as per my briefing until you park in the village square and think how you are going to explain your actions to the headman and impress him with your professionalism at the same time. Good luck. Continue as ordered. Do you understand?"

"Yes, Sir." the PC mumbled, obviously aware of his mistakes.

"Carry on." Mac breathed deeply, regaining his composure, and then remembered to jolt the PC's action a little.

"As you move, tell your men to shape up. The Turks aren't very impressed with your performance so far. Savvy?"

"Yes, Sir. I savvy."

"Move out. Now!" Mac started walking back. Somehow, he didn't want to be in the village when the PC arrived and started talking to Mustafa, and he knew he'd receive a full report with all the gory details from John.

----

[142]

On his arrival back at the village, Mac made straight for John.

"What was Mustafa's reaction when they met?"

"He ran around flapping his elbows and clucking like a chicken. He's such a uniquely enigmatic character and the world's worst diplomat." John chuckled.

"What about the PC? What did he say?"

"He stood there, looking confused and bloody stupid. I had to step in, make the introductions, and sit them down to talk. It's ominous that Mustafa did not offer them brandy or food. He had the last lot for us cleared away before the PC arrived."

"Well, John, my old mate, we must make this Regiment and the sector Turks come to some understanding. I think we'll leave, and recommend to the powers that be to put this PC in a different area. We'll tell them there is a personality clash or something. I'll take Mustafa on one side and tell him I will arrange another PC for his sector, a man with experience, which should pacify him. This PC's in the shit, I'm afraid. He may be a good soldier, which I doubt, but he must be a policeman, diplomat, and bloody politician on this job. Any other ideas, or am I correct?"

"You're right, Boss. I wouldn't want this PC with me if we had a firefight on our hands."

"Right. That's it then. We'll leave them talking now until the "polite hour" is up, then we'll take action. I'm going to skip the other villages. We'll only have to come back with another PC. What do you think?"

"I don't know, Boss. The local nationals have all been told by radio and newspapers the UN take over today. Maybe we should let them see the Panhards and flags, even if we don't stop."

"Okay then, that's what we'll do. I'll keep pointing things out to this PC. You never know, maybe the Van Doos will kick our recommendations into touch anyway, and the poor bastard will find himself back here again, having the piss taken out of him by Mustafa and his cronies." Mac sighed.

[143]

Their plans decided, Mac and John walked casually up to the table to join the PC and Mustafa. They were talking quite calmly and seemed to be concentrating on each other's point of view, but that could have been because of difficulty in understanding the different English dialects. Mustafa was a good mimic, because when he spoke to Mac, he imitated a Canadian drawl.

"Dawg on Fraaanki booya, dang gowd tows see yow."

"Fuck off, you Turkish Canadian bastard." Mac retorted, and Mustafa went into another one of his mad fits of laughter, spluttering out to the villagers around him what had been said, and they all joined in this crazy laughing contest. It was infectious. In seconds, everybody was rolling over with unleashed glee again, including the Van Doos. Mac and John had to join in, and even the village dogs started howling, as though they too understood what the fun was all about.

It was close to the "polite hour", so Mac decided it was time to move, whilst everybody was happy. Relationships must have improved somewhat, because Mustafa ordered brandy and proposed a toast to everybody without doing his chicken imitation.

The UN presence was made known to the locals while they slowly patrolled the rest of the sector which was to become the Van Doos responsibility. On Mac's orders, the troops waved every time they saw a local, and in the vicinity of the small villages, they cheered and shouted greetings. By the time they started on the return journey to base, everyone in the southern Kyrenia Range knew the UN was now the force responsible for security, law and order in the area.

Trouble arose when they drove back into the northern outskirts of Nicosia. When they approached a traffic island at Ayias Sofia, they were confronted with a long queue of cars. Mac drove past this build up, pushing oncoming traffic over to one side. When he passed one car, the occupants were shouting "Get the bastards, mate!" and "Sock it to 'em!" and other such phrases of genteel British language.

The problem was the Greek irregular roadblock mentioned earlier. Mac took the situation aboard in seconds; eight gun-toting Greeks had formed a barrier with two cars. They had left just enough room between the cars for one vehicle to pass at a time. These activities were completely illegal, and Mac debussed with John, telling the PC to show men manning weaponry, but to stay put.

Mac and John approached what seemed to be the leader of the group, and told him in no uncertain terms that he should stop this block now and leave, or be disarmed and arrested. Unfortunately for the Greek, his response was to stick his Sten gun in Mac's stomach, and shout in Mac's face that they were the law in this area, and the UN could go away. Mac leaned forward, looked the man directly in the eyes; an almost mesmerising look, and, sliding his hand forwards, pushed in the Stem's magazine release catch, deftly removed the magazine from the weapon, and hit our brave Greek on the head with it, knocking the man out.

He then casually walked back to the PC's Panhard, handed up the magazine and said to the PC. "One down, seven to go. Use your authority, disarm, and arrest them. Understood?"

"Yes, Sir," spluttered the PC.

Mac walked back and sat in his Land Rover to watch the fun. It was obvious to Mac that these Greeks were trying it on to see how far they could push the UN before any strong retaliation was used. For the past four weeks under British control, they had been as quiet as lambs.

They knew that if they tried something like this with the British, they would be disarmed, more than likely beat up in the process, and arrested. After arrest, a six-month prison sentence was the normal punishment, often combined with a hefty fine.

The PC and his patrol dismounted, while two weapon men stayed put, showing their heavy firepower capability. Under the PC's orders, his men split up and, taking one man each, they started talking. With the language barrier, this would never work.

[145]

"PC, concentrate on the leader. Make him give orders to the others. I've knocked him out. You frighten the bastard to death. Make him work. I want their guns, or I want their bodies. Understood?"

"Yes, Sir." He answered, in a high-pitched voice.

He doesn't like this job one bit, thought Mac.

The PC brought the leader round and started shouting and bawling at him, holding him by his jacket at the scruff of his neck, waving his gun under his nose. All very intimidating, but the Greek knew he wouldn't shoot him, so it was wasted effort.

Oh, well, Mac thought. He's plenty of time to learn. I'll let him learn the hard way.

Then it happened - a perfect demonstration of control by an open top Land Rover with four UN troops in it, which screeched to a halt at Mac's side. They instantly leapt out of the Rover, dashing forwards to the nearest Greeks, and grabbed the Greek's weapons with one hand, while hitting them with truncheons held in their other hand. At the same time, they bundled the Greeks to the Land Rover. They forced them to lie down and snapped on wrist ties. Once accomplished, they dashed out again to get the remaining Greeks.

These sensible chaps promptly stuck their hands in the air, dropped their weapons, and rushed to lie down with the others before they received a beating. It was over in twenty seconds.

A British Parachute Regiment Sergeant came over to Mac, stood to attention, and said, "Sorry, we were late on scene, Sir. We were dealing with another bunch of naughty bastards down the road. You'd have thought these clowns would have learnt their lesson by now. Thank your men for keeping them occupied until we managed to arrive. We'll stick these in our sector cooler for now with the other bastards. We're nearly full, you know. Isn't it funny how they've started being shits again after we've kept them quiet for so long? Do you want a copy of my report on this incident, Sir?"

"No thanks, Sergeant. You came at a perfect time. I've been given the job to make these Van Doos internal security field operational. Your demonstration of clearing a roadblock and effecting arrest couldn't have come at a better time. Thanks a lot. Write me down

[146]

your name, and give my regards to Warrant Officer Waldron. Tell him WO Mark Hudson SOG commends your actions. He can confirm that at HQ."

Even though these four men were wearing the blue berets, cravats, and shoulder patch of the UN, they were different in dress to other UN forces in that they wore maroon material as a backdrop to the UN hat badge. They had been involved in the troubles as the Parachute Regiment since early January. After the RAF Regiment and Royal Green Jackets, they were the first troops into the fighting. They would have been in with the other two Regiments on Christmas Eve had not their second battalion just moved out of Polymedia Camp in Cyprus to act as a garrison battalion in Sharjah, down the Persian Gulf.

When the early morning handover to the UN took place, they very reluctantly took off their red berets and put on the light blue ones, as they became a part of the UN contingent. The Battalion had stirred up so much shit about losing their red beret that the UN Command gave in, hence the maroon cloth backdrop to the UN badge. They also wore their Regimental belts when not in light fighting order. At least it gave them all the blue and white stripes of the UN Medal as compensation for changing the beloved red beret.

Mac and his team stayed while the Paras waited for their 'Golly Wagon,' as they called it, to come and pick up the Greeks, who were still lying tied up on the ground. The Sergeant obliged Mac and told his men to answer any questions put to them by the Van Doos.

"We might as well use the time as training time. God knows these people need it. Although, I think they do their best. It's just lack of experience of this type of soldiering," Mac told the Sergeant, tongue-in-cheek.

It turned out the local area, including Trachonas (the sniping and ice factory), were in the Para's sector. He started to tell Mac about some nutcase who had gone into the Ice factory alone and physically threw out five hundred armed Turks, killing three of them with his bare hands in the process. At that point, the "wagon" arrived, so he had to break off and load his beauties aboard with their weapons.

[147]

Mac thought that was a pity, because he would have liked to hear the end of his story.

Isn't it amazing how things become blown out of all proportion, he thought.

Once the Paras left, Mac instructed the PC to mount up and they continued their journey. The Van Doos had taken over the vacant hiring facilities belonging to the RAF as their accommodation in the field. Essential back up, such as the sick quarters, a dentist, clothing, bedding and fuel stores, were all on the RAF Nicosia Camp. Therefore, Mac had to detour to the camp and show his protégé their locations.

About eight hundred metres from the camp gates, to the right, was a large area of open shrub land. To Mac's amazement, he saw a large oil barrel bouncing up in the air. It then sped along the ground, rose up in the air again, and then skidded across the ground again. This was followed by the banging of gunfire in rapid succession. Now, Mac was experienced, but he'd never before seen an anti-aircraft 40mm Bofors gun firing ground to ground. This was the weapon's secondary anti tank role, with a mixture of armour piercing and explosive ammunition. It was a superb demonstration of accuracy. The gun was positioned at the camp gates on its wheels and hooked up to the back of a three-ton RL vehicle. Three men were on the gun, two on hand wheels, and one holding a clip of four rounds. There was also an ammunition feeding chute that could be seen with ammunition in it.

Mac assumed the man standing was the loader. One Corporal stood on the ground, giving orders. Once again, the gun fired four rounds at the barrel target, blasting it all over the place with each shot, and the shots were fast. Mac discovered afterward that the gun fired four rounds per second, or two hundred and forty rounds per minute. It could be powered by a generator, and one man could operate the entire electrical control system, including firing. He would have hated to be on the receiving end of that big baby.

He made a point of finding out why this gung ho gun display was happening. In the early stages of the fighting, the Greeks, as part of the pre-attack preparation, had welded armoured plating on to bulldozers. This was not news, because Mac had seen these innovative weapons himself in Omorfita. What he didn't know was that the Greeks had threatened to use these armoured bulldozers to smash through the guardroom gates at RAF Nicosia, with the intention of causing damage to Motor Transport Fuel compounds and parked aircraft.

Their intention was to inflict as much damage as they possibly could if the British gave the Turks any assistance or interfered with the Greek operations. The answer to this threat was three of these 40/70 Bofors guns plus the 14th 20th Hussars heavy weapons, which in themselves could cause the bulldozer crews a severe headache. These three guns were always hooked up to the towing vehicle and loaded, with standby crews at instant readiness, 24 hours per day.

Only four ways into RAF Nicosia were possible for a bulldozer, including cross-country, and these could all be covered in a few minutes by these weapons. With a ground range of over 1400 metres, they would thwart any adventure by bulldozers quite easily. A few questions later and Mac had found out that the guns had come up from Three Wing at RAF Akrotiri, and were manned by No 2 Parachute Squadron of the RAF Regiment. These men had completed a crash course on how to handle the weapons in their anti-tank role just for this emergency, their main job being field infantry roles.

Needless to say, the Greeks never tried any of their threatened bulldozer-come-tank antics against these deadly accurate formidable weapons.

The Van Doos patrols eventually arrived, and the PC tried to explain his decision-making process, referring to his crew's exit from the Panhards to a "ditch flag waving episode," his excuses were a barrage of pure blustering bullshit, and Mac told him so in no uncertain terms. After a few moments kicking the problem about in his head, Mac decided to give the unit commander, JRM (who was in charge of all special forces), the basic facts and let him decide how much of it should be sent back to the Van Doos. Mac told Kennedy his decision, and he agreed with Mac's outlook, especially when Mac expounded one of his many philosophies.

[149]

"After all, that's what officers are there for. They do fuck all else but socialise with their Regimental counterparts anyway."

"They can't have much time for socialising in these times of chaos can they, Boss?" asked Kennedy.

"You've gotta believe it! Ask Scouse. We went to 14th 20th Hussars about a week ago to organise a sweep with their duty officer. It was 2 o'clock in the afternoon. A Duty Colour Sergeant dealt with us, as all the officers had put on their mess kits for midday lunch and wine. They leave the Senior Non-Commissioned Officers to run the unit until 6 p.m. After that time, they are responsible for what happens to the unit, but leave all operational decisions to the SNCOs because they've drank too much fucking wine with their dinner!" Mac had a smug look on his face while he was disclosing these anti-officer corps facts. Secretly, he wished officers would fuck off all of the time, but then admitted to himself that on occasions, like now and his Van Doos PC problem, they could be handy to do a task he himself didn't want to do.

Mac and his crew stayed on Field Advisory duties to the UN forces until the end of May 1964, when they returned to their little base on the Akrotiri Salt Flats for a long earned rest. From Christmas Eve until the end of May had been an extremely long five months of very hard work, work for which the unit was well rewarded in medals.

Because no war or state of emergency had been declared for this operation, British troops involved received no decorations. If they were part of the UN Force deployment, they received the blue and white striped medal ribbon, plus the medal of the UN. Because there was no British medal or GSM Bar awarded, men who received Queen's Commendations or Mentioned in Dispatches (The highest awards issued for this operation) the Oak Leaf had to be worn on a regiment's uniform background cloth, for example the RAF blue background or Army khaki background.

After two days E and E (Equipment Examination and Maintenance), the unit took a ten-day block leave. Apart from a small administration and maintenance party, everybody takes leave. Mac,

John, Scouse, and Fred jumped a lift with the RAF on an Argosy Aircraft back to RAF Nicosia.

The intention? To spend some time with friends from the Parachute Regiment and Army Air Corps who had become part of the UN force and based on the RAF camp. Now was a fantastic time of piss-ups, lounging round the station swimming pool with an abundance of females, WRAF, WRAC, and WRNS plus married quarter's daughters and a few accommodating wives. Some days, a trip to some exotic place was organized; these activities had to be coordinated through the UN Command HQ. By this method, the UN could keep control of any force's activity in areas where there was possible danger.

One of these trips was for twenty-eight mixed Airborne and Women's forces to an old, quaint wine cellar bar in Kyrenia Harbour. On the day of departure, the party all met at the camp gates at 10 a.m. and climbed aboard the RAF bus for the journey.

The UN had advised the party that they would provide an escort, because the situation was still fluctuating in the Kyrenia Mountains. One hour passed waiting for the UN escort, and then, much to Mac's crew's hilarity, the UN escort arrived in the shape of two Van Doos Panhards with our useless PC sticking his head out of the lead vehicle turret looking the epitome of Rommel himself.

When our luckless PC saw Mac and John clutching their stomachs and laughing with tears streaming down their faces, he ducked into the turret and closed the hatch. That was the last time anybody set eyes on him for the whole outward and return journey. He sent his Corporal to give the party the escort discipline briefing.

This trip was one of many. It really was a great time to be in Cyprus chilling out and letting the UN do the work.

The time came all too soon to end this revelry and return to unit. This itself was done in a rather novel way. During the break, along with AAC and Paras, Mac's crew had made a few free fall drops over RAF Nicosia with AAC American TU parachutes. Sergeant Major Kearny of the AAC came up with the idea when they were standing at the Sgt's Mess bar. Mac mentioned that leave was over and they had to

[151]

go back and scrounge a lift of the RAF Air Movements Section to get his crew back to Akrotiri on any aircraft flying that way. SM Kearny suggested dropping in.

"We have an RAF Liaison Sycamore flying to Episkopi tomorrow. I'll lend you four of our chutes. You drop in over the salt flats. We'll call in to see you on our return and pick up the chutes. What do you think about that?"

"Perfect, me old mate. Will you radio drop clearance with Akrotiri? I'd hate to bump into a low flying Canberra Bomber."

"Shall do. Leave it to me. Take off is at 9am, so time to get hammered one last time. Let's go for it. Nothing cures a hangover faster than a free fall from eight thousand feet."

"Agreed completely. I'll go tell the crew and see you back here in one hour for human destruction juice. Okay?"

"Okay. Out."

With that, they went about their respective business whilst building up their inner strength for a drinking competition. They were both experienced enough to know what would happen. Physical challenges would be flying thick and thin that night, and Mac was determined to win, especially the "Dance of the Zulu Warrior".

For the uninitiated, the "Zulu Warrior Dance" is famous in every Regiment of every arm of the military. Challengers for the dance strip naked, then adjudicators tightly roll up newspapers, usually The Sun or Daily Mirror, and stick these into the rectum of the contestants who by now should be performing a red Indian war dance on top of tables, singing with the audience, "I JIGA JIGA ZUMBO ZUMBO I JIGA JIGA ZUMBO ZUMBO ZAM." At this stage of the dance, the newspaper 'monkey tails' are simultaneously set alight. Contestants keep dancing as long as they can whilst the papers burn down and eventually burn the dancer's arseholes. Some men suffer excruciating pain, and carry for life badly scarred backsides attempting to win this duel. The winner is the last man dancing with the burning paper in his arse.

Some people were famous for their dance achievements. One friend of Mac's often won, because he had a special way of farting while he was dancing, a sneaky fart that blew the flames away from his arse. He could also relight a paper on the point of the flame flickering out with this methane gas infusion. It was a great night. Everybody drank to the extreme, competitions galore, and four separate "Zulu Warriors" took place.

Mac didn't win a thing, but initiated the midnight swimming competition; everyone staggered to the station swimming pool, and most took part in the Nicosia Water Olympics. The party continued all night, but Mac managed to creep away about 2 am and grabbed a little sleep before his flight at 9 am.

The next morning, a motley, a horrible looking bunch of hungover crew paraded at the helicopter pad. All of them were trying, unsuccessfully, not to show their suffering. Gingerly, they fitted parachutes and said nothing, silently regressed into a little world of their own.

Their chute types were known as TU, an American piece of equipment used by "smoke jumpers," the maniac fire fighters that jumped into and fought forest fires in the States and Canada. They were held by the AAC for British Special Airborne units, such as Para Medics and SSTs (Special Safety Teams), who might have to jump into small mountain drop zones, to rescue downed aircrew or retrieve something politically sensitive from a crashed aircraft; nuclear warheads for example, anywhere in the Middle East. They could also be used on any other job where a degree of steerage was needed.

These were the chutes used in the hostage rescue affair with very high winds at the Island of Castelorizo, off the coast of mainland Greece, when the Greek Sacred Heart Squadron (SAS) combined with our SOG to affect the rescue and kill the Libyan terrorists in February 1961.

With the crew's hangovers, it was a good job that they had such a large drop zone, the salt flats, to land on that morning. Mac carried out equipment checks and ordered the crew to mount, in order to meet the exact 9 am takeoff. Just after takeoff, an AAC passenger handed out the standard service 'plastic egg sandwiches,' cold and covered in grease.

For the uninitiated, the plastic egg sandwich comprises of regular hen's eggs cooked in the station of departure Sergeant's Mess. They are prepared in bulk (forty at a time) on a large aluminium tray that had been slightly greased on the bottom and the eggs broken on top. They are then finished off in a low heat oven until the aircrew needed them, which could be more than one hour. This left the white of the eggs fairly well cooked and rubbery and with the yokes seemingly untouched. These eggs were often referred to by the troops as a 'portion of piss in the snow.

Cyprus was given a good layer of British vomit fertiliser that morning by men hanging half way out of helicopter doors, a terrific downpour that was spread round by the helicopter rotor blades downdraft. The sight made Mac laugh like a spotted Hyena, because he felt fine. The crafty old bastard had been shamming a hangover on the airfield tarmac.

The flight path taken to Akrotiri that morning made use of a ravine type valley through the Troodos Mountain range. Large, pine covered cliffs loomed up high above and on either side of the aircraft for most of the trip. This caused a lot of turbulence and tail swing, only ending when they suddenly came out of the railway cutting effect onto the Southern Plain. All of these flying hazards added to the misery of the spew fertiliser production machines inside the fuselage.

"Check equipment, you poor bastards. Time to make like Peter Pan, which should be no hardship for you, you fucking fairies."

Mac was enjoying himself, but it didn't seem the WRAF Squadron Leader on board was very impressed with his language, or with the professional vomiting demonstration given for most of the flight by his crew. But as though given an adrenaline injection, everyone came instantly alive and aware of their surroundings again, as it came close to the moment to jump. Parachute descents give people that type of buzz and are definitely are one of the finest, quickest hangover cures available to man.

"Follow my leader and stack on opening. Go on my exit."

This, in short, was Mac's instructions for his team to follow him out of the aircraft, one at a time, and copy his free fall direction. Then

[154]

they were to stack up, one behind the other after opening their parachutes, and follow Mac into his selected landing target area. A thumb up from everyone confirmed the team's understanding of what was needed of them. Now the wait until Mac calculated when to jump. Wind speeds and directions at five hundred foot intervals (Blue Met Information) had been given to him by the pilot to help him to decide his release point.

Leaning out of the aircraft door, Mac spotted their base, seeming the size of a matchbox from that height, and made his calculations when to go. He then gave the Sycamore Load Master the thumbs up sign; indicating that he should tell the pilot over the microphone that they were leaving, thank him for the ride, and goodbye.

With a final wave to the WRAF officer, he French Frog positioned out of the door, his team following in quick succession. It was a glorious, refreshing ride, until he opened his parachute at 2000 ft. He had steered himself well upwind of the target before opening the chute, leaving the team an easy downwind drive, before a wheel back into the wind to slow down the speed just before landing. All copy book stuff that they had done hundreds of times together, mostly at night following a pinprick of light on the back of their jumping helmets.

On landing, all signs of hangovers had completely disappeared. No one could ever have guessed the state they were in a couple of hours before. The chutes were quickly rolled up, and, after a short two hundred-metre walk, they were back in the base having a mug of tea.

JRM called for a SNCOs brief on the second day back from leave. All the first day was taken up with full E and E, degreasing weapons, testing radios, range firing, and testing individual weapon zeros. Then came general administration, store trips to the main camp, personal hygiene checks, doctor and dentist visits (athlete's foot was a problem), and worn out personal clothing and boots had to be changed after five months of working in the field. After one day back at base, Admin and Equipment informed Mac he was able report to JRM that the SOG was fully operational in its equipment, with no loss in manpower because of sickness.

[155]

That is the datum line set by the British for Special Forces and comes under the often used phrase in a written operations order or verbal briefing, "Recuperation Time Allowed." Most often, this is followed with "Minimal, even if any time available". JRM's brief was a breakdown of unit personnel deployments, with immediate effect. Eight of the sixteen four-man field teams were to stay on site with a double-headed task.

Firstly, they were to train and act as a Middle East SST with parachute capabilities against the advent of an air crash with nuclear weapons on board. Their aim, if this happened, was to parachute into whichever country the aircraft crashed in without permission, and recover any warhead or other sensitive secret equipment on board. They were to fight, if necessary, to carry out these tasks.

In support of this unit was a Gulf Communications Flight Argosy aircraft fitted out with special equipment and passenger oxygen banks for them to use in a HALO (High Altitude Low Opening) plus Commando carrier born Wessex helicopters for recovery. The Commando Carrier HMS Bulwark was somewhere in Middle Eastern waters, but they did not need to know where. The fact that she would help them out of a tricky spot was enough reassurance for all of the crews.

Second support would come from air strikes if needed, but that was up to the RAF. Naval gunfire backup would be available if an incident was within range, and of course, the most important, the Commandos on board the Bulwark would be ready.

Their second task was to maintain a field interpreter back up to the UN forces in Cyprus, if they were called upon in any deterioration of the situation. Mac was to stay with this element, a command decision that made him happy, for once. He liked Cyprus from a service point of view. A number of men were to go back to the UK for formal training courses to keep them in the promotion qualification range. Four highly mathematically qualified men were to go on a new course for the SOG, the Long Gunnery Staff Air Defence Course. Eighteen months in duration, this course took place in a number of locations, including the Outer Hebrides, but mostly at the Royal School of Artillery Larkhill, near the Salisbury Plains.

Apparently, it was the hardest technical weaponry course in the British forces. Indeed, men who passed this course at certain grades were promoted to Warrant Officer Two. Subjects covered in this course would bring them up to date in teaching gunners to fire any air defence system, guns, or missiles; not just the British equipment but that from any country worldwide, when equipment was captured.

Additionally, they would learn how to sabotage missiles and associated radar systems so the enemy could still fire them with confidence but never be able to hit anything. This last ploy was pulled off with the Tiger Cat Missile System used later by the Argentines in the 1982 Falklands War. The diki fix "safe to fire" on the missile launchers were set in such a way that they could not launch a missile below a certain degree of elevation. The RAF was informed of this, and they flew their Harriers below this elevation. The RAF destroyed targets and the Argentine's missiles could not be fired in reply to these low-level attacks. Unfortunately, the British soldiers didn't manage to sabotage the anti-aircraft guns in time, and the Argentines scored successes. Well, that's another story.

A man, we'll call him KJ, became an expert operator in this field, (he eventually knackered the Argentines), and his exploits around the world were legendary among the SOG operatives, and certainly among the very high ranking officers who were involved in the dirty tricks brigade. KJ's schemes were so underhand, and sometimes ugly, that the involved personnel nicknamed him 'Ugly'.

Back in 60's Cyprus, SST training involved certain personnel having to complete a course of nuclear accident training with the RAF School of Fire Fighting and Light Rescue. During this training, they learned many different skills, all orientated to an accidentally crashed aircraft with nuclear weapons on board and possible radiation hazards. They mastered how to predict radiation fallout pattern and its range of dispersal. Protection, advice, and control were skills they needed to help the friendly local populace.

They used 1320x Radiation Detection Meters to ascertain if, and how much, radiation was present. White, yellow, and downwind monitor duties, and much more, all to be passed on to the SOG SST when they returned from the course. The one thing not covered by the RAF School were the actions to be taken if British or NATO aircraft crashed in hostile territory. This was a book to be written by the SOG. These SSTs were already operating with the Middle East Para Medics and RAF Regiment support parachute elements, but were now being given a higher priority. This was due to a couple of American crashes and a large area of radiation contamination involving a multi-million dollar clean up, and decontamination operations, which had taken place in southern Spain.

The Americans kept this incident secret for a long time, admitting a crash between a refueling tanker and a B52 bomber had occurred, but they did not mention the fact that four hydrogen bombs had crashed within a small area near Torremolinos in southern Spain. Three of the bombs landed on terra firma and two gave off a radiation spill, even though the nuclear warhead had not exploded.

One bomb dropped in the sea and involved a major, very expensive, naval operation before it was recovered. In the initial crash and detection of the radiation spill, the British were involved, but once the gigantic American clear-up started, they returned to Cyprus. Nearly five thousand large barrels of topsoil were removed and sent for disposal in America. Every minute piece of the aircraft found was sent back also. All local crops were torched and farmers compensated. It was a monstrous operation and involved the whole of the American 6th Fleet.

An example of SST cover in the 1960s by the British would be as follows: an aircraft would take off in the UK, heading for the Far East. A UK team from RAF Brize Norton would be airborne and responsible until the aircraft reached the Mediterranean, regardless of the route taken. Approaching the changeover point, the Middle East SST from Akrotiri in Cyprus would be airborne and assume responsibility. On reaching Diego Garcia in the Indian Ocean, the Far East SST from their RAF base in Singapore would be airborne and responsible.

It was assumed that only the Middle East Team would be involved in a hostile territory crashes and may have to fight to remove the warheads. Personnel involved in this side of the operation received extra training at Aldermaston. British involvement against certain dissidents in that theatre led to this conclusion, and that assumption proved correct.

Libyan-Egyptian relations had never been good, and the strained, tense atmosphere was blown up, or escalated into a near war footing, when one of our aircraft strayed into their sensitive border airspace and our SOG went to work. This escapade has been one of the best-kept military secrets since the end of the Second World War. Many times, the aircraft involved in the transportation of nuclear armaments were RAF Transport Command freighters. These aircraft carried replacement parts for weapons stockpiled at various staging posts around the world. People have the image of a nuclear bomber, fully armed, carrying evil destruction when a nuclear bomb is mentioned. Not so. In most cases, the load is maintenance parts.

Akrotiri in Cyprus is a good example of this. The base had a large, very secure bomb dump where nukes were stored, serviced and maintained. Certain parts of the bomb could not receive the full maintenance at this dump, because special equipment and areas were needed to carry out the work. These units had to be replaced with new or refurbished parts from Aldermaston in the UK. These items were carried to Akrotiri in large 6 by 6 by 6 foot fireproof and heavily reinforced containers on board freight aircraft, mainly Britannias; the very safe long distance "Whispering Giant".

Usual SST procedures were carried out, even when only parts of a bomb were carried; it was treated just as though it was a complete, live device. When a Britannia landed at Akrotiri, the SOG carried out the unloading, with SST equipment, instruments and clothing in use in case of an accident. Once on board low loader trolleys for road transport, RAF Police and Regiments escorted the containers to the bomb dump. Items being exchanged were then escorted back to the aircraft and loaded by the SOG for the return trip to Aldermaston.

Often, if a piece of equipment was travelling to Muharraq, or Sharja in the Persian Gulf, or Khormaksar in Aden, an Argosy aircraft from 104 Gulf Communications Squadron would collect the item straight off of the Britannia to complete the journey. When this occurred, the SST would be airborne, flying in a holding circuit, just outside of Libyan air space. It could then go north if the Britannia was in trouble, and southeast if the Argosy came to grief. In the million to one chance that both aircraft had a problem, the UK SST would go airborne earlier than was the norm.

On one occasion, a 104 Gulf Communication Argosy was flying low over the Southern Egyptian/Libyan border, near the temporary desert prison camp of Kalifranarias. The pilot misjudged slightly and clipped a wing tip into a sand dune. The jockey lost control for a second, but recovered to land the plane with only minor damage to his craft and used his back ramp as an 'air brake' in the sand. Fantastic flying skill really, but frowned upon, because he shouldn't have been trying to imagine he was a fighter pilot. There was no fire; only minor bruising of the crew, and the cargo was intact. Because they had been low flying, there was a good chance they had not been seen to crash by any radars, meaning the crew and cargo were retrievable without the Egyptians or Libyans knowing.

The entire rescue plan was scrambled to all units involved, and the cavalry charge began with the SOG SST airborne element in the lead, with its Argosy going down to wave top level again to avoid foreign radars. Mac and the SST made a final operation rehearsal of their tasks, based on the latest information they had received on the scrambler. They also elected to jump at low level using X type parachutes, which were kept onboard the aircraft as well as their Para Commando free fall rigs. Chute X types were vintage equipment that the user clipped onto a cable running the length of the aircraft, and this pulled the rigging lines out of the parachute sack, and lastly, the canopy to give a very safe opening for the jumper. These X types had been doctored with special features. All writing, chute numbers, and instructions of any form were in Arabic, and some in Swahili, to confuse anybody picking them up after a drop. The men would always

[160]

try to bury them, but sometimes time was simply not in their favour, plus the possibility that winds and shifting sands could expose them after a short while.

Limited steering was available with these canopies, but nothing compared to the Para Commando. In this case, a large and forgiving drop zone, in case of mistakes, meant the X type was the chute for the job. Accuracy would be no problem with the drop, because the crashed aircraft's Search and Rescue Beacon was guiding the pilot, and drop zone information was open desert and high sand dunes.

"What height for us to jump do we all reckon?"

Everyone began to give their opinions at once, "500...800...400...500...500...600...500."

"500's have it. No reserves."

This meant, because of the height, they were not going to use reserve parachutes. It was doubtful if they would open in time if they had to use them, especially taking into account the fluctuating sand dune heights and air density.

"I'll select Release Point, Loadmaster. Okay?"

The Loadmaster was responsible for loads and jump disciplines onboard all RAF fixed-wing aircraft and helicopters. He must be consulted about all operational decisions involving the airborne chariot.

"Fine by me mate. You're the Dickey." A Dickey was the jump commander. He gave Mac the universal recognition of compliance – the thumbs up signal.

"We all know how we stand. We get this right, we go in and out, or we risk capture, and that is not acceptable as an option. I personally don't want to die. I'd rather fifty other bastards go first. That's the only option for you mother fuckers. Retrieve the warhead, gather the crew like Bo Peep did her sheep, and rush south like fuck. If our people pick us up en route, fine. If not, we fight all the way to Sudan.

"That's it. Prepare for it; condition for it; and let's do it. Anything back, anybody? No? Good. Let's face it, you bastards, there's no fucking soldiers out of that fucking door can hold a fucking candle to us. Am I fucking right?"

[161]

They all screamed in unison, "You bastard; you're fucking right."

By now, with the winding up and excess of adrenaline, they were screaming, maniacal killing machines, with a technical job to do: retrieve the warhead and save the air crew. Seconds later, the Loadmaster buzzed Mac, and he lay down, hanging out of the door looking for his target. Everyone and everything was primed, psyched up, and raring to go.

Suddenly, the crashed plane came into peripheral vision. Mac hit his helmet, and the Argosy emptied from rear and side doors as though by magic. Men were actually jumping over his prostrate body on the aircraft floor. He was the last to jump. In training for this, most of the men stamped on his back when they went for the door, their way of having fun and taking the piss. On this occasion, not one man touched him; they cleared him, meaning their heads had to be near their own chest height to avoid banging them against the top of the door when they went through. Of course, rear exit men didn't have to perform these contortions.

Two scramble motorcycles were also dropped from the rear ramp on supply chutes. All landed safely and in a very small area, because of the speed of exit from the plane. Later, Mac estimated thirty men exited in ten seconds flat. Two men rushed downwind, with 1320xs instruments to see if any radiation spill was present, and then ran toward the aircraft, still checking, until eventually declaring the "No Spill" signal on the inside body check.

Medics were busy checking out the air crew and found them in good shape, and fit to walk. Two men on the scramble motorbikes dropped by the team sped off into the direction of the border to see if they had company from any direction. A boundary weapon defence was already established to protect the team against anything and everybody, and they would maintain this perimeter protection, even on the move. Considering the small size of the team, they had tremendous firepower and state of the art equipment.

'Clockwork' was a statement often used to describe a well-run efficient sequence of events in military jargon. Many times this claim is exaggerated; to allow a commander to gain a little praise for himself, maybe earn him a medal or two, and sometimes a minor award for one of his staff. However, this operation did run like clockwork in the real sense of the word. The carriage container for the nuke parts was only slightly damaged. The warhead retrieval crew opened it quite easily with the three sequential keys carried by all operational SSTs on take off. A detailed search of the plane and area was carried out. Two containers were once again checked and found radiation free and placed in two Bergen Carriers for backpacking out. These packs, along with the aircrew and a bodyguard, immediately galloped off at a fast rate of knots on a dispatched route South, following a compass heading that would make a helicopter lift from RAF El Adem possible.

All aircraft documents were likewise collected. Radio and radar navigation and the new GPS, or Global Positioning System, were smashed beyond repair. Fuel was drained from aircraft tanks. The chutes were collected and placed in the aircraft. After a report of 'no enemy' from the bike reconnaissance unit, explosive charges were set on a one and a half-hour delay. This would ensure the men were well away from the site before the smoke from the burning aircraft gave the position away.

Now came a backbreaking march due South to confuse any enemy, then a swing to the East, and then North again in order to arrive at a point close enough for a helicopter lift to El Adem. The team did it in style. Closer to El Adem, they broke radio silence and scrambled a 'collect' message. In half-hour intervals, they landed outside the RAF Camp gates. Their Argosy was sitting on the far west edge of the runway, away from prying eyes, fuelled up and ready to go.

That's just what they did; welcome plastic egg sandwiches and bacon butties with hot mugs of tea were downed abundantly on the way back to Nicosia. The only thing that left a bad taste in one's mouth about this operation was the insistence of detailed and long drawn out custom inspections by the RAF Police when they landed at Nicosia.

The aircraft at Kalifranarias was on the Libyan side of the border, but neither side had picked up their aircraft radar signatures. Egypt had purchased a number of modified Argosy transports. When the Libyans found the burnt out aircraft hulk, there were some chute fragments left with Swahili instructions on them and later some Arabic material markings were found. The Libyans accused the Egyptians of airborne aggression, backed up by Sudanese Paratroopers, and so the political chaotic scene was set.

The radio airways told us about Armoured Brigade movements up to, close to, and sometimes over the respective borders. This may well have been the first time the truth about all this tremendous military activity in that theatre of the Middle East and the escalating war possibility has ever been told. The outcome of this operation became the textbook for future Airborne SST tactics, and so it should be, a complete success - job evaluation and resources application were perfect, and most importantly, no casualties. It was a classic.

Cyprus was still suffering its ethnic separation, and it is very doubtful if these problems will ever be resolved completely. There are too many savagely bitter memories on both sides. Even now, Greek and Turkish Cypriots are taking each other to the International Court of Law over a multitude of wrong doings.

One example of a more recent row was, 'Who should dig an archaeological site at Salamis ten kilometres north of Famagusta?' Before the Turkish invasion, there were two archaeologist teams working Salamis, the Cyprus Department of Antiquities and the French University of Lyon. The Greek Cypriot representative to UNESCO said the Turkish Cypriot regime was attempting to recruit new teams and had also made representation to Lyon University to carry on the digging, all of these units refused because they said the action would be illegal.

The Turkish Department of Antiquities from the University of Ankara decided they should carry out the work and started in August of 1998. Declaring they were inside international law, they blamed everybody who had refused to participate in the dig as biased and on the side of the Greek Cypriots. Many students who went to the site, took hundreds of photographs showing the digging in progress, and made these photographs available for lawsuits by the Greek Cypriot Department of Antiquities. The Greek Cypriot Ambassadors to UNESCO and the Minister of Education and Culture had informed all international bodies about this illegal activity on be part of the Turkish Cypriots.

There have been many such problems on the books to solve at UNESCO. The Turkish invasion in 1974 partitioned the country and a United Nations presence has been in place on that beleaguered island ever since. In 1983, Northern Cyprus proclaimed its independence, but this was recognised only by Turkey, and the Greek Cypriots continue to control the only internationally recognised government. Both sides publicly called for some sort of settlement and the establishment of a new federal system of government.

The Turkish Cypriots created their own constitution in 1975 and a new one in 1985; negotiations have intermittently taken place to revise or create a new constitution for the Island that would improve relations between Greek and Turkish Cypriots, but at the time of writing in 2012, little has been resolved.

Some day in the future, agreements may be made and politics may be forgotten. At the time of writing it seems unlikely. A pity, Cyprus is such a beautiful place.

Book THREE –THE BLOODY WAR OF ADEN

CHAPTER 1

Aden 1966-67

Mac's arrival in Aden in 1966 for his second tour of duty in South Arabia would have blown the mind of any man, regardless of experience, regiment, or strong personal qualities. He was met by the infamous John Buchan AFM, DSO. Buchan was waiting for him at Khormaksa airport, not in the arrivals lounge, as one would expect, but on the tarmac at the bottom of the Britannia aircraft steps. Buchan did not offer introductions, unless his "follow me" could be classed as an introduction of some form. In ten minutes, the crazy fun began when John Buchan, or JB as he was known, spun round and raced through the lounge, straight through immigration & customs, with a wave of his hand to the duty officers, with Mac in tow, dragging along his kit, plus rifle, ammunition, and parachute.

All the Britannia passengers were military personnel, and most had cross-decked from the VC10 'moon ship' from the UK to Bahrain, as was the normal practice. Everyone called the VC 10 the 'moon ship' because it brought out to the Middle East white humans with white knees called "moonies," because they were not suntanned.

Because the shuttle had only a third of its normal passenger capacity, the passengers carried their personal kit and suitcases on the aircraft. Loading bay facilities were full of more important and much needed items for the camps in Aden, such as Tenants beer cans (with gorgeous, nubile models printed on the sides) mail from families, and newspapers.

"Get in and hold tight, watch and observe for Grenadiers. You'll see a large hotel called the Red Sea on the left- opposite is a block of flats on the Ma'alah Bandar turning. Watch there for snipers. Questions when we arrive at Steamer Point. Understood?"

"Understood".

With that, he leapt the long wheel based Land Rover forwards with a screech of burning, acrid smelling, smoking tyres. He drove like a madman, but expertly and with complete calm. Mac knew this display was for his benefit, and did not mind. A fairly comprehensive and detailed briefing about JB had come his way before leaving the UK from Harry Smith, his Aden post predecessor.

Buchan's appointment in Aden was Officer in Charge of the RAF Steamer Point Fire Section, Station Ground Defence Training Officer, Station Security Officer, Station Bomb Disposal, and Demolitions Officer during bomb scares. If time allowed, the Army Bomb Disposal Teams were called in, but JB appeared to want to do everything himself. He was old for his rank of Flight Lieutenant, and highly decorated. His courage was beyond question, though bordering on that of an impulsive, irresponsible madman. He had blasted many people of high rank in the past and this was still happening in the present, so much so that promotion was out of the question. But JB didn't give a shit about that or what anybody thought of him.

One small example of his attitude to rank and position came when a staff car carrying Arab dignitaries pulled up outside the fire section gates and the occupants went into the RAF Police and Special Branch HQ across the road.

JB saw the vehicle and shouted "Corporal Carmichael, go and get that posh car's tyres down".

"Yes, Sir. You are aware it's a VIP car and there are some Arab bigwigs with it?"

"Their hard shit, Corp. Do as you are told".

"Right away, Sir".

All his staff knew better than argue with JB. If they did so, they would suffer. He was vindictive and carried a grudge forever.

The Arabs finished their visit and returned to their car to find the tyres flat. At first, they were confused, then angry. JB casually strolled up to the gate and looking at the Arabs, shouted to Sergeant Brooks over his shoulder.

"Sgt Brooks, it seems these dim-witted fucking Arabs and their driver can't read the 'No Parking' sign we've displayed in four languages. They've blocked the fire engine entrance and now, if there's a bomb or a fire, we can't make our exit to deal with it. I wonder how many poor innocent people could die, including Arabs, because of these thoughtless, selfish morons?"

With that, he turned on his heel and walked away, with the stutters, screams, and gesticulations from the irate Arabs bouncing harmlessly off his back.

Twenty minutes later there was a telephone call telling JB to report to the Station Commander immediately. JB climbed in his long wheelbase, which was rigged with crash bars for ramming small roadblocks, and shouted. "In for a penny, in for a pound!" He drove at speed out of the compound, ramming the front near side of the staff car knocking it out of the way. Half an hour later he came back (by now the remains of the staff car had been towed away) with a huge grin spread all over his face.

"I enjoyed that Sgt Brooks, but it will cost me some money I'm afraid, at least a round of drinks in the Officers Mess and two for the Station Commander and his wife".

Back to Mac's arrival.

They approached the Red Sea Hotel at a fast rate, and all Mac's concentration was on the block of flats opposite, scanning for snipers. Suddenly, JB swerved right, across the central reservation, and into the road at the side of the flats that ran through the Ma'alah Bandar.

[168]

This side road joined the major road called the Ma'alah Main near Tawahi on the road toward Steamer Point. Huge signs were displayed in English and Arabic on each side of the road and on awnings stretched over the top of the track, stating that this route was strictly out of bounds to all traffic, including military vehicles.

To top this off, 'Danger Mine' signs were everywhere. JB simply smashed his way through, knocking over old corrugated iron sheeted 'Kochi huts,' (temporary Arab dwellings) bins, and anything else he could use his roadblock crash bars on with good effect. He was laughing a maniacal scream of a laugh as he wrought this destruction.

"Watch out for crowds of kids". He shouted over the roar of the engine, swerving to the right in order to deliberately knock over a bicycle parked at the side of the track.

"The terrorist uses kids as a cover for grenade attacks. There's a crowd of kids; we slow down for them. The kids all hit the ground; a grenade comes from behind them. Motto? Run the kids down. Kill the grenadier behind them. Understood"?

"Understood".

This little revelation was not news to Mac; his brief from Harry included this terrorist ploy, and it had been used on a number of occasions, killing four British soldiers and injuring eight. As they continued on JB's stock car racing practice circuit to Steamer Point, Mac, even though very entertained by JB's antics, had time to reflect on why he was sent here and what he had to do in the future months ahead. He had a licence to ignore politics and protocol, plus military rules and regulations, and employ the terrorist weapons and tactics against the terrorists themselves, using 'Misinformation and Psychological Warfare' to its and his maximum potential. Why he was here was caused by a short but recent history of political events, which would lead to the British military withdrawal from Aden.

Aden is situated on a peninsula at the southern entrance to the Red Sea, between Arabia and eastern and north-eastern Africa, and acted as a commercial station for neighbouring states. It gained even more commercial importance after the opening of the Suez Canal in 1869, and as a result of oil discoveries in Arabia and the Persian Gulf, this superb natural harbour was thought vital to safeguard the sea routes to trade in India and the Far East. Aden was at the centre of the British Colonial trading system. Ships stopped there for fuel en route between Europe and the eastern trading ports. It was still a loyal imperial outpost in 1953 when the newly crowned Queen Elizabeth paid a visit during her world tour.

During the 1950s, Aden became the busiest port in the world after New York. Another great boost to its trading potential came when BP Oil refineries were built in Little Aden, located on the West Side of the bay to process oil from the Gulf. The British enjoyed the good life in this little Rahj. Pampered by Arab servants and catered for by Indian traders, they felt safe in their imperial backwater. Throughout the 1950s, when the British Empire was being dismantled, Aden's economy boomed. As a free port, it was raided by thousands of cruise ship tourists from around the world. Lost in time, British rule continued in the old colonial style.

Around the Aden colony, was a wilderness larger than England and Wales, called the British Protectorates and ruled by feuding tribesmen. When the British grabbed Aden there was had no interest in these lawless territories, other than as a defensive zone.

Tribal rulers such as the Amir of Bahrain were persuaded to sign 'Treaties of Protection' and to accept British political advisors into their sheikhdoms; the few British to enter this medieval world could do little to change it. Major-General Sir James Lunt, Commander of the Arab Army from 1961-64, gave an example of this backward place in the arrival lecture.

When he was coming back from a visit "up country" he arrived at a village and heard a scraping and clanging noise at his feet. Looking down, he saw an iron grill embedded into the ground with a blurred human face pressed against it. He asked his Arab hosts who the man was, and they were very evasive.

General Lunt ordered the man released and upon coming out of his dungeon, he saw a man dressed in ragged shreds of clothing, caked with filth and excreta, a beard down to his knees, finger and toe nails like eagle talons, and exceedingly emaciated. Sir James asked how long the man had been down there and nobody could remember. Apparently, he had been shackled, hands and feet, and these shackles were now thick with rust, and he'd been imprisoned many years before and had been there ever since. Sir John ordered the shackles to be removed and the man set free. Far from being grateful for Sir John's intervention and his release, the man complained profusely that he wanted to go back, because if he were free, nobody would give him food anymore. Such was the law in this backwater as late as the early 1960s.

In the Protectorates, approximately half a million people scratched a living from the soil. Unlike their neighbours in Saudi Arabia, their leaders did not have oil revenue. Britain bought them as allies for a few rifles and a small amount of money. The Aden Protectorate Levies were formed; a small Army of Arabs under British Officers which brought the British and the local Sultans into closer alliance.

The colonial power also had a more modern system of controlling the tribesmen: Air Power Policing or APL. If a village or a Sultan caused any trouble, leaflets were dropped from aircraft, warning them they would be bombed and at what time, if they didn't hand in hostages to prove their good behaviour in the future. If this instruction was not complied with, they were bombed. They were ordered to move everybody plus their livestock out of the village, and at the precise time, the village would be bombed into oblivion. This was found to be an excellent, fast, cheap, and cost effective way of controlling a large number of people spread out over a large, almost inaccessible area of land.

Aden became self-governing in 1962 and joined the Federation of South Arabia (FSA) in 1963. The FSA linked the feudal sheikhdoms that were lying between Yemen and the coast with the urban Aden Colony. Opposition to the British presence increased after the Suez Operation during November 1956.

Nasserism, the political ideology based on the concepts of Egyptian President Gamal Abdel Nasser emerged via inflammatory broadcasting on radio Cairo and later, to a lesser extent, from regional broadcasting stations, such as Taiz in the Yemen. For the first time,

Arabs had an outspoken leader, speaking for all Arabs, against colonialism and supporting nationalism everywhere throughout the Arab states.

This antagonism toward the British increased with the establishment of the Middle East Command Headquarters on the colony of Aden. The Sultans were so extremely worried by the increase of nationalist propaganda from Radio Cairo that they were persuaded by the British to join a Federation of South Arabian States. In 1959, this Federation was established, and eventually, most of the Sultans joined.

Britain built a "Whitehall in the sand" and palaces for the Sultans. In the new Federal Capital Aden, the Sultans performed a charade of parliamentary government. One of the few Sultans with a formal education acted as their spokesman, Mohamed Farid, Federation Foreign Minister, 1962-67. When he was questioned by ITV on his thoughts on the Federation, he said something to the effect of, "Before the Federation, we Sultans had a system that worked. The tribal leaders elected our Sultans and that, by Western concepts, may not be democratic, but by our concepts, it was, and it worked. We believe it is no good trying to adopt the Western system in our country, as it has failed in every country in the world, and led to nationalists calling for freedom from your colonialist rule. If I am wrong in my words, ask yourself, where has your Empire gone?"

Wow. Did he pack a punch?

The absence of elections and the autocratic rule of the Sultans did not allow us, or the Sultans to understand the depths of nationalist feeling among the people in the New Federation. Saleh Musleh, a prominent NLF guerrilla leader said to Mac, "The Sultans were our enemies. The imperialists set up the Federation. We felt nothing had changed since their ancestors had signed the protection treaties with the British colonialists".

In Aden, prosperity had attracted a huge influx of immigrant labour from all over South Arabia. They joined trade unions that took up the Nasserite anti-imperialist cause and opposed the Federation with strikes and demonstrations. The authorities ignored the nationalists and gave full backing to the Sultans and the Federation. The British military was really very short sighted in those days, and seemed incapable of reading the writing on the wall.

An Army-led coup overthrew the hereditary ruler of the Yemen, the Iman, in 1962 and was backed by Egypt. The new republican government of Yemen initiated a revolution by its brothers in the South. Aden and the Federation did join in, and the battle against colonialism began. There was now an undeclared war, involving two colonial powers: Britain against Soviet backed Egypt, with a horrendous battle ground of pure desert, sand, silt, lava, and volcanic remains, criss-crossed with deep wadis and mountainous territory with peaks of up to 9000ft. Britain backed the guerrilla royalist Army of the deposed Iman, as did Saudi Arabia. This Army was supported by mercenary troops, mostly comprised of so called ex-SAS "veterans" operating out of bases in the Aden Federation.

The British had two problems to contend with; putting down the tribal uprising in the Radfan adjoining Yemen, and highly organised urban terrorism in the Aden Colony itself.

In July 1964, Harold Macmillan set 1968 as the year for the Federation's self-government, but with a continuing British presence in Aden. This statement helped to accelerate the nationalist cause to push Britain out by military force. Yemeni, Egyptian, and Adeni nationalists, as well as paid mercenaries continued bringing weapons, mines, explosives, and grenades across the border for the use of border tribesmen, who viewed guerrilla warfare as a way of life. These ordinance items were mainly ex-British equipment that had been left behind when the British evacuated the Canal Zone, Egypt, in late 1955.

Later on in the struggle, when more Aden terrorists received Marxist guerrilla training by the Soviets and Chinese, more and more high tech Soviet weaponry began to appear on the scene.

The emergency was declared in December 1963, coinciding with the new outbreak of severe fighting in Cyprus, which tied up Middle East resident garrison troops. An attempt to subdue the Radfan was made by a force of Arab Federal Regular Army battalions, supported

[173]

by British tanks, guns, engineers, and other specialist corps. It failed, at the cost of five dead and twelve wounded.

As soon as this force withdrew, the tribesmen moved back into their old stomping grounds and carried on, attacking traffic on the Dhala road that links Yemen and Aden. The Federal government asked for additional British military aid, and they were supplied with a mixed force of Brigade strength and support aircraft.

These force's rules of engagement forbade them to bomb or attack areas containing women and children, so they dropped leaflets warning the local nationals to move out of harm's way. They could retaliate with maximum force if the troops came under fire.

The Paras and Marines carried out this latter job to great effect. At the time of Mac's arrival on the scene, the British government had announced its intention to withdraw from Aden in 1968, breaking their previous promises to maintain a military presence after independence. As a consequence of this political blunder, or gaff, as it has been called, the narrow streets of the Aden townships were the scene of a bloody civil war between the National Liberation Front and the Freedom for the Liberation of South Yemen.

Britain was between the two factions and under attack by both. These two antagonists were trying to prove to the local populace who was the strongest, and who should be the party to rule Aden. Even though we, the British had said we were pulling out, they wanted to claim that they threw the troops out instead.

In this bloody war, British soldiers were killed in a land that was no longer of any interest to Britain, and for reasons that no one in Britain could understand.

On the plus side, because the Aden colony townships were small and in close proximity to each other, surrounded and dominated by overlooking volcanic high grounds, they were easily controlled by troops and air support. Only a limited number of troops were needed for normal battalion internal security duties. It gave the British an ideal training ground to practice special operations tactics and use new weapons and develop an individual's various skills. New technology was given its proving base here. Intelligence gathering techniques were a top priority, and combined service SOGs were tasked with that side of the game, and issued with all the latest night surveillance equipment and specialist cameras, bugging and tracking devices that the military may have purchased. They had a readymade operational test bed for them.

Mac's job as a TWATT member (Terrorist Weapons and Tactics Team) was another embryo organisation to develop in this theatre. One can imagine the piss taking they received from other Special Forces with a name carrying that sort of abbreviation.

It was hilarious in a way when you met someone, especially a supercilious officer who pompously asked, "What are you?"

You would reply, "I'm a TWATT".

On actual operations, they learned the job, tested equipment, and produced brilliant results. They were allowed access to SOG information, which was invaluable as a tool of war. So too were the SAS (Keenie Meenie) squads, the most dangerous job of all. These very brave men lived as Arabs among the Arabs. They dressed in Arab clothing and were armed only with their Browning High power 9mm pistols, rooting out and eliminating terrorists in their own back yards. The rabbit warrens and Kochi's were behind the main road running by the sea. Here, the terrorist felt safe and ruled supreme. They were in complete control of their own area of terror.

Many tales have been told about these silent, crazy men and quite rightly so. They deserve it. Consequently, because of this "use" of the war, a lot of original anti-terrorist ideas were welcomed from even the lowest ranks and were tried in a true combat situation. Some paid off, some didn't, and some had hilariously funny results.

Finally, after a few more Daytona 500 like occurrences involving many cursing Arab taxi drivers who were also infamous for their one arm out of the window driving, JB pulled up in the Steamer Point fire section yard.

He sat behind the wheel for a few silent minutes, then said, "Welcome to my empire. You'll find I'm strict but fair, and will listen to ideas. Just don't try to be too clever, or I'll screw your arse so far into the ground even ants will look down on you. Do I make myself clear?"

Mac grinned, "Yes, Sir. Would you brief me as to what you feel my duties are? I want to get started and make the time go by quicker".

"Your job is to be part of the GDT Section. You will run the Cemetery Valley CQB (Close Quarter Battle) weapon ranges. You will lecture on the military situation in South Arabia to all new arrivals to the colony, including turn around battalions. You will lecture and demonstrate captured terrorist weapons and the tactics behind their use. You will keep abreast of all newly found arms caches and liaise with the brigade ATO (Ammunition Technician Officer). With the ATO, you will devise methods of combating the weapons you encounter and if possible, turn the tactics used in their employ back on the terrorist himself. Is that clear? Have you any questions?"

"Just one, Sir. Who am I answerable to? You? Brigade Major? Senior ATO? Just so I don't make any chain of command balls-ups, you understand. It's a little confusing at the moment. I received a briefing in the UK outlining my duties; you read me another set of instructions. Nobody informed me about CQB ranges or history lectures, so who is my boss?"

"I am. You report everything to me. I take it up the chain of command. In that way, you have a buffer and shield between you and some of the supercilious bastards at Command HQ. They are a right toffee nosed bunch of twats up there I assure you. Is that clear enough for you?"

"Yes, Sir. For now. When do I start?"

"Straight away. Follow me. I'll introduce you to the team".

With that, he heaved himself out of the Rover, and started walking down a long concrete yard, passed the two large fire engines and the crash rescue Land Rover. Homemade wooden shacks appeared around the edge of a wide area of sand forming some semblance of a training area, with one large marquee in the middle.

This area took Mac by surprise, because it couldn't be seen from the road. Behind it was a sheer volcanic cliff face, and this cliff curved, forming a semicircle of protection against prying eyes. The boundary not covered by the cliff was enclosed in barbed wire, eight double rolls of Danet Razor Edge. Quite a fortress. Three separate training groups were at work on weapon training. One element was carrying out dry runs on different firing positions: lying, kneeling, and standing with the Lee Enfield Mark 3 Rifle. A second was carrying out stoppage drills with the 303mm Bren light machine gun, and a third group was involved in the load/unload and firing positions with a collection of Mark 2, 3, 4, and 5 Sten guns.

The instructors were all stripped to the waist, dark skinned and sun-tanned, and wearing green bush hats and desert canvas boots. They looked exceptionally fit and were screaming instructions like madmen at the luckless trainees. The trainees themselves were obviously new arrivals. They had sickly white skins compared to the instructors, and were made up of males and females of all ranks of the three services.

"Why are they training with these obsolete weapons? Don't we have any SLRs (Self Loading Rifles) or Stirling submachine guns here?"

Mac believed the training weapons being used had gone out of service years before.

"Steamer point is an RAF station, with RAF Headquarters and Administration setups covering all three services posted here, command pay accounts, hospital and maintenance units are all combined service organizations, for example, but run by the RAF. The RAF is still issued with old Second World War, and pre-Second World War weaponry. Everybody posted here has to carry out their own unit guard duties, including a station guard duty at least once a month. Station policy is to train the new arrivals on the weapon they will use when on guard. They then carry a card saying they are competent to carry that weapon. They have to fire a set practice every three months to keep this card stamped, signed, and up to date. If they fail to do

[177]

this, they are charged and fined. That means we keep the Cemetery Valley Range open every morning of the week from 7 a.m. till 1 p.m. We may fire as many as 150 people every morning. Can you see now why we need you on the range?"

"Yes, Sir. But if I'm on the range every day, how do I fit the other jobs in?"

"You lecture to new arrivals on the history, terrorist weapons, and tactics on Monday and Tuesday mornings. Then you're on the range the rest of the week. Your dirty tricks stuff comes in the afternoons and night. You've no time off here my old son".

"Those three instructors, is that our full complement?"

"Yes. The fire section is a separate entity, fully manned by RAF crews, but on top of their usual work, they run the Arab labour force. We have to employ the bastards, because of political agreements, so we give them all the shit jobs, such as putting up barbed wire fencing, cleaning fire engines, and a dozen other jobs".

"I'm surprised we have Arab labour in this terrorist hotbed when we're involved in fucking them up. Surely they won't work with my side of the schedule?"

"You have two levies that help out on the range. Corporal Carmichael, filing magazines, opening ammo boxes, and cleaning weapons, closely controls them. You're too busy running the show for those types of things. You must concentrate on running the different weapon firing practices".

"These two Arab weapon experts we've trained, they go back to their Arab Quarters and run night classes on weapon training for their friends, I suppose?" Mac couldn't help sounding just a little sarcastic at this news.

"You've a lot to learn about this rat hole. Everybody here is your bloody enemy, the local Police, Customs officers, Federal Army, they're all climbing on the side of the NLF (National Liberation Front) who is appearing to be stronger than FLOSY (The Front for the Liberation of South Yemen). If they don't, they're dead. Your two men are FRA. The bloody British government has put us in a terrible, impossible situation we'll be lucky to survive, let alone win. I'll

[178]

introduce you to Hugh Boyle. He'll update you on all the devious, underhanded skullduggery so called politics that's going off here, and something we can do fuck all about".

Hugh was a fit, tough, experienced character, full of a broad calm and peace, which possibly came from his upbringing in the Western Isles at Benbecular. When he spoke, his voice was deep, but profoundly clear and concise in its punctuation and sounding vowels. His handshake was strong and positive, something Mac looked for in introductions. He hated insipid, limp handshakes, and carried an instant distrust for people who had them. He normally found people's character reflected their handshake. He instantly liked Hugh.

"Welcome! I won't ask if you've had a good trip. I'll bet you a tenner the last three miles on Buch's dodgems were the best". With that very true remark, he grinned, shrugged a follow me sign, and headed for the opened marquee in the dust bowl centre.

"Sgt, Boyle. I'll cover your duties. It'll keep my hand in weapon-wise. Fill Mac in with everything you know and two hundred percent of what you don't know. Take what time you need".

Buchan wheeled out the tent like an imitation of some glamorous Sheikh from "The Arabian Nights".

"Ah-hem! God help the poor wee trainees with that bastard loose on them". Hugh laughed a loud, raucous explosion of sound, seemingly far too loud for his size. Mac soon noticed his thoughtful "ah-hem" came out as the sound of a throaty cough, screened behind the back of his hand, and was a habit that indicated that he was thinking of, or considering an answer to any question, or contemplating what he was going to say.

"Ah-hem, I heard you were coming about two months ago, and no bullshit, it was great news. We need your know-how here on the terrorism side. All the team are slightly pissed off that you have to be included in the defence training side. We're so pushed, though, that's the only way out to keep the station personnel able to draw and use weaponry on guard. I'm sorry".

Mac's brief had stated Hugh was a straight to the point merchant, so this introduction and compliment didn't surprise or embarrass him in any way.

"It did give me a bit of a kick in the balls when the Buch told me about ranges and lectures, but I can see the need, and I don't really mind, as long as I can get the other side of the job done with satisfactory results. I received a brief in the UK, but I'm going to drain your mind of everything you know about this fucking place during the next few days, especially now I've found out that I have to teach all new arrivals the military history of the bloody place. Are there any more surprises like that waiting for me?"

"Ah-hem. No. You lecture in the main lecture rooms above station HQ. I'll take you to see the place shortly. You have all the training aids you need for the history side, maps, news reports, and intelligence daily data tickertapes, OHPs, (Overhead Projections) DeBrie 16mm projector, Pathe News clips about Aden that's made the world news, and the station library WRAF girl keeps these updated. Ah-hem. You have the new arrivals for history on Monday at 7 a.m. till 1 p.m., then your own terrorism thing on Tuesdays, same hours. You'll have a mixed bag, both genders, of all ranks and services, possibly one hundred per week. The station supply lecture room cleaners and personnel will lay the room out with chairs and so on just as you dictate. You also have secure lock up facilities for your equipment downstairs in the Station Orderly Room. Is all clear so far?"

"Yes. No problems, but Hugh, just spell out to me why the powers-that-be want new arrivals filled in on the history of the region. They are here to do their own particular work. They follow orders on security as they change day-by-day. Why this emphasis on fucking history?"

"Ah-hem. We only assume that somebody up there in the command 'gin palace' has had a dream that everyone will be better little sailors, soldiers, or airmen, if they know why our Arab neighbours fucking hate us and are trying to kill us! Who knows?"

"I can see the need for terrorist weapons and tactics for all ranks, especially with them all doing their own individual unit guards and searching Arab workers on the way into work. They'll be able to recognise even small parts of a device if the Arabs try to smuggle them inside their compound, and then assemble the parts together later into a complete bomb".

"Mac, you've got it in one. Ah-hem. Your side of the work is very necessary. The history might be interesting, though its value is doubtful, but ours is to do and die and all that shit. Come with me and I'll show you our private club. We'll have a cold drink".

Hugh stood up, knocking over the folding flat table they had been sitting at. With a grin, he bent down and pulled a small tape recorder bugging device from the underside of the table held in place with tape. Putting it close to his mouth, he let out a high-pitched whistle, then a scream, and then put the device back, and put the table upright. "Ah-hem. That should blow the Buch's eardrum out when he decides to listen to that. He wears earphones to listen to his baby bugs. He plants them everywhere to see if people are breaching security regulations. I knocked the table over because he sometimes plants spray bombs to test for alertness. The only problem with them is you can't get the spray off and it stinks to high heaven. What a screwball he is. Have you met one like him before?"

"I can't say that I have. Thank fuck. I'm a great believer in that characteristic called 'trust' when it comes down to your own men. If I find him fucking me about, he'll have bloody problems on his hands, like real booby traps not bloody pretend ones".

Mac was pissed off with these new revelations of Buchan's character. He had once laid an officer out unconscious who he caught trying to catch sentries out at night. That type of stupidity takes the men's eyes off the real ball and doesn't help at all in combat situations.

CHAPTER 2

The Crows

While they were talking, Hugh and Mac had been walking past the back of the homemade wooden buildings between the barbed wire and the volcanic cliff face, and Mac couldn't help notice the large numbers of crows perched in the nooks and crannies of the gnarled, blackened rock. He mentioned this to Hugh, and was led into a world of observation of which he had never even dreamed.

"They're clever bastards. Look at them sitting there, all silent, not one bit of noise out of the lot of them". Hugh had taken Mac into one of the shacks backing up to the cliff, and they were observing the crows through a screen of brown Hessian cloth that acted as a combined window, fly net, and sunscreen.

"Ah-hem. Just keep quiet, and you'll see them in action".

They stood in silence for about fifteen minutes, when a starling landed on the barbed wire between the building and the crow's cliff. It hopped and stared about in a nervous bobbing manner, and then just as suddenly as it arrived, it flew off. Over the next ten minutes, there were a few more starling sorties following the same pattern. There was still not one sound or movement from the crows. Mac now began to see what was going to happen. The starlings wanted to feed on the figs and attendant insects, all in profusion in the trees growing over and shading the shacks. Soon, about fifteen birds had lined up on the barbed wire, ready to begin a mass feeding foray into the trees, where, no doubt, they would be joined by the rest of the flock, when – Bang! It happened.

As though actioned by a starter pistol, the crows launched and dived on the starlings, screaming like Stuka dive-bombers. It was murderous. The victims, trapped between the cliff and buildings with the crows diving from above had nowhere to manoeuvre. A full body impact behind the stabbing beak of the crows and there was soon a ripping, tearing, noisy feast in progress. These crows were savage. Over the weeks, Mac saw them feast on many different varieties of prey, including an injured cat.

"Here we are at the 'Exclusive Club,' ah-hem, our very own private bar, with the coldest, cheapest, largest range of beer in Aden. Officially open with barman from 13:00 hrs. till our senior member on the night decides to close. Guests by invite only, except females, they are welcome all the time".

CHAPTER 3

The Aviary

The club was contained in a large building, made up of two adjoining rooms, each one big enough to hold three full size billiards tables. One room stepped up above the other, and contained wicker armchairs with matching tables.

The lower room held the bar running the full length down one side, whilst at right angles to it was a huge aviary forming the outer wall, full of hundreds of tropical birds, dozens of beautiful creatures that were brought in by visiting aircrew from around the world. The collection must have been worth thousands of pounds in those days.

"Mac, this budgie here is called Whisky. Watch this". Hugh held a glass of whisky up to the wire netting separating the birds from the bar, tilting it inwards slightly. A yellow breasted, blue winged male strutted sideways across one of the many perches, tweeting and nibbling at different females, he spotted the whisky glass and immediately flew down, settling on the glass rim, and began to drink.

After a few good swigs, the character flew back to the perch, mounted a female, gave her a good fettling, and then flew back to the glass for a pit stop. Mac could not believe his own eyes. This drunken, rampant, buggering budgie (it tried to mount males on some occasions, probably too drunk to tell the difference), performed the drink and screw operation nine times in succession.

Two WRAF Corporals on leave were club guests for a day and claimed they watched him perform twelve times in quick succession. Eventually, on this Mac debut, after the last drink, this fantastic epic, bird just managed to land on a lower nearer perch, and finished hanging upside down, grasping the perch with one foot and fell asleep. What a character. He made a repeat performance at least twice per day.

"Ah-hem. Our section owns the club - it is famous throughout Aden. It is secure, with armed guards on the section perimeter towers at night. Gate guards check all entry. We let our own section invite their own guests, as many as they like. We keep our profit margins low, and sell our drinks cheaper than the NAAFI. The bar staff are from the fire section personnel on a rota basis, and they get paid for their work. We never have a shortage of volunteers if one is off sick or something. Ah-hem, every member can buy and wear the club tie, which is dark blue with a single white logo of the 'Saints' top hat, monocle, and bow tie. At the end of a member's tour of duty out here, we present him with a silver tankard engraved with his name and the same logo and the dates he was with us. Can you see why we're so popular?"

"Too right I can. If the work setup is as well organised as this, I'm going to have a good time here. That's if I manage any time off, that is, which seems very fucking doubtful".

After a couple of ice cold drinks in the club, Hugh took Mac to his accommodation to give him the chance of a shower and settle in before beginning work on the ranges the following morning. His hopes of a good posting rose again when the Land Rover pulled up outside a normal looking service three-bedroom house, surrounded by alfalfa grass lawns, and bordered with geraniums and bougainvillea flowers. The house was part of a crescent of similar houses and within the secure confines of the camp itself.

"Here we are Mac, your humble abode, ah-hem, compliments of the RAF Officers married quarters. You are now in a place called Tarshyne, overlooking Telegraph bay, and the Cable and Wireless Complex. Because of the emergency, many married families have gone home to the UK and not been replaced because of our impending withdrawal, so the quarters are vacant and used as SNCO single barracks. A good break for us, what?"

"It sure is for me, old mate. Things look rosier every minute".

"Ah-hem, come and have a wee look at the view".

They walked into the back garden and found it terminated about thirty metres from the house on a steep cliff. This cliff was crisscrossed with footpaths, twisting their way down and leading into a large circular bay. Surrounding the bay were volcanic cliffs on three sides and the other opened out into the Indian Ocean. Large radio masts crowned the top of the cliffs as part of the Cable and Wireless Communication Centre HQ.

"One warning for you about this place Mac, ah-hem, if you go swimming, watch out for sharks the Sassenachs, an officer's wife was taken by a Great White in this bay and she was only standing in about nine inches of water. An Arab fisherman tried to beat the thing off her with a boat oar, but it was too late to save her. The poor wee soul died. Secondly, keep well away from the radio masts if it looks like a storm, they attract lightning bolts by the dozen".

Suddenly, the place doesn't seem so rosy after all, mused Mac.

The married quarter was of standard design found in Middle East areas. All had high ceilings with large bladed fans in every room. There were no carpets; these were substituted by bare easy-to-mop tiled floors. The rooms were spacious and lightly furnished with just the basics, but with a monstrous sized fridge freezer. The whole structure was cool and easy to clean, essential factors in a place where temperatures soar into the high nineties and hundred plus degrees during the summer season. All the windows had fly and mosquito screens, as did the door porches. Curtains were surplus to requirement. The kitchen was equipped with a cooker, washing machine, toaster, electric kettle, and fruit juicer, so there was no need to go out to the mess for meals if one didn't feel like it. Everything was in the home. From the sitting room balcony there was a great view of the Steamer Point football pitch and sports track. By leaning out from the balcony a little, Mac could see a panoramic view of the sea running into the port of Aden and the P& O Shipping Lines HQ at Tawahi.

A large, semicircular shark net enclosed the small bay in front of the Steamer Point NAAFI, which had a white sandy beach running down to the clear crystal water. A small metal jetty ran from the beach and into the sea for some fifty metres, and this was full of budding deep sea fishermen, after Leopard Ray or Shark for the dining room cooks to make into a fish and chip supper for them.

I can put up with this, was the predominant thought when Mac finally crashed on the bed and fell instantly asleep.

CHAPTER 4

Aiwa

"Bang, bang, bang! Morning Master killer trainer!"

Mac was sent bolt upright in bed by this 05:00 hours start to his day. "Chi, Master, chi, here now, you drink hot".

Standing by the side of his bed, carrying a big brass jug, nearly as large as himself, was a four-foot tall, black-skinned, Nubian-featured Arab boy, with a shock of pitch black hair and a grin that spread right around his face, exposing large pure white molars. He was dressed in a one-piece white Galabia come Futah, held in at the waist with a rope belt, from which hung a dozen or so green tin mugs.

"Chi now Master. Your Dhobi boy 'Aiwa' here every day with chi, and take washing, clean very good, make very good starch, keep Master clean, very smart Master, clean boots every night, Master very big man, I keep Master very smart".

While he was talking, he poured a large mug of tea, and was ferreting around among Mac's kit to find dirty clothes to take away to wash.

"Aiwa take clothes to laundry for Dhobi every morning, bring back clean and starch every day five o'clock with afternoon cold lemon drink. You like this Master? You pay Aiwa one Dinah every week, for chi and lemon and ten piasta every piece of clothing wash. You like?"

"I like, but first I question. How did you get into my house and my room?"

"Master Dhobi man has key all houses. Give keys to Dhobi boys when come to work in morning. Take keys off Dhobi boys when go home at night".

"Your master Dhobi man, is he soldier?" Mac didn't like the idea one little bit that somebody had access to troop's accommodation in

[188]

this fashion, especially in a theatre of terrorist activity that was escalating every day that passed.

"No master, Dhobi master is Mr. Patel, the Pakistani master of all the Chi and Dhobi in all the camps in Aden. Mr. Patel, he very big man. Very much money. Pay English government much money".

"Okay, Aiwa, you keep me clean with my washing. What day do I pay you?"

"You pay me one Dinah start of week, like now, you pay me Dhobi everyday five o'clock when I bring and you see it is good and clean and good starch".

"That means I have to carry many piastas every day. Why don't I pay you Dhobi once per week?"

"Maybe terrorists kill master after two or three days and Aiwa no get paid for Dhobi. You pay every day".

"Okay, that's fine by me". Mac thought what an honest, straightforward, no nonsense, little Arab bastard this boy Aiwa was. Mac liked him.

He also decided to make a thorough check on Patel and his organisation; maybe a fresh mind here may spot something wrong that others had missed by their familiarity with the day-to-day happenings.

After morning ablutions were over and he was ready for the day, Mac headed up a very steep, winding hill, toward the Sgt's Mess and breakfast. The hill was known as Barrack Hill, and did contain troop barracks, Sgt's Mess accommodation, Public Building and Works HQ, and right at the top was the RAF Steamer Point Hospital. The back of this hospital gave a tremendous view down the volcanic cliff face leading to the white Arab dwellings of Tawahi. Unfortunately, it also gave a panorama of the poverty, the corrugated tin and cardboard box Kochi dwellings scattered up the hillside, with their rivers of open sewage flowing down toward the hard surfaced roads in the township below. Between these temporary dwellings were passages no wider than three feet to traverse one's way through them. Accurate navigation through this Arab quarter was nigh impossible, because the layout-changed every day with some dwellings erected and some

[189]

disappearing. This was the rabbit warren of terrorist activity, from which they would attack targets in the main streets and commerce centres bordering the harbour. This area was soon to be the nightly haunt of Mac and his crew.

The Sergeant's Mess at Steamer Point was a large, double story structure, with the usual mess facilities found in all messes on the ground floor. It sported a huge upstairs bar and dance hall instead of the usual accommodation, although the dance hall was not used for its original purpose, due to the shortage of women of SNCO rank and the exodus of married personnel.

Mac discovered that the room was now famous for indoor rugby matches between visiting messes. The accommodation was adjacent in single roomed, one-story barracks, protruding like fingers at ninety-degree angles to the main building.

The kitchen was staffed with Arab cooks, under the supervision of an English Sgt Mess Steward, with a Cpl assistant. Food was self-service, and as much as one wanted, though lacking in choice somewhat in comparison with other messes. There was always plenty of fish of various types, caught by the members themselves in Aden harbour. Another unusual item often on the menu was Gazelle and Ibex mountain goats that were shot by Army crews moving north up the Dahla road to the Radfan, and by helicopter crews on the way to the up-country airstrip at Thurmier. A good breakfast of eggs, sausage, beans, and fried bread washed down with another mug of tea, set Mac up for the start of what was to become the five times per week shooting gallery mass shoot.

CHAPTER 5

Cemetery Valley

As per pre-arrangement, Hugh turned up at the mess with the unit Long Wheelbase Land Rover to collect Mac. Hugh never took breakfast himself, he felt he was putting on too much weight, therefore he subjected himself to a diet of one evening meal, mainly steak, and about seven pints of lager per night.

First port of call was the armoury. Hugh walked up to the small wire screened window of the duty armourer and handed over his service identity card. A few seconds later, the sounds of locks and bolts being removed from a side door heralded the appearance of an RAF Policeman and a bloody great fearsome looking Alsatian dog that kept a mean eye on Hugh's balls.

"Ye dina ha tae be bothered with these wee canine ladies. They're well trained to kill Arabs but not us wee Brits".

It was a mark of Hugh's apprehension at the presence of the beast that he broke into his Highland lilting dialect.

"I'll be taking the usual range detail please, ah-hem".

"Sign here mate", came the voice of the still invisible armourer behind his screen, as an A4 sized document was passed through the aperture.

Hugh read aloud, "Twelve SLRs, Twelve 303 Enfield, 6 Smith and Wesson 38mm, 6 Browning High Power 9mm, 2 Greener 16 gauge, 4 Shotguns 12 bore, 4 mk2, 4 mk3, 4 mk5 Sten guns, 6 Stirling SMGs, 6 Bren 303mm LMGs, 6 CS Grenades, 6 Smoke grenades. Ammunition, all weapon types in full sealed containers, count and sign for on return and acceptance of used empty cases. One pack of fire control orders - Rules for Engagement Aden. One pack new weapon authorisation cards. One-pack pens. Two unit stamps and ink pad. One first aid pack. All correct. Thanks a lot".

With that, Hugh signed the form, and signalled Mac back to the Land Rover. The RAF Policeman was opening a side gate to the armoury compound. While they drove through, Mac observed two more dog handlers watching them with the animals straining at their leashes. Hugh drove up to a large metal door just starting to open, allowing two men to push out a four-wheeled trolley full of the weapons and ammunition.

Loading the Land Rover was a second security check; Hugh ticked off another list called 'Weapon complete and cleaned,' as the men loaded them on the Rover, after presenting the weapon for inspection by Hugh and Mac.

"We do this every range practice, ah-hem. After firing, we clean and well oil all weapons. On return, these men clean again and dry off excess oil before we collect them. The weapons are rotated with others every seventh range to even out wear and tear".

Everything loaded and forms signed, Hugh drove out of the armoury compound, leaving the mean-eyed police dogs looking pissed off because they had just lost some humans to chew.

Cemetery valley was so called because it housed an Arab burial place from as far back as anyone Mac met could remember. The graves themselves were really shallow scrapes in the volcanic rock, with a cairn of volcanic stones on top. They were carelessly constructed, and it was a common occurrence when driving to the range in the mornings to disturb the 'piard' (wild) dogs away from the graves, carrying bones in their mouths.

On the few occasions when heavy rain fell, some of the bodies were washed down the valley into the shopping streets of Tawahi. The dogs numbered hundreds and lived in the nooks and crannies of the 'Shamsan' volcanic mountain at the head of the valley. They were a bastard enemy in their own right, when one was on patrol at night. Not only did they 'pack' attack, but also the noise they created when they heard a human movement virtually made covert operations impossible.

One of Mac's first decisions was to take out his crew with 16 gauge guns and eliminate the dogs on the west side of Shamsan, which overlooked his main area of operations. These animals were clever. After a couple of days being shot at, they moved to the eastern side of the mountain, which was fine with Mac. However, he and his crew still carried silenced pistols in case of 'Pack' attack at night.

On the way to the firing point, Mac saw the laundry facilities owned by Mr. Patel. There were huge, clothes lines full of sheets, shirts, shorts, trousers, towels, and any other washable material items which seemed to stretch for at least three miles. Twenty-foot diameter concrete bowls built from the ground was the start of the wash. They had wood, lava, and gas fires burning underneath them, heating the boiling soap and water they contained. The finest fuel used in these washing boilers was crushed volcanic Magna, reheated with a gas lance until it was glowing red liquid, giving off tremendous heat. Once melted, it could be left heating the troughs for hours. To reactivate it, oxygen lances were pushed in the base of the fire, and, in no time, it was melted lava again.

It was very rare to see any new fuel material added. It seemed to last forever. Into these boiling cauldrons, everything was thrown in after sorting. Underpants in one, whites in another, colours in another, and so on.

After boiling, clothes were hung on an aerial conveyor belt running under recycling water to rinse. It seemed that all the people from the Indian subcontinent and Pakistan were employed at this establishment, but Mac discovered, as part of his investigations, that Patel had to employ 50% of his workforce from the Arab NLF HQ to keep his contract. What a security thorn for Mac to try to pull out of the British backside.

The range consisted of a 25 metre firing point and twelve metal target holders in the ground. All firing was done on figure targets, normally number 12s. There was no backdrop to catch the rounds after they passed through the targets, just a few boards and a scrape of earth and stones. Most bullets just ricocheted their way from stone to stone up the slope of Shamsan Mountain. The whole setup was one of complete well-organised, rule breaking efficiency.

[193]

Weapons were laid on the firing point, at the ranges the men may be expected to fire them. A brief appreciation without presenting argumentative pros and cons was as follows: Smith and Wesson revolvers 10 metres, Browning High Power 15 metres, SMGs 20 metres, Rifles, Brens 25 metres. All the weapon magazines, except the 38mm revolvers and 303mm Enfield rifles, were pre-loaded to lend speed to the operation. A folding flat table and chair was situated at the entrance to the firing points, and this was the domain of Cpl Carmichael.

When a person arrived at the range, his service identity card and weapon proficiency card were checked. Both carried a photograph, and these must match. The service identity card was handed back, whilst the weapon proficiency was held back for a unit stamp and signature on completion of firing. The person for qualification had their name, weapon, and the date entered into a large foolscap sized book.

They were then allowed to enter the range to the back of the firing points, carrying with them the appropriate magazine or number of rounds for the weapon they were due to fire. It was nothing short of a mass conveyor belt, but it worked. The station could maintain its security requirements with everybody carrying out their fair share of duties and maintaining high standards of weapon safety. Not one man was charged with accidental discharge of a weapon during the last two years of the emergency. Personnel only fired the weapons they would carry on duty. For example, Officers fired the 38mm revolver. RAF police and some Warrant Officers, plus Army Officers, fired the 9mm Browning. SNCOs fired the various Sten SMGs, as did RAF driver trade group. Junior ranks fired 303 Enfield or SLRs if they were Army. Ambush teams fired the Bren LMG, and Riot Control Teams fired under CS gas and Smoke concentrations, wearing their respirators during the last half-hour of the daily range.

There were a few exceptions to the normal weapon allocations, mainly the Internal Security Special Patrol Teams who operated in the Arab Kochi's at night. These characters fired everything, including captured terrorist weapons such as Kalashnikovs AK47. Then, of course, the specialist units took over the range in the afternoons to carry out their own thing, without any spectators. SAS 'Keenie Meenie' teams were shooting their particular style of double tap close quarter combat practices nearly every day, with a variety of weapons.

Hugh had a style of his own when it came to giving men incentive to fire well and with enthusiasm. Even though it was a range shoot, he managed to create an air of authenticity in the practice, as though the men were actually defending themselves against a terrorist attack. Everybody stripped to the waist, wearing just shorts, bush hats, and desert Bondoo boots. Even senior officers were briefed by their aides about these uncompromising actions, which took place every day in Cemetery Valley.

One day, Mac witnessed a slight hiccup take place, not because of a failure in safety procedures, but because of a combination of fair skin, freckles, and sunshine. Admiral Sir Michael Le Fanu was affectionately called 'Ginger' by the men, because of his very ginger hair. He and his staff came to the range, displaying all the rank emblems, medals, and gold braid. This led to the much-talked about incident-taking place.

"Good morning, gentlemen. Welcome to the range, ah-hem. You will notice everyone here has removed all clothing displaying rank or other awards. You will remove your jackets and other symbols of rank and position now!"

He waited whilst the reluctant party removed their clothing.

"That little action makes us all the same: a human body with human strengths, weaknesses, housing fear, bravery, and all the many other little things that make us the most complex but effective animal in the world. When we strip down to the basics, we are not mentally conscious of being protected by the abstract power that our uniforms displaying rank afford us. We are aware of being vulnerable. We are bodies that can feel pain, get shot, and die, or we can kill the murderer first. When we are dead, we will decompose. Ants and flies will creep into every orifice of our bodies, lay their eggs, and their young maggots will eat us until we are nothing but bleach white bones without marrow. We will never see our loved ones again. We are

[195]

nothing. We do not exist. We must train hard to prevent this from happening. We must kill the terrorist and his employees first".

Hugh coughed behind his hand, his sincerity in what he was saying, and the emotion in his voice was mesmerising the shooters. You could see them physically change into a potentially aggressive person, rather than someone having to fire his three monthly range.

"This state of affairs, gentlemen, is brought about by the terrorist. He avoids placing himself in danger if he can. He very often uses children to do his dirty work. He will give a nine-year-old Arab boy a gun and a nine pence value 9mm bullet and says 'Shoot a white man'. He explains to the boy that a person with a lot of badges on his clothing, or people around him protecting him, or one who shouts, points, and gives orders is an important person, therefore a better person to shoot. He explains that the boy can earn two Dinah for shooting the important 'master' instead of the one Dinah for a normal man. Did you know you are valued at 5000 Dinah, Admiral? We have to work especially hard to stay alive, don't we? No going around patting kiddies on the head out here, Sir. They might fucking kill you!"

Hugh had a way of his own, and he didn't give a shit what rank to whom he was talking. His facts were correct, and it was his job to make people aware and help keep them from falling into a terrorist trap.

"Ah-hem, we cannot effectively train against these types of attacks apart from maintaining our vigilance and never trusting children, any child, regardless of age. Although this goes against our nature. The terrorist knows this and that's why he employs them. He knows our weaknesses. The bullet fired by this boy is travelling at the same muzzle velocity as the one fired by our terrorist and will do us the same amount of damage. The only little thing in our favour is the boy is, more often than not, less accurate.

"The daily incident reports are full of shooting attempts, missed targets, and child arrests, with them carrying the weapon. Are there any questions so far? No? Fine, let's continue.

"The attack we are going to train against today is the increased number of professional assassin incidents. We know that there are at

[196]

least three of these bastards operating in the townships of Crater, Ma'alah, and Tawahi. We know the weapons they use and the weapon movements. This information comes from the Special Branch. It has been put together with the knowledge of the places they have killed and resultant forensic tests on the bullets and cartridge cases. We also know the modus operandi of these budding James Bonds, and their days are numbered, but you have to be aware of how they attack and what you must do about it, in case you bump into them before our boys have eliminated them. One of them, we believe, is an East German; so don't trust any Arian looking Kraut. The other merchants are Arabs, sent to the Soviet Union or China, and trained to fuck us up. Their technique for assassinations is to head kill. The first indication you may get of your death is seeing an Arab with a gun pointing at your head. This is how they are trained to kill. Your instant reaction if you are lucky enough to observe the attack, or if a buddy yells, 'target,' you drop below the terrorist point of aim. Do not forget, he is frightened. If he is aiming at your head and you disappear from his line of sight, he is confused. He is concentrating on your head when, suddenly, it disappears. Drop gentlemen, below his line of sight. He then has to correct his point of aim. We do not allow him the privilege of the easy, calculated shot, with all the time in the world to steady himself for the kill. He has been trained to work this way; it is the Modus operandi they use".

While Hugh was making this psychological and mental build up in the men's minds, he was walking around casually, with a 9mm Browning high-power pistol in a holster on his right hip.

"Notice those six targets behind me? Imagine they are the enemy, and now watch this". With that statement, he'd turned around the 180 degrees, dropped onto one knee, and fired at all six targets inside six seconds. He then stood up and casually placed the browning back in its holster.

"What I've just shown you gentlemen, the enemy can do, you must be able to beat him, and can you do that now? No? You will be able to by the time you have finished with me today. Let us go and look at the targets". They walked down the range together, and stood

[197]

in front of the six figure targets, each target had a single shot in the belly button.

"That is what we must do, gentleman, place every shot in the centre of the main target mass. In this way, we are giving ourselves the biggest possible target. This should ensure our opponents are hit, and the enemy will die. What's more, he knows he is going to die when you hit him in the stomach, but it will take him a while and give us a chance to interrogate him and find out where he got his weapons from, who he worked for, and any more information that we need. This will not cost us any money for a hospital bed for him; we need them for the British soldiers. When a man is hit in the centre of the stomach, he knows he's going to die. He is in terrible pain. If you offer him skilled medical aid and the promise that we will make him better, he will talk his head off. That is not cruel, gentleman, that is fact".

For the next twenty minutes or so Mac and Hugh tutored the shooters on the move, the need to shoot up the length of the body, because it gave them the approximate 5' 6" height of the man to hit, instead of the 18" width of his body to hit if they traversed across the body. They all quickly achieved the two handed triangular firing position, and, after firing a few CQB (Close Quarter Battle) practices, they were hitting targets in the centre of main target mass in less than a second. They were amazed at their own progress, but were continuously spurred on to better results by the amazingly enthusiastic Hugh and his war chant, which he had them all shout while they fired the two shot double tap practice.

"You are firing two shots at a time at a Golly. You are trying to hit him in the area of the balls or just above. For the first two shots, shout 'Gol'-'ly' to the rhythm of your firing. For the next two shots, shout 'Bol'-'locks'. Got it? First shot shout 'Gol', second shot shout 'ly', third shot shout 'Bol' fourth shot shout 'locks'. Rhythm men. Let's practice, 'Gol-ly Bol-locks'. Again, 'Gol-ly Bol-locks'. And again, 'Gol-ly Bol-locks', and again 'Gol-ly Bol-locks'. That's good rhythm men, rhythm, come on my lovely Golly Bollock hunters, shout, louder...louder!"

It was epic. Every man on the firing point and the spectators behind were screaming at the top of their voices, "GOLLY BOLLOCKS!"

to the rhythm of the shooting. Talk about mass hypnosis. The Admiral Commander in Chief and his staff were screaming loudest. It was at this time that Mac noticed the Admiral was turning a definite shade of pink. At first, he put this down to the exertion he had been involved in, but then realised that with him being ginger haired and very light skinned, he was probably beginning to get sunburned.

"Are you feeling okay, Admiral?"

"Yes, I'm fine. Thank you, Staff".

"Be careful of the sun, Sir. It can catch up with you very quickly; before you realise it, you could be badly burned".

"I am beginning to tingle a bit. Maybe you'll give me permission to put my shirt on again?"

"Of course, Sir. Put your shirt on now".

That was it, and that was the mark and the calibre of the Admiral. He was very badly burned by teatime of the same day. His brigade Major came down to the Cemetery Valley Range with a letter for the staff.

The Admiral had written:

"Let no one blame you for my condition, especially yourselves. I should have known myself that I was beginning to burn and told you as such. You're doing a brilliant job there, and must have saved at least battalion strength of lives with your very effective and irregular style of training. Thank you very much. I'll come for some more 'conditioning' soon"

Signed, Le Fanu.

How many Senior Officers would have thought and gone to that sort of trouble?

He was a great man.

CHAPTER 6

Golly Hunters

Today was to be a special day. While Mac had been in the UK having his brief about the job from Harry, he had been given two large rectangular boxes that Hugh had asked for. It now came to light that these boxes contained the little Golliwogs you used to find on the side of Robertson's Jam. These had been requested from Robertson without any explanation as to their use, so they were very good to send them really.

Now, the idea behind this silliness was simple. They were intended to be a morale booster for the men who had to keep coming on to the range and qualify to use their weapons. Once they had passed their shooting qualification, they would be given one of these little Golliwogs to stick on a material wrist band and wear it as if it were a marksman's badge. The badges would be signed on the back by Corporal Carmichael, and carry the letters QGH standing for 'Qualified Golly Hunter.'

They were an instant success, and everybody wanted one. There had never been so many volunteers for range practice in history. Considering the number of people who attended the range every day, it did not take long to see hundreds of people walking about with Golliwogs strapped to their wrist.

Some do-gooders among the Headquarters personnel were frightened of what the Arabs would think about this new British emblem of lethality, and tried to have the practice stopped, even issuing threats of formal disciplinary action against Hugh and Mac if the issues continued. They were politely told to "do their worst and fuck off".

It was also believed then and still that somebody with mega power was backing the practice up behind the scenes. Buchan possibly, or Le Fanu? Who knows?

Taking into consideration the heat, the dust, and the sweat caused by the horribly humid climate, Cemetery Valley was a place of many good memories. One could wonder how many men out there now reading this story will have kept their little Golliwog. There must be literally thousands. The original supply of two boxes had 1,000 Golliwogs in each box. These were used and the re-supply was tenfold. Thank you very much to Robertson's Jam. All of these badges were issued to men who had actually fired on the range and qualified; no one received one for nothing!

One morning, when on the Valley Range, Mac heard the Cur-rump, Cur-rump of mortar bombs, exploding and spreading across the Aden peninsula. This was a regular thing for the Arabs to perform. For some reason, they always fired the mortar bombs in banks of seven, and you could count them off. They were so regular, you could tell if the attacks were finished or not. These Arabs never fired more than seven bombs in one salvo. On this particular morning, only five exploded.

Mac had to rush in the Land Rover from the range to discover where the bombs had landed and what had happened to the mysterious two that had failed to explode. As it happened, they were two-inch mortar bombs that had been fired and two had landed near the hospital and the Sergeant's Mess on Barrack Hill without exploding. Buchan arrived on the scene at the same time as Mac.

"Stick the fucking things in the Land Rover," Bachan said, and promptly drove away at a very fast rate of knots with the two unexploded bombs on the back seat.

He took them into the fire section compound, stuck a little bit of Nobel's 808 Plastic explosive on them, and with only five seconds delay on the time fuse, dropped them in a roll of unopened barbed wire and strolled away. He had two Arabs working twenty yards away, but did not tell them to get out of the way.

"I bet these Bastards tell their mates in Tahwahi that we nearly had them killed, don't you think?"

What can you reply to such a question?

Now to finish off the story about the Golliwog saga. Many strange things happened related to the golliwogs that were hard to believe. The Royal Navy often called into Aden Harbour as part of the Gulf patrol. When HMS Sheffield arrived, someone noticed a person wearing a Golliwog and asked him what it stood for. On gaining the information he requested, he rushed back to the ship and told the crew who turned up en mass at the ranges to shoot for the coveted QGH. They even brought their own weapons and ammunition with them. When they left Aden, they called in at Bahrain and told the crew of HMS Eskimo, who promptly bombed off south to fire at the range for a QGH.

Our British Navy has never been short of being adventurous. It was unending. Aircrew flying from the Far East made it a number one priority to fire and earn the emblem of British savagery. This 'Symbol of Deadliness' had also changed in stature, there now was a QGH 1st Class, QGH 2nd Class, and QGH Marksman.

Mac and Hugh folded up in fits of maniacal laughter when they heard a group of Sergeants arguing vehemently about who had rated the best QGH when they had fired that day. They were so heated in this argument that they didn't see Mac or Hugh stood there. When they finally noticed them, they proceeded to lace them with drinks trying to wheedle another QGH out of them. Of course, they were unsuccessful. No way would our stalwarts give the QGH away in a bar, Sergeants Mess or not. They refused to lower its value and importance, which made it an even more desirable piece of kit to possess.

CHAPTER 7
Terrorist Weapons and Tactics

Mac soon commenced the other side of his work. His first port of call was the Ammunition Technician Officer headquarters in Khormaksa. The first meeting there was with the Senior ATO, a mature very professional Warrant Officer, Jonathan Griffith. It was rewarding; the Warrant Officer put him at ease straight away, and made it clear they would be working together, sharing all information, keeping nothing from each other.

When it came to Mac bringing up the seven bomb mortar patterns, the Warrant Officer had a theory. He believed that when the terrorists went to train in Russia and China, they were given demonstrations on a seven Katushka rocket system.

"They've assumed this was the norm, seeing their instructors using a seven-bomb pattern".

Another theory was the fact that most of the attacks took place between ten and twelve AM, so they needed a timing device that worked best in the heat of the morning sun.

Strange things had been used as mortars, such as the British 94 Energa grenade, which was used by Mac's men as a rifle launched anti-tank weapon. They had left behind thousands of these in the Canal Zone. When kicking about the attacks, it became clear that bombing by the Arabs, regardless of what type of weapon or launcher was used, was dependent on the morning sun, since the climate was very hot between ten and twelve, and all attacks came at this time.

The long and the short of it was that the Warrant Officer and his staff were too busy taking apart bombs and booby traps that had been planted, and one of Mac's special jobs was to attempt to solve the seven bomb mortar pattern dilemma.

Mac's next port of call was at Ballycastle House in Khormaksar to see the SAS and ask for their support in locating possible mortar base plate positions. These had to be hidden and camouflaged in the Kochi huts behind the main streets of the main towns. This area was the SAS's domain of operations and Mac felt it was much wiser to let them know what job was needed in these rabbit warrens, rather than try to do things himself.

This was partly due to the sad fact that two Royal Anglians on undercover duties in Arab clothes were killed by the SAS as suspected terrorists, because they had not been informed of the Anglian's activities. If the SAS located any of the mortar base plate positions, it was suggested they do nothing; just report their location, and then inform Mac, so he could then work out how to play dirty tricks on the Arabs.

SAS activities were at a peak at this time. In the urban townships of Aden, as well as up-country, they were very stretched in manpower, but they agreed to assist Mac as much as possible without making his request a 'Special Activity.' They would assist in other ways. One way was to let Mac go up into the Kochis with his crew on his own to carry out searches. This concession came with certain provisos. They must wear uniform and inform the SAS where they expected to operate and the approximate times.

They gave him a radio call sign to allow direct contact with them. His activities were to be combined with the Duty Officer's program of the resident battalion patrols and activities from the Operations Room in P&O's Shipping HQ in Tawahi.

Resolving the seven bomb patterns was only a fraction of the other work he was expected to perform. Grenade attacks were increasing all the time. Different types of grenades were showing their ugly heads with the increasing supply of Russian and Chinese F1 and RG 42 contact grenades and other equipments. These needed to be investigated and a solution found to limit their effectiveness. Attacks against guard posts and sniper attacks with high velocity weapons were on the increase with the large arms smuggling trade from up country supplying the weapons. Ever more sophisticated mines and booby traps with high tech timers and delay devices were being used with the equipment coming from the same source, although many of the booby traps were of second world war vintage, but still just as lethal to the unsuspecting. The Arabs were also very good at improvising booby traps and explosive devices.

It is common knowledge in an internal security situation that the normal activities of a local government's duties suffer, for instance refuge clearance hardly ever takes place, if at all. Sewage systems break down; drain leakage increases, resulting in deterioration in hygiene, and with this, the smell and increase in flies and disease. This was the case with Aden. With no refuse clearance for many weeks, rubbish was piled high on street corners. It was in these heaps of waste that the Arab used to hide their weapons to attack the patrols on the streets.

The Arab male does not carry the weapon. It is the female and the curse of our policy overseas does not allow the British soldier on the road to search women. This must be done by our own women's services in properly prepared roadblocks with private searching facilities for the work to be performed. So, an Arab woman would walk down the street with the grenade under her clothing. She would wait for the opportunity to place her weapon load in the rubbish heap on the street corner. The Arab male could be searched for weapons a dozen times an hour by passing patrols, but of course, he would be clean.

When the 'tail end Charlie' passed by, (the last patrolman), the Arab would delve into the rubbish, bring out the grenade, and throw it after the patrol. This was a common practice. By the time the patrol had taken evasive action, either upon seeing the grenade or hearing a firing pin strike or a warning shout from a patrol member, the Arab is on his way into his pre-planned escape route and the safety of the Kochis. The patrol would, by now, have dived away from the grenade, with their feet toward it and their hands over the back of their heads. One had a little more time to deal with a grenade attack if it was the British Mills 36 grenades, because these had a four-second fuse, and a seven seconds fuse if it was launched from a rifle.

Most of these grenades were thrown, not rifle launched, so there was the chance of four seconds to do something about it. Once the

[206]

Chinese and Russian grenades were in the theatre, they were using the standard UMF fuse, which only gave a 1.5 second delay, and the contact grenade gave no warning at all, unless it was seen coming. This UMF type of fuse also gave off a loud explosion, like a pistol shot when it detonated, so the drop action against the head shot pistol had to serve as the instant reaction defence against the grenade. A number of men were killed because of this.

Mac began to work on these problems, and, within a few months, he and the team had overcome a lot of the difficulties and turned their method of attack and weaponry back onto the Arabs.

To carry out night searches of the suspected base plate areas, it was necessary that the team put together specialised night operations. For this, an internal security section at Steamer Point came into being. A number of people were available for night time patrol activity, and Mac approached some of them spelling the problem out. They were asked if they would like the opportunity to do some extra work against the Arabs at night in the Arab's nest. These men were informed they must have special training, very hard training at that, strict discipline, and complete obedience to orders. What they were about to take part in was not a boy's club; it was a lethal force in which they would have to kill or would be killed.

Within the first week, after word of mouth approaches to people Mac thought might be suitable, over 70 men had volunteered. Of these, Mac selected 30 of the brightest and fittest, and the training began.

The first phase of all training was weaponry and the ability to fire up all weapons, including captured terrorist equipment at night, and in Close Quarter shooting situations. These weapons were already available from previous captures.

Mac could not really take up the range during the day because it was taken up by those needing to get their three monthly qualifications. A time sheet was worked out for afternoon and evening firing to achieve their shooting capabilities, and they also practiced night firing with torches that Mac knew the men would need in the Kochi rabbit warrens at night. Very little night surveillance equipment was available at that time, although once again, the SAS came to the rescue and lent Mac some of their equipment.

Calculations were made on possible ranges of the improvised mortar launches to be able to select certain areas in the back of the townships from where mortars may have been fired. Mac spoke to as many people as possible who had worked with him in Egypt during the Moslem Brotherhood terrorist situations, and particularly in Palestine. His idea was to pool everybody's knowledge and see if the Aden Arab was using the same techniques as had been employed elsewhere. Mk5, Mk7, Mk10 anti-tank mines, Mills 36 grenades, Energa 94 grenades, 38mm Smith and Wesson revolvers, Sten guns, 303 Lee Enfield rifles, Gun cotton, standard issue explosive such as Nobels 808 plastic, 33 electrical detonators and much more besides, were in the Arab arsenal. All that the British had left behind in ammo dumps on the Suez Canal.

It made sense for the Arabs to use them, and, it did help in a way, because the British knew of the weapon capabilities and could work against them. The new team followed a heavy schedule of fitness training, often running up the volcanic slopes of Shamsan Mountain, and then finishing off with a Close Quarter Battle shoot out on the range.

Mac insisted on the centre of main target mass hit in half a second, even after extremely strenuous exercise. It was surprising how quickly the team came around. They had a goal. They knew the terrorist was killing and maiming British troops, and they knew they could do something about it, albeit in a slightly unorthodox manner. This appealed to the majority of them. Very strong team morale soon built up, and even though Mac was biased, he had to admit to himself that the team, for the limited night operations expected of them, would be as good as any regiment in the province.

In selecting the members, Mac had ensured that he would get at least one year's work out of each person before they were due for repatriation to the United Kingdom. Details of the fact they were working at night in an area where street lighting was very sparse and rare, Mac ensured the men were issued with a Lovat green light weight uniform, which made them hard to see at night when they were camouflaged. Because they had a lot of climbing and mountain work to do, the uniforms were easy to move about in and keep cool.

In three weeks from its conception, the 30 man team was ready for its first introduction to the Kochi areas in the back of Tawahi, Ma'hala and Crater.

A further method of gaining information about possible base plate positions was by the use of helicopters. Every time the helicopters delivered troops up country to Thurmier, they would make a circle around the camps out to about 4,000 metres, taking photographs. These photographs were then compared to previous ones by the photographic interpretation unit, and if they noticed any changes from the previous day or two investigations would proceed. One sortie returning to camp photographed what appeared to be seven holes in the ground, spaced about a metre apart. Upon checking up on these, it was discovered that they were 3" diameter pipes about one metre long embedded into the ground with homemade mortar bombs inside them, modified French 66mm weapons, and they were timed by a watch timer to go off at 10 a.m.

They would have landed on Khormaksar Airfield.

This particular cache of weapons could not be turned and used against the Arabs. They had been buried deep and, as such, attracted a lot of attention when removed from their position. The Arabs would have noticed this, and therefore, any surprise element would have been lost.

Later on in the campaign, the Royal Air Force helicopter crews managed to get infrared imaging photography. This allowed them the extra benefit of seeing a heat reflecting source. Metal that had been exposed to sunlight all day, for instance a mortar barrel, cooled down at night at a slower rate than the surrounding earth. This left a clear whitish heat halo around the end of the barrel. Therefore, the photographing was done first thing in the morning, to see if there had been any movement or placement of weaponry during the night, and photographs were taken again at last light, or just as dusk was setting, to get an infrared image if there was one. Of course, in the form of backup there would also be checks performed by the patrol on the ground during the night. It worked. After a while, devices were being found, turned around, and used against the enemy.

CHAPTER 8

Energa Improvised Launcher

A device similar to that mentioned in the last chapter was found by the team ground patrol on the third night of duty. It was novel, if not bordering on genius, with its simplicity. The patrol observed two Arabs involved in placing some sort of construction on the back slopes of Tawahi, just below the Steamer Point Hospital. All the hospital lights were clearly visible, and one could hear singing from the Sergeant's mess. That was how close it was; quite off putting, being so close to home, yet still in the midst of bastards trying to kill you.

Remember, the British patrols were in uniform, and when the Arabs spotted them, they melted into the shadows. The men moved forward carefully, in case a little booby trap was waiting for them somewhere in the darkness. Instead of a booby trap, they found a seven bank salvo of 94 Energas being prepared for launch. The Arabs had nearly completed their work, so, at long last, there was a device to analyse. A quick study on the spot showed that the ingredients for a bomb cocktail were there, but they had not been finally connected for launch. The seven bombs were modified to fit on tubes eighteen inches long and approximately two inches in diameter, and had a simple wooden base plate with wiring taped to it, plus a battery with an open clothes peg and electrical contacts, held apart with a solid piece of beeswax as the delay device.

It was now obvious that the 10 a.m. – 12 p.m. attacks came because the hot morning sun melted the wax which completed the electrical circuit. The parts of the device were split up and carried off by the patrol members for a detailed breakdown later with the ATO.

The men were jubilant, and Mac had to kick arses to keep their minds on the job in hand and remind them that they were still in the middle of a very dangerous place.

Two men were left at the base plate position as an ambush party in case the Arabs returned, whilst Mac rushed the find to the ATO's branch. After detailed inspection, it was found that the tubes contained a Russian low explosive powder similar to the launcher solid fuel found in the Katushka rockets. The Arabs had ground this down to use in their own improvised launchers. The tail fin, which gives the 94 Energa directional nose-first flights, fitted perfectly on the end of the launcher tubes. Energa grenades were armed after thirty feet of flight, due to two forces: 'Set Back,' which happens on the initial acceleration of launch; this action frees the firing pin, allowing it to initiate an explosion when the Tungsten steel tip on the nose of the weapon impacts. The second force, 'Creep Forward,' settles the firing pin in the correct position for flight when the 'Set Back' recedes.

Mac and the ATO soon worked out an evil scheme to give the Arabs some of their own medicine. They emptied out the low explosive from the tubes and refilled them with a mix of Pentolite and RDX explosive. This would still launch the bombs, and still ensure 'Set Back' took place, but on launch, it should blow the tail fins off. This would mean the bombs had no directional flight, but were armed. After a period of climb, the bombs would fall back on the Arab Kochi huts and explode; and they wouldn't have the faintest idea why. From now on in, if launch pads were found when they were about to attack, they would be bombing themselves. It was imperative to take the weapons back to the base plate position before first light. The heating rays of the sun were required to melt the wax and set them off that morning, otherwise, the Arabs would come looking and possibly notice something amiss. Our two field men left at the scene did not report patrolling, and our Height Observation Group at the Steamer Point hospital yard, which overlooked the launch site, had seen no Arab roof observation activity. Quickly, the weapons were moved back into place, disguising any sign of intrusive presence as much as possible, and the men headed back to Steamer for breakfast before the fun started.

It was absolutely epic.

[212]

By 9 a.m., the British had a long range photo and video crew unobtrusively in place under the Steamer hospital barbed wire perimeter fence. Everything was filmed to help make any further adjustments to any more devices found.

Hot, humid stickiness started to build up while the globe of the sun climbed in the sky, turning from red to yellow, then white. The temperature build up in South Arabia is fast and breathtaking. Very soon, the base plate position area was covered by a shimmering screen of ground heat, which slowly rose in height as the day became hotter and hotter. There was a little apprehensive and conjecture as to why the bastard thing hadn't blown. Had it been wired right? Had too much wax been used? Was the impedance of the wire too high for the battery power? Was the improvised explosive mix going to work? Many more horrible tantalizing ideas for possible causes of failure were being knocked about, when suddenly, at 10:20 a.m. exactly...

Whooomf...Whooomf!

The bombs were being launched. Within five seconds, they were all in the air, clearly visible, spinning and tumbling, not having any directional flight. They were completely out of control. The cameras and videos worked double time as the bombs (now counting seven) reached their peak of trajectory and seemingly lazily, started to fall back to earth. They tumbled nose first, because of the slow pull of gravity against the tungsten steel impact tip. Then...

Vawoom...Vawoom!

They began to explode on the ground in an estimated 100 metre radius of the launch pad position, right in the middle of the Arabs Kochis. What a tremendous, roaring success. The British had begun to beat the bastards at their own game. The Arabs were running around in complete confusion; they would never know what hit them.

At the sound of explosions, the follow up action was automatic and carried out by the Royal Anglian Regiment. They instantly blanketed the area of impact with troops, carried out detailed searches for any forensic evidence, and took endless photos of the bomb craters and bloodstains found in the area. The Arabs assured them that no human deaths had occurred, that the bloodstains were

[213]

of donkeys and dogs. When questioned about the possible cause of the attack, the Arab spokesman believed it was an attack on the Marxist-Leninist NLF by the other terrorist group FLOSY, who were Nasserist.

This was great news, because it gave Mac the chance to exploit the situation by playing one terrorist group against the other in tit-for-tat reprisals.

A new era of operational procedures had been born.

CHAPTER 9

Attack on FLOSY HQ

Mac's first move in this new direction followed the same night. He had the intelligence support unit to produce leaflets in Arabic, blaming the FLOSY for the dastardly attack on the NLF at Tawahi against innocent women and children, and called on all true Arabs to support the NLF in their fight against this danger from within. Therefore, to show the people their strength and determination, it was the NLF who blew up the FLOSY HQ that night.

Leaflets ready in advance, Mac gathered the team together, and he drew a captured Brant Blindicide Rocket Launcher and two bombs from the ATO stores and set off for Sheik Othman and the FLOSY HQ. This equipment was dangerous to fire, because one often gets a flame flash back. Therefore, it has a chain mail face guard to stop you frying yourself. This makes seeing the target difficult. To compensate for these limitations, one must get very close to the target to ensure a hit. Mac positioned his crew in such a way as to ensure a safe withdrawal route when the shit hit the fan and commissioned four groups to distribute leaflets by throwing them from the roofs of houses en route to the target, and also in Sheik Othman Township about fifteen minutes after Mac's arrival.

Weapons armed, Mac with Mike Rourke as his no 2 loader with the second bomb, slowly crept along between the piles of rubbish. They managed to find a good fire position about thirty metres from the FLOSY HQ, and at exactly 12 o'clock fired the first rocket into the building. Vicious sheets of flame shot back from the antiquated launcher and roared, while the rocket seemed to spiral in flight toward its target.

Wahoom!

The whole building was enveloped in flame. The second floor instantly collapsed onto the street facing, while flames shot fifty meters into the sky, and then explosion after explosion literally blew the building and the next two houses into obliteration. Mac, withdrawing from the scene as fast as possible, was burned on the hands and face by the searing heat emitted from the inferno. It was obvious that the initial rocket had set off a chain reaction of explosions of the FLOSY weapon arsenal stored in the buildings. Mac, in his wildest dreams, could not have imagined the devastation that ensued caused by one single rocket.

Arab activity was stirred up into a hornet's nest within twenty minutes of the big bang. By this time, they were reading the leaflets and calling on Allah to punish the NLF infidels. They were soon in a frenzy, performing self-flagellation and other forms of mass Arab self-torture, in the hysteria to take revenge on the perpetrators of this heinous crime. Mac and company were pissing themselves with laughter at this Laurel and Hardy performance that was taking place around them. FLOSY Arabs were so intent on finding NLF Arabs that they never spotted the sneaky British perpetrators in the shadows.

Mac finally managed to arrive back at base, just as first light was breaking, He felt content. He had completed a mission against the enemy and successfully blamed it on the other enemy, and because of the way of the Arab, his next plan was made for him. He now had to blow up the NLF HQ as a reprisal from FLOSY. Things were getting easier, and the dim-witted locals had no idea who was behind it all, nor did Mac or his crew let on to anybody else, only the ATO and the SAS at Khormaksa knew the details.

Keep it hot, Keep up the momentum. Don't give them time to think and appraise the situation. Keep their hatred and blood lust for each other on the cooking stove. Hurt them as often as you can, in as many ways as you can, in the shortest possible time. Allow them no time to think. Such were the continuous thoughts rushing around in Mac's head the following morning.

The die was cast. From now on, in a series of events that took place in quick succession, the men had the idea in which direction to go to make the enemy's life a misery.

Aden had always been an unpopular posting with the Army and, even at the best of times, was commonly referred to as 'South Arabia's Arsehole.' Reasons for this unpopularity were not hard to find. The country was a wild and inhospitable place that offered few attractions to the Army's young recruits. Its people showed no affection to the troops. Some soldiers unlawfully used excessive force and methods during frequent and usually violent demonstrations against the British government's decision to include Aden in the Federation of South Arabia.

If the troops disliked Aden in general, they reserved their greatest hatred for Crater. It was in this teeming town that most of the terrorist attacks by the National Liberation Front and their rivals, the Front for the Liberation of South Yemen, philosophically and militarily took place. Jagged volcanic cliffs on all but the seaward side surrounded Crater, nestled in the crater of the volcano known as Jebel Shamsan. The town was the most hated hotbed of terrorist activity, and a nightmare to patrol. During the sixties, it was excruciatingly hot by day and bitterly cold at night. The surrounding cliffs only served to extend this heat and cold and help to contain the numerous obnoxious smells rising from the open sewers, which ran down many of the town's narrow streets except at two points. The first point was a fortress, where the slopes of the volcano denied access to or exit from. This was located to the east of the town. Marine Drive ran between the rock and the sea before passing along the waterfront. On the harbour side to the west, another road climbed to a break in the cliffs known as Main Pass. After the pass, the route descended into Crater to become Queen Arwa Road.

It was an ideal ground to wage a protracted terrorist campaign. There was a maze of tortuous streets and small narrow alleys, all far too small for a military vehicle to traverse. It provided a perfect base from which the NLF, unforeseen, could launch their attacks from a safe haven on British security units, using their group's large arsenal of grenades, small arms, mortars, and rocket launchers. Often, the terrorists would orchestrated riots to bring the troops within range of snipers.

CHAPTER 10

The Pac Vac Mine

After the NLF began its urban terror campaign, it became increasingly difficult for security forces to maintain their grip, because the number of terrorist attacks grew to almost unmanageable proportions. This was the time when a new weapon came into the NLF armoury. This little expedient was known as the Pac Vac mine, a terrible little device no bigger than a 50p piece, but with enough explosive power to be able to blow a man's foot off. It was so small; it was easily smuggled into bases and camps. It could effortlessly be sprinkled in the sand at the side of the roads and short pathways. A group of Arabs would gather on the hard tarmac of a path, and force the soldier off the path onto the sand and, Bang! He would be minus one foot.

They also placed them under toilet seats and any other convenient location where they could do damage to our British soldiers. Not only were these devices damaging, they were very demoralising to the troops, because they could be hidden almost anywhere due to their size.

They were Czech by source and had arrived along the smuggler route from Yemen over the mountains. Armed with this small amount of intelligence, the ATO arranged through Command Headquarters for the upcountry special troops, such as the SAS and the Parachute Regiment, to make special efforts to ambush troop convoys coming in from the Yemen and try to get their hands on some of these Pac Vacs for their own use. After about three months, they did manage to acquire some. So began the little operation, to return the Pac Vacs to the Arabs on their own ground, tenfold in quantity.

During the night in the Kochi areas, it was very quiet, and in the narrow alleys, there were no hard surfaced roads. Everyone who lived there seemed to congregate in the main village square, where there was plenty of light. Arab food stands were present in profusion, cooking exotic aromatic dishes that would give a Brit the shits for a month if he was foolhardy enough to eat them. The weird Arab music and street performers provided some form of entertainment. Within 30 metres to the side of the square, there were no lights, no hard surfaced roads, only silence and shadowy figures. It was in these alleyways between the Kochi, that the Pac Vac quota was paid back to the Arabs.

During the same night, every single township in the colony of Aden received a fair share of the captured presents, all placed in sand and walkways away from the main streets and right in midst their terrorist playground. The morning intelligence reports on the ticker tape from headquarters told the story. Every night, Arabs were carried into local hospitals with injuries relating to explosions, obviously caused by our little friends, the 50 piece sized bomb. After this successful blitz on the Arabs with this tiny weapon, they ceased to use it against the British soldiers.

CHAPTER 11

The Mutiny

1967 was a very black year for the British Army in Aden, and it was in this year that the Argylls began their tour of duty. They couldn't have picked a worse possible time. They were due to replace the Northumberland Fusiliers in Crater. Just five days before the takeover, British forces had suffered their heaviest losses of the entire campaign, 22 men killed and 31 wounded in a series of ambushes and mutinies.

The first mutiny occurred in the former headquarters of the Federal National Guard, now a training centre for South Arabian Police. On hearing rumours that the Federal Army was being attacked by British troops in Lake Lines, the local police set ambushes that killed eight and injured a further eight men from 60 Squadron Royal Corps of Transport.

Later, the same rebels inflicted casualties on British troops in nearby Radfan Barracks and on troops sent as a relief force. When two British Land Rovers passed by the Aden Armed Police barracks on Queen Arwa Road, the police opened up with rifles and machine guns, killing a further eight troops, three of which were Argyll and Sutherland Islanders due to relieve the Northumberland Fusiliers. A further patrol of four men sent out to investigate what was happening did not return and were never seen again. Three more attempts to send in rescue parties were driven back by murderous crossfire, and a Sioux helicopter was shot down at one stage injuring everyone on board. A total of 22 British servicemen were killed, and many more injured on that never-to-be forgotten day.

When nightfall came, British troops were withdrawn from Crater and its immediate area, but now came payback time. During that night, covert SOG and SAS patrols saw grizzly examples of what these local Arab bastards were capable. Armed police issued rifles and weapons to all comers, members of the NLF and FLOSY. Plus, local criminals released from jail all became gun owners.

Stupid farcical mock trials of the dead British soldiers were held amongst great rejoicing. Then their bodies were mutilated, ritually hanged, and burned. Some were nailed to doors. Now was the time for some fast decisive action, and it happened, but not on the orders of the British High Command, who were quite happy to seal off Crater and contain the mob. Individual covert operations made the Arabs pay tenfold for what they did that day and night, and paved the way for a very successful return of the British troops to Crater in the splendid musical march of the Argyll's back into the town.

British snipers ringed the volcano rim surrounding Crater. These men were drawn from all Regiments and shot anything that moved on a rooftop. The official version says they were ordered to fire only if they saw an armed person, and in fact, the figures state that they killed ten terrorists armed with AK47 assault rifles. This, in truth, is a load of bollocks.

Mac and Hugh lay side by side on the crater rim with 303 Enfield sniper rifles and a range spotting telescope between them. They also had a detailed grid map and Arial grid photographs of Crater. Over the next five days, it was like being on a Bisley Long Range Competition. If either one saw anything suspicious move, a grid reference was checked and passed on to whoever's turn it was to shoot. They were talking all the time. They observed hits and kept score sheets, shooting in turn at any opportune target that presented itself.

During the dark, under the starlit Arab sky, the borrowed SAS night surveillance equipment kept them going and abled them to observe and shoot the enemy. Sandwiches or soup, coffee, pep pills, and adrenalin tablets to keep them awake arrived at last light. They fired a total of 4,700 rounds and calculated a 98% successful hit rate. One can see a lot of Arabs died because of their atrocities to the British men. Over and above this sniper work, SAS and SOG units worked in the warrens of Crater at night and took out a lot of known terrorists who had been clever enough not to expose themselves to the sniper fire.

All this specialist work was 'kill by knife' and each kill had the index finger cut off for print identification on who had died. Nearly all known terrorists had print records. Before they became terrorists, many had worked for the British, and were issued identity cards. A lot of Arabs died this way, because they were known and deliberately targeted.

On one night's sortie, an operative brought out a bag that he had carried between his legs under his Arab Fut. He tipped out the contents- a total of 40 finger tips, on to the Brigade Intelligence Officer's desk and calmly said, "Here you are mate. Earn your fucking money. Who have I 'molested'?"

The IO, smart in his starched shirt and highly polished Sam Brown belt, vomited down his shirt. A further simple method for targeting suspects was simple deduction. If an Arab was running uphill, he was running away from a crime he had committed on one of the main streets. The Arab walks uphill with head bowed in deference to Allah. If he's caught running uphill, 'neck' him was the order of the day.

Known Koch areas in the back of town that intelligence had indicated were HQ areas, or meeting points for terrorist groups were simply razed to the ground by sustained General Purpose Machine Gun fire, and this, of course, meant anybody in that area went to hell as well. All in all, payback time for the Arabs was a very costly procedure.

Mac knew this. He interrogated a few captured specimens later, who admitted they lived in fear those few days; they never believed Mac and his men would do what they did, because they had been so soft on them before because of British politics.

If only the British politicians, once a decision had been made for use of military force, could keep their noses out of it and let the services get on with the job, Britain, as a nation, would have been much better thought of and respected around the world at the time.

CHAPTER 12

Mad Mitch

The coup de grace of these Crater activities was the reoccupation of Crater and the follow up operations by the Argyll's and their Commanding Officer, Lieutenant Colonel Colin Campbell Mitchell, or 'Mad Mitch' as he was commonly referred to by the news media.

Mitch joined the Argyll's late in 1945 and saw some action in the PO valley campaign in Italy. He served in Palestine, Korea, Cyprus, Kenya and Borneo. He was wounded by terrorist action in Palestine. Therefore, he brought to the theatre of terrorism in Aden a high level of experience, but this was tempered by a panache, or flair, that did not endear him with his command peers. In particular the General Commander of Aden Forces, Major-General Philip Tower, so much so, that Mitch found after Aden, promotion prospects were non existent, nor was he awarded the customary DSO that normally graced the uniforms of all senior officers in charge of units on completion of a campaign. One supposes that some compensation for this lack of official recognition was the affection and high esteem he was shown by soldiers who served in Aden, and also by the press. Television and the British public in general, bestowed on him his title, 'Mad Mitch'

Mitch was appalled at General Tower's soft approach to the Crater problem. Especially galling was the flaunting of NLF flags and open showing of rifles by the terrorists in Crater before the sniper teams sent them to ground. These taunts were infuriating to the Northumberland Fusiliers who were responsible for Crater, and the Argylls who were to relieve the Fusiliers on the 25th June, especially considering the great loss of life suffered by both battalions when the mutinies took place.

Historians have written much since the retaking of Crater and the infighting between Mitch and General Towers came to light. Mitch's plan was for a bold, aggressive, two-pronged night attack, carried out by the Argylls, and his own night patrols, as well as the SAS patrols. Mitch thought this strategy would cause a little trouble. Tower argued that a 'bit by bit' type of less aggressive action would cause less Arab casualties and avoid the chance of another mutiny by Federal Forces. Mitchell's horror at this suggestion and scorn for its conception is well recorded and was openly televised at the time. His argument was this method would allow the enemy to consolidate each position after the 'nibble' and force his men to fight dozens of battles against people dug in and prepared for defence.

As history shows, the Argyll 'Stirling Castle' plan was eventually accepted by Tower, and brilliantly carried out by the Argyll's and armoured cars of the Dragoon Guards, who flew the red and white Hackle of the Fusiliers from their radio aerial masts. The Argylls went into Crater to the piper's strains of Moneymusk, the tune that had preceded every Argyll attack for generations.

Crater came back into British hands with no further British casualties during the attack. The Arabs in Aden were awakened by the Argyll's pipes and drums playing 'The Barren Rocks of Aden' from the rooftop of the Chartered Bank, which Mitch had commandeered as the Argyll's Headquarters and renamed 'Stirling Castle.'

The firm hand taken by the Argylls against the Crater Arabs made the place one of the quietest and safest places to be in the colony. Armed men who used the local mosques for protection were wheedled out and eliminated. Because the Arabs lost this sanctuary, they had nowhere to go after an attack and soon decided it wasn't worth their deaths. Unfortunately, there were a few British casualties. Some were very unfortunate, like the Corporal killed by a 2" Mortar bomb that landed on the small roof of the 'Stirling Castle'. That bomb could never have been aimed with accuracy at such a small target, a lucky shot for them, but a loss of life nonetheless.

CHAPTER 13

Grenade War

During the month of June in 1967, things began to reach fever pitch, both militarily and politically. The two terrorist warring factions were now at open warfare. Apart from fighting each other, they were still making even more effort to prove to the people that they were the party throwing the British out of the colony. Grenade attacks were happening more often, with a greater variety of grenades being used as their supply from the Yemen increased.

The British dirty tricks brigade now had some very hard work on their hands. The British Garrison troops carried out more frequent and thorough searches through the rubbish that had built up on street corners looking for grenades. When they found one, they left it in situ and called a code signal to Mac's organisation, which then turned out to remove the timed fuse from the grenades. For instance, the 1.5 second fuses from the Russian F1 grenades, and the 4 second fuses from the Mills 36 grenades, were replaced with instantaneous fuses. As a result, any Arab trying to set off these grenades removed himself from the face of this earth, instantly.

It was almost amusing to see the ticker tapes reports coming into the GDOC in HQ stating Quote 'Grenade attack number 3 street Tawahi, no known target. Casualties, one local national male.' The RG 42 impact grenade was a little more troublesome; this consisted of two explosive charges, each with individual firing pins and detonators, separated by 40 feet of copper foil. Mac's grenadier would put his finger in a loop at the start of the foil, and then throw the grenade. It was safe, because the foil paid out, but when it finished, the moment one of the two charges touched anything, even a glancing blow, the weapon would explode. Mac did eventually defeat this device by taking off the foil and replacing it with narrow strips of toilet paper, and then disguised the last four-foot with the original foil. Often the terrorist, when he used this weapon, tried to stay out of sight of the patrol at which he was throwing the grenade. He managed to do this by bouncing the grenade off opposing walls or off a rooftop. He was safe doing this while he had 40 feet of foil to play with. Once we had replaced the foil with toilet paper, he was not safe, because the toilet paper did not have sufficient resistance to stop the grenade explosive charges from striking the detonator pin the moment they touched anything, so he could now blow himself up with the grenade jut four feet away from his body.

One of these grenades caused Mac problems in July of 1967. A patrol sergeant of the Prince of Wales Own Regiment of Yorkshire saw a Mills 36 grenade lying in the road with its striker lever stuck to its own body with adhesive tape. He quite rightly believed this was a booby trap, and called Mac on the unit code. On turning out, Mac observed the grenade through binoculars. Mac thought it might have been a case he had seen before when the terrorist had used adhesive tape on striker levers to hide and or avoid fingerprints. Somehow, he assumed this tape had become stuck to the main body of the grenade. Taking the usual precautions, he instructed the patrol sergeant to make sure he had height snipers covering the object, and then he slowly made a cautious approach to the grenade. When he was approximately 6 feet away from the grenade, an RG 42 grenade came over the wall at the side of the road and exploded right between Mac's legs. He was lucky, because the grenades position blew him straight up in the air away from shrapnel, which moves outward and upward. He lay on the ground in a dazed and confused state, before slipping into unconsciousness.

The next thing he remembered was coming round in Steamer Point Hospital with a nurse leaning over him with a blue cape over her shoulders and squadron leaders badges on the epaulettes. She was a member of the Princess Mary's Royal Air Force Nursing Service. When this lady of mercy noticed that Mac had come round, she said to him, "How do you feel?"

"Am I OK?" Mac asked her.

[227]

"I hope you are not planning on having more children?"

The grenade had caused quite some damage to Mac's left testicle, and he now appeared to only have one ball or 1.5 at best. What a fucking diplomat that nurse would have made. She certainly missed her calling.

Mac had everyone in fits of hysterical laughter a couple of years later when he told the story of the final outcome of this disastrous event for him. If a man is married and has children, he is not entitled to any disablement pension for the loss of his testicles. If a man is single and has not procreated, he could claim a pension for the loss of his balls. All they will give the married man with children is a pair of synthetic balls made from a substance similar to what women have as breast transplants. The cosmetic effect was supposedly good for moral.

When Mac eventually went to Central Medical Establishment in London to see about this cosmetic implant, he was taken into a small room on the fourth floor, a very dingy musty smelling place. In this room, there were shelves of balls on the wall display. Lo and behold, the size of balls one could have issued depended on rank. For example, a private or an aircraftsman would have a pair of balls the not much bigger than a marble. A Warrant Officer could have a pair the size of golf balls, whilst a Lieutenant Colonel could have a pair the size of cricket balls. Mac decided against it. It was silly verging on the point of ridiculous, and he would not play the game.

One good thing came out of Mac's forward planning on his approach to the suspect weapon; the Prince of Wales Own Regiment's height snipers killed the Arab grenade thrower.

Another very slender victory was won against the terrorists. This was with a supply of the AK 47 assault rifles, which came in from the Yemen. These weapons were of Chinese manufacture and someone, no one knows who exactly, but it is believed that the SAS played a very important part in this, interrupted the weapons at source and modified them by a small sliver of metal placed under the rear sight. This made the weapon fire 10 ft high at 100 yards range. The terrorist had no ranges to practice on, because the British had closed down both the FRA and the police ranges, so they had no chance to zero their weapons and find out whether they were accurate or not. The final result of this intervention was 500 inaccurate weapons in the hands of the NLF.

They were very brave now and openly showed themselves to fire at British checkpoints and patrols. Of course, with their shots going 10 ft high at 100 metres, they were hitting nothing and this also made them a sitting target for the British squad. This new development was kept secret from the squaddies, because we did not want them becoming complacent. The NLF never seemed to catch on as to what was happening with their weapons.

CHAPTER 14

Land Mines

A new development that occurred toward the end of July early August '67 was the increase in land mine attacks against vehicles. Previously, land mine attacks had been on the main road to Dhala, the main route to Yemen. Now, attacks were happening on the beach roads that ran through the colony past the old Army barracks such as Radfan Camp. In a way, the British were fortunate, because the landmines they were using in profusion were British Mark 5s and the Mark 7s from their arms dumps in Egypt. They were very familiar with these and worked out a strategy to defeat them. The British produced a document on old paper, saying 'Instructions for use', and emphasising that these mines should be buried at arm's length underground. These instructions would be placed into any arms caches, and left in places like cafes, where terrorists could pick them up and gain this valuable information on how to plant a mine and blow-up the British infidel.

The dear enemy took note. There began a spate of mine attacks on vehicles and light armoured personnel carriers where the explosion was happening after the vehicle had passed. This was what was expected, because the pressure from the front wheel passed over the mine caused a compression, initiating the explosion. Because the mines were so deep, their vehicle's rear wheels were already past it when the thing went off.

The British just changed convoy procedure and gave vehicles wide area spacing to prevent a following vehicle running into the mine debris. Once again, they never did catch on to this clever ploy, and for the rest of the time in Aden, the Mark 5 and Mark 7 mines were planted at arm's length.

[230]

The British were lucky. At the end of October, Chinese and Russian rigid plastic mines began to show up in the colony in large numbers. There would have been a bigger problem with these mines, but as the men were leaving in early November, they didn't care. A few of these things had always been in Aden, but they were very rarely used.

All matters in the colony were now becoming chaotic. Every day and night one heard gunfire, machine gun fire, and explosions. This, of course, was the battle between the National Liberation Front and the Front for the Liberation of South Yemen and a few daring skirmishes with the British, but with the new supply of inaccurate AK 47s they always lost.

HMS Bulwark the Royal Marine Commando Carrier was now in Aden harbour, with twenty-four other ships to assist in the withdrawal, if needed. The Commandos of 42 Commando had taken up positions as a perimeter defence around the British troops, with special emphasis on the airfield at Khormaksa. It was quite funny, in a way, that the Commandos received a very warm welcome from the NLF. When their helicopters, with the large slings underneath carrying their equipment, approached the shoreline, the NLF decided to use them as target practice from the rooftops in Tawahi. The marines instantly put in ground forces and started house-to-house clearance, whilst their helicopters were still flying overhead delivering stores.

Mac's group sat on top of Barrack Hill, overlooking the rooftops of the hundreds of flats in number one, two, and three streets in Tawahi, picking off the red and black checked turban terrorists, who were firing at the marines. It was a Turkey Shoot.

At this time in the debacle, approximately thirty thousand troops had been evacuated, and their personal goods and belongings had to be left behind. Cars were abandoned everywhere, some with fuel and the keys still in them. Most were in immaculate condition, because the hot climate helped to preserve them. It was sometimes the policy for patrols to jump in one of these abandoned cars to use as a patrol vehicle. This was excellent for the terrorist. They now had a new way to get at the British and started to booby trap the cars left lying about. They gained quite a few casualties this way.

[231]

Orders instantly went out for troops not to touch abandoned cars, and Mac and his group blew every ownerless car up that they came across, except some they booby trapped for the Arabs to use after the British had left, regardless of value.

One helicopter pilot at Khormaksa had a beautiful white sports car. He was heard to say that 'no fucking Arab' would have his car. Together, he and his friends attached the car into a sling underneath a helicopter, and flew it to a selected site and deposited it on top of a high mountain point in the range of hills that surrounds the British Military Cemetery in Silent Valley.

Even to this day, civilian pilots flying into Aden from a certain direction use this car as a reference point for landing.

CHAPTER 15

Paperwork Madness

The preparation for withdrawal from Aden was now at a frantic state. One of the major tasks that had to be performed was the unloading of the giant arms dump, situated at the junction of the Mhalar Main and the Mhalar Bandhar. It was during this operation that Mac nearly got himself court marshalled. The Royal Air Force, at that time, was armed with Second World War weapons, 303 Lee Enfield rifle, Sten submachine guns of different marks, and 38mm Smith and Wesson revolvers. Some members, for instance the RAF Regiment and the RAF Police, did have SLR, Sterling's, and the 9mm Browning high-power pistol. When the bomb dump was emptied, it was taken for granted that everything would be thrown into the deep water harbour. Mac noticed that the working party of a Marine Logistics unit was loading boxes of SLR rifles, Stirling submachine guns, and the Browning 9mm, plus tons of ammunition for the same, on to freighters for the trip to the deep water channel.

Mac had a word with a Colour Sergeant in charge of the working party and pointed out the ludicrous fact that the Royal Air Force was using antiquated Second World War equipment and here the men were throwing away modern arms and ammunition. It would be a good idea if they took a lorry load of the good weapons to the Royal Air Force at Steamer Point and brought back the old weapons and threw them into the sea instead. This seemed to be a commonsense thing to do. The sergeant wholeheartedly agreed. A quick radio message to his unit at Steamer Point and a four-ton RL vehicle was quickly on its way.

Whilst they were waiting for the vehicle to arrive, Mac and the Colour Sergeant had a very interesting conversation about what was happening around them at the dock and at the bomb dump.

Apparently, everything could not to be moved in time, and a party of Royal Engineers and a Bomb Disposal unit were very busy booby-trapping the large bombs, such as thousand pound aircraft bombs, and large artillery shells. The sergeant said the bomb dump would be a blowing up for the next 500 years. Mac decided the Arabs may be having their moment, but they would have nothing left when the British finally made their exit from that bloody hellhole.

The vehicle arrived from steamer Point, and Mac ordered the crew to instantly load up the new weapons and ammunition. They set to with a will and had nearly finished loading when an Army Major came up and asked what was happening. Mac and the Colour Sergeant explained the process in hand.

"You can't do that. Where is your paperwork? Who gave you the authority? If the Royal Air Force wanted these weapons, they should have submitted a requisition order. Well, answer me!"

"Am I correct, Major, in saying that these weapons are going to be thrown into the sea?" Mac was having control difficulties.

"It's immaterial where they're going. Show me your paperwork, now! For all I know, you may be selling these weapons to the Arabs. You look a shady character, to say the least".

"No wonder the British Army is in the shit like it is at the moment, with stupid bastards like you as Officers. These weapons are going to the Royal Air Force at Steamer Point. Don't try to stop me or I'll fucking shoot you. Check with the Royal Air Force that they have received the weapons. Oh! By the way, I'm bringing a load of second world war weapons back so you can play at throwing things in the sea".

"Colour Sergeant, arrest this man. Arrest him instantly! He is not to leave these docks with any weapons. He does so over my dead body. Arrest him, I tell you, now!" He was turning an even brighter shade of red and dribbling from his mouth.

"Arrest him yourself, Major. There is no way I'm to tangle with the bastard, and after all, what he's doing is only common sense".

"Place yourself under arrest Colour Sergeant. You are disobeying my direct orders. This would never have happened in India in the old days".

"Go and fuck yourself, you stupid old bastard" was the Colour Sergeant's final remark. He walked away to continue the work with his Royal Marine 'Loggies' who had watched, with humour, the whole incident, waving to Mac when he left.

Mac finished loading the wagon with the equipment he felt necessary and, ignoring the arm waving and idiotic gibberish and screaming from the Major, he mounted the vehicle and headed to Steamer Point armoury. Now came Mac's second big surprise. On arrival at Steamer Point, the Armament Officer, a Royal Air Force Flight Lieutenant, refused to accept the weaponry and ammunition, because there was no paperwork with the reference numbers of the weapons on it. Mac went nearly blue in the face trying to explain the situation. Under no circumstances could he make this Officer understand just what the Royal Air Force was gaining.

After a while, a very frustrated Mac drove to the Royal Air Force fire section and saw John Buchan. Buchan switched on straight away.

"Bring the fucking things in here, store them in the back room, and we'll sort out the details later. Meanwhile, I'll go down the docks and educate this fucking Major about how to fight a war".

"Thanks a lot. Sir. I just can't understand where these Officer's minds are. They're obviously living in a very different world to me".

"That's the trouble; peacetime amateurs only out for a civilian type job and a living. If they have to fight for the fucking money they're paid, they wouldn't earn two bob a week. The only thing to remember is that these twats have no minds of their own. The only thing that keeps them going is paperwork and more paperwork. Combine this with the rules and regulations and they don't have to think any more. This is what we have to put up with nowadays. Anyway, I am going down to the docks to piss this Army idiot off. See you later".

The outcome of this saga turned into quite a complicated affair. The Army was filing charges against Mac, the Marine Colour Sergeant, and Buchan. Luckily, some high-powered Royal Air Force people managed to calm things down. All charges were eventually dropped. The weaponry and ammunition were packed into crates, labelled as MT spares, and sent to the Royal Air Force Regiment Ground Combat Training section at Muharraq, Bahrain.

At Muharraq, the majority of personnel finished work at one o'clock lunchtime, and many of them went to the 25 metre ranges in the afternoons to fire unit competitions for crates of beer prizes. The weapons used on these sporting afternoons was the ex-Aden supply of SLR rifles, Stirling submachine guns, and the Browning 9mm high-power pistols. Thanks to Mac and Buchan, and a few unsuspecting Argosy pilots and their crews who flew the 'goodies' up the Gulf, hundreds upon hundreds of Royal Air Force, Army and Navy were trained and fired the new weapons with unlimited ammunition, thanks to SAS assistance. No questions were ever asked as to where the goods had come from. They were not kept secure in the armoury, as is the usual practice, but resided in the RAFR target store behind the range stop wall. This practice was still taking place when Mac left Bahrain in April 1968.

As for the finale of this story...

The Royal Air Force packed and sent all its Second World War weapons and ammunition to their RAF stations such as Salahla, Masira, Sharja, and Muharraq in the Persian Gulf. (Mac still wonders who made that brilliant decision). Imagine the humour and comments when the equipment arrived at Muharraq.

CHAPTER 16

Rescue the Jews

Mother Nature came to the British forces assistance at this confused and critical time in the most unnatural way. A freak, thunderous, heavy rainstorm slowed all terrorist activity practically to a standstill. Mudslides crashed down the sides of the Shamsan volcano, washing away everything in their path. The dreaded Kochi huts disappeared into a twenty-foot high, one-mile long heap of twisted tin, cardboard, and other rubbish along the Tawahi main road. Graves from cemetery valley were washed up, along with arms caches stored in them. It was a devastating blow to the terrorists. The rain was continuous for two days. Walls crashed down under the pressure of the weight of the water. It was a common occurrence when wading waist deep from the resulting flooding to find skeletons from the graves floating by, and strange to be able to pick up rifles, mines, and other weapons at the water's edge.

The British used the quiet time after the storm to evacuate the Jewish refugees under their protection in the Kumara Hotel in Tawahi. During the Arab/Israeli Yom Kippur War in June 1967 (the six day war), the Arabs in Aden savagely attacked Jewish enterprises, schools, and religious buildings. The British rapidly fought their way in and rescued these people from the mobs of marauding, half crazed, looting Arabs, but not before a large number had been killed or injured.

It was a myth that Moslems and Hindus forgo the use of alcohol, because these rioting Arabs had looted supermarkets of all the booze. They were drinking the stuff and screaming around the port area pissed out of their minds. Many British soldiers, with the full knowledge of their superior commanders, took advantage of the Arab looting to look after their own wives and families and snatched watches and jewellery that were small and easy to carry.

"We're being fucked about here with these Arabs. Let's give ourselves a bonus. Why leave it all for the Arabs?" Was the general train of thought.

That frame of mind and thinking process made sense at the time. The soldiers loaded the Jews onto the impounded freighter, the 'Stainless Carrier,' and sailed them back to Israel. These thankless, although provoked, people were screaming insults at the men the whole time, because they hadn't saved their stocks and therefore their livelihoods. It was obviously not in the British soldier's interest to show them any watches or other goods we had looted from them.

All these goodies were kept at base and out of sight.

As a side note, it is worth mentioning the Norwegian Captain of the rescue ship was later shot twice in the back of the head outside the Chartered Bank near P&O Wharf.

CHAPTER 17

The Rains Continue

One strange sight Mac watched during these storms and resultant flooding was at the football and a sports stadium at Steamer Point. This stadium was approximately six hundred metres from the swimming beach at Steamer, and shark nets protected this beach. The floods covered the land between the stadium and the beach, and the outward rush of water to the sea from the hillsides washed the shark nets off their anchors and out to sea. Whilst sitting in his billet, Mac actually saw six shark fins circling round and round in the sports stadium. Storms such as this one were extremely rare in South Arabia, and consequently building planning and buildings themselves were not made to withstand these types of rains.

Many military buildings collapsed because of these factors, and a tremendous amount of improvising by the Brits took place to maintain operational efficiency. The drainage systems could not cope either and streets became open sewage channels.

Mac saw a skeleton float by him once with a big, thick turd of shit sticking out of its mouth, just like a cigar. Desperate as the situation was, one cannot help but keep a sense of humour when confronted with such a sight.

True to form, when the floods receded, the Arabs asked the soldier's to help them clean up the mess, the cheeky bastards. They were trying to kill them one minute, and then wanted their help the next.

It doesn't take much guessing to understand what the soldiers did, being British; we helped them, of course. The Royal Engineers had to drop all they were doing in preparation for our withdrawal, and bulldozed everything away from the streets, assisting in the building of temporary accommodation, gave them a fresh water supply, and reinstalling electricity and power. The British medical staff had to deal with hundreds of casualties. They put out field teams to spray the area to prevent mosquitoes breeding and causing outbreaks of malaria. Helicopter spraying prevented outbreaks of cholera and typhoid fever.

The RAF supplied locals with food, financial aid for damage to businesses, and basically put them on their feet again. But by the time it came to the end of October, the Arabs were trying to fucking kill the British again. Only the British would be so stupid and soft with an enemy who doesn't give a shit.

Mac still wonders who made the decision to spend the British taxpayer's money. If you were to ask Mac what he thought, he'd tell you, "Whoever it was should be hung as a fucking traitor".

The excuse for these endeavours given by the military command, were that it was necessary to perform these functions to protect ourselves. What a load of bollocks. Inside the bases, everything was working perfectly. They did not need to carry out these 'Fairy Godmother' activities on behalf of the British soldiers stationed there. No, the British did it for the Arabs, full stop.

CHAPTER 18

Blow the Oil Tanks

When starting up their terrorist activities again, the Arabs brought in a new dimension. Surprisingly, they began to blow up and rocket the fuel storage tanks in the scattered depots around Aden harbour. This caught the British by surprise, because they were destroying their own future income. These actions were never predicted by our intelligence services for that very reason. Why they were doing this self-destruction exercise, no one could begin to understand. One of these storage tanks was situated on a lava flow that ran from Shamsan to the sea between Tawahi and Mahler. This unit towered approximately 50 ft above the main road.

During the night, the terrorists had fired a Brant Blindicide rocket at the base of the tank. Fortunately, the tank did not explode, but the very large gash in its side allowed the contents to run freely down the hill, across the main road and dockyard, and into the Aden harbour. The slick of oil running down the hill was approximately 100 metres wide and 2 feet deep, and obviously, with gravity assistance, it was flowing very fast indeed.

Buchan and Mac turned out to inspect this incident, after an assistance call from GDOC. On arrival, Buchan made a decision. He simply knew in his gut feeling that the fuel would not ignite and equipment held in the dock store compound on the other side of the fuel flow would assist in diverting it, making the flow narrow and therefore easier to control.

"Mac, get your arse across that fuel flow, and get the ship oil leak safety equipment out, and start using it from the other side", he took charge and commanded.

This equipment was used to contain oil spills from ships if they accidentally leaked oil into the harbour.

[241]

"You must be fucking joking! What happens if the Arab fires an incendiary bullet or another rocket into the middle of that lot?" Mac asked.

"They won't. They're too fucking stupid to think of that, and the stuff wouldn't fire up anyway. It's shit Arab fuel". Buchan replied calmly.

"Okay then, wise guy, you wade through it and do the business if you're so sure. I'll wait here for you".

"That's no good. I have to wait here with the radio and keep updating the powers that be, plus stop anybody else from trying to cross".

"Why don't we just let the tank run dry? The damage to the sea and the harbour are already going to need a major cleanup operation. A little more oil won't hurt or change the situation. Why take fucking chances now?"

"Because, if we act now we can save thousands and thousands of gallons of valuable fuel. Get over there and do the job. It's expected of us", Buchan answered, growing irritated at the questioning of his orders.

"I know what your game is, Buchan. If you save some thousands of gallons of oil, you will be looking for some back pocket money from the oil company at my fucking expense. Whatever you receive, I want half. Okay?" Mac knew what he wanted, and he wasn't afraid to ask for it.

"Okay. Now get going. You're losing hundreds of dollars a minute".

Mac gingerly started to wade through the oil slick. Its consistency was similar to cod liver oil, blackish-brown in colour, smelt exactly like petrol, and gave off pungent fumes and vapours that burned the eyes and throat. The contact on the legs burned like hell. Half way across, Mac started uncontrollable vomiting. His lungs were burning; they seemed to be on fire. His eyes were streaming, and he had difficulty keeping them open. His legs and feet were like lumps of raw meat.

A thought crossed his mind, and he was muttering it aloud to himself for the rest of the way, "70% to 30% to me Buchan, you bastard. Fuck you and your 50/50!"

[242]

This chanting gave him a second lease on life, and he eventually came out of the other side of the slick. A large ship spray cleaning hose and high powered water was available on the dock side. The first thing Mac did was to strip off all his clothes and liberally spray himself with the water, trying to remove as much oil as possible from his legs and feet. Free from oil, but still burning badly, Mac recruited some local Arab dockyard workers and began to position the leak boom in place. So far, there had been no fire threat, and Mac's confidence was beginning to rise when he saw a sight that made him freeze in his tracks. Buchan started driving the Land Rover through the oil slick, with a hot exhaust.

Mac screamed and yelled at the top of his voice, "Are you fucking crazy or something? Don't you realise that exhaust will set the oil on fire?"

No answer. Just a rigid-like a zombie with a fixed, determined expression on its face, Buchan kept driving, creating a large bow wave of oil as he did so.

Mac grabbed his workmen and anybody else in the area and ran about 50 yards to get out of the way, in case Buchan fired the oil, guessing all the time at Buchan's motive for this madness, and expounding on the stupidity of British Officers, and the college and university system that bred such strange beings. Buchan was one of the better ones, of course. Eventually, Buchan drove the out of the oil with fumes and steam coming from the exhaust pipe.

God only knows how the oil did not ignite.

When Buchan dismounted from the Land Rover, he gave Mac the stupidest grin and said, "I came to give you a hand, old chap. I thought it looked a bit too much for you myself, and I remembered the fact that I have used this equipment more often than you have". Mac was close to bursting point.

"Buchan you twat! I have come to a decision about you. If you had another fucking brain, you would have a total of one".

With that, he mustered the workforce and continued to channel the oil with the boom. He dare not speak anymore, or he would have eliminated the stupid grinning Buchan. Eventually, the boom principle

[243]

worked, and it channelled the oil into a fast moving slick, about 10 feet wide, and this was directed into a large lighter, tied up to the side of the dock. Buchan was correct; they did save thousands of gallons of oil. However, Mac never saw a single penny in commission for his efforts.

CHAPTER 19

FLOSY Dilemma

As all these mad little schemes were taking place leading up to the British withdrawal, the Arabian political scene sunk further into a state of chaos and madness. The FLOSY leader, Abdullah Asnag, who had all of the union support from the docks, was finding it very hard to stay in contention with the National Liberation Front. He left for Cairo to try to persuade the Egyptians to give him more support. He had been receiving help from them for three years, but insufficient in quantity for the escalation of fighting. Unfortunately for him, Egypt, with its economy screwed up, could not afford to give him any more money or weaponry. The NLF, being stronger and better financed, undermined Asnag's FLOSY with superior strength, not only in the townships, but also in the guerrilla wars being fought against the Sheiks up country.

Meanwhile, in an attempt to 'broker' some concessions from the NLF, Lord Shackleton went to Aden in an attempt to meet the terrorists, much to the annoyance of the Colonial Office. Mr. Sam Falle, a Foreign Office advisor, made arrangements for the Lord to meet with the NLF in a house in Crater. He offered to release the NLF prisoners and to recognise their party. Lord Shackleton was told 'No Deal.' The NLF insisted that no truce or ceasefire was negotiable.

The NLF became stronger and British intelligence became weaker, because no Arab would speak to the British, or to be more correct, no Arab dared speak to the British soldiers, for fear of death. The British troops became very frustrated and began to be tough. They were rounding up Arabs and sticking them in barbed razor wired compounds where hooded informants, who had been taken from 'Death Row' at Fort Morbet jail, picked out known terrorists. The propaganda machines were full-time against the soldiers. Broadcasts over all the Arab state radios emphasised the tales of British brutality in Aden. An independent assessment was made by the International Human Rights Committee, which agreed that the British were brutal in our interrogation techniques and arrest procedures in that unfortunate colony.

They should have tried running the show themselves and seen what the men were up against. They may have sang a different tune if they were being shot at, murdered, blown up, and mutilated. One thing that was never explained and caused a lot of outside concern, even after intensive interrogation by these international bodies, was the complete disappearance, without trace, of a large number of known terrorists captured over the last three years of fighting. One case, in particular, was the disappearance of two terrorists who had been shot and sent for treatment to Steamer Point hospital.

The British gave a reason for these disappearances, stating that the people in question had died in captivity and had been cremated with the remains being buried in unmarked graves. This was a very logical explanation, and it made sense. However, rumors upon rumors were beginning to circle around the townships that the British were up to some very dirty tricks indeed.

For years, the British had grown their own pigs for their supply of bacon and pork. To do this, they had established a number of pig farms on the sand stretches leading to the sea on the coast road past the Army camps. Waste food from all of the kitchens and Messes was collected twice daily, and delivered to pig farms for the pig's consumption. When the British troops began to withdraw, the food from the remaining camps was in excess of the small supply needed to feed the few animals that remained. This excess was loaded, still in its dustbin containers, onto helicopters and flown out over Aden harbour and tipped into the sea. This practice carried on for weeks, and eventually, it was quite easy to see the large influx of shark's fins swimming around the food supply area. The sharks seemed to have a built in clock. They arrived in their numbers at the same time every lunchtime and evening, just after dark when the load was being tipped into the harbour.

After the oil spillage into the sea due to terrorist activity, there was great reduction in the number of sharks. There were also many corpses discovered, and even though the bay was tidal, with water rushing in from the Indian Ocean, there was still a lot of damage to the fish and the ecosystem. The rumours had it that it was not only the excess slop from the Army camps that went into the sea for the sharks, but also terrorists who had given us problems, and who could cause more problems in the future, politically. This was a good way to get rid of them. A common saying by troops in Aden at that time, if they were talking about someone they had just arrested, depending on the severity of his crime, was, 'this one is shark bait, mate'.

Nobody ever proved if it this exercise was actually happening or not. Helicopters were often seen late at night, flying out to the deep water channel, (the bait area) and then returning to land again. It will remain a mystery whether the British were guilty of this.

The Sultans began promoting Federation officers from the Army and the police force, hoping for assistance when the NLF came to power on the British soldier's exit. It came to be understood that the mutiny and slaughter of the British troops in Crater in June was the beginning of the end for the Sultans and the Federation. Twenty-four hours after that mutiny, the Emir of Dhala was deposed, and within a few weeks, the Sultans fell, one by one, to the Federal Army and the NLF.

[247]

When the final days before the British exit came to a close, the British patrol activity and terrorist baiting practically ceased. They had a number of fixed defensive machine gun positions and 42 Marine Commando was acting as the perimeter protection force for the withdrawal. The British had ships out in the harbour, some of which could give naval gunfire support if the men were really in the shit. Basically, most people stayed on their bases until such time as they were allocated either to an aircraft or ship to bid their final farewell to the Colony of Aden.

Quart an al Ashabi, the NLF commander, was now openly holding press conferences, explaining to the International Press the intentions of the National Liberation Front once they had got rid of the British infidels. He was invited to London and was wined and dined, and treated very well by the British Government, and all this was going on whilst the NLF was still committing terrorist atrocities against British troops in the 'Arsehole of South Arabia.'

The situation wasn't all rough going; some lucky troops were really living in a paradise situation. The Sergeant's Mess at Barrack Hill in Steamer Point had closed and been relocated at the beach NAAFI, which was a single story rambling building on the beach in Steamer Bay and 20 yards from the edge of the sea. There was a marvellous dining room, television rooms, reading room, and bars in idyllic settings, with a swimming pool on one side of the complex in case you did not wish to risk having a limb chomped off by a shark in the sea. Remember, the shark nets had been washed away after the flood.

With the troops having a lot of free time now, there was not much work to do in the form of patrolling and anti-terrorism. Having a protective circle of Marine Commando all around them, they had little to do but lie about on the beach and sunbathe, have a swim in the pool or go to the bar, watch television, and read or fish from the beach or volcanic rocks surrounding the bay. In fact, they still had the same laundry and servant facilities as before. All of them had now moved into vacated married quarters.

Yes, this was a paradise setting and a comfortable time for the men who remained.

CHAPTER 20

Embassy Protection

Mac still had plenty of work to do trying to slow down as much of the terrorist activity as possible. Also, he had the task of ensuring the security of the staff at the British Embassy, which was located in Steamer Point Station itself, and making sure they embassy workers understood the terrorist weapons and tactics, and how they had used them against the soldiers.

He was to take them to the Cemetery Valley Range to make sure they were proficient in their personal protection weapons and the heavier weapons available to use for the protection of the embassy building itself. This was necessary because the embassy was staying functional after the troops had left.

This was one of the strangest embassies that Mac had come across; because it was the only one he had seen without serving troops acting as protection. Security elements at this embassy were civilian guards, mainly men in their late 40s and 50s, ex-servicemen, recruited on completion of twenty-two years of military service, and then, after application to the Civil Service, selected for embassy security duties.

Mac spent as much as four hours a day with these people over the last five weeks of occupation. They were very good men indeed, especially in close quarter combat. They were armed with their Browning 9mm high-power pistols as their own personal weapons and, of course, had the standard British weaponry in the Embassy, including general-purpose machine guns, which were very few and far apart in the British Army at that time. To make the last few weeks even more enjoyable, from Mac's point of view, were four female British secretaries at the embassy, plus some local typists. The situation outside of the camps did not lend itself for people to go out to bars, restaurants or hotels to enjoy themselves. Consequently, when Mac offered the ladies invitations to the Exclusive Club where they could drink in safety and have a good time, they agreed wholeheartedly.

There seemed to be a lot of last war abandon present at the time. Everyone lived by the hour and enjoyed each other. The girls went for sex as though it had just been invented. The lady who latched herself onto Mac could have won the Miss World Competition, and she had a rampant sexuality about her, which could not be ignored.

It was quite obvious that the SAS Keenie Meenie squads were still very active in the Kochi areas of the townships. One could always tell when they were about doing their dirty business if they were refused permission to enter any certain patrol areas. Sometimes a soldier went into the patrol headquarters of the Prince of Wales Own Regiment of Yorkshire for a briefing by the duty officer, and he would indicate areas that were out of bounds to patrol.

That meant the SAS was in that area, and they were no doubt up to mischief.

CHAPTER 21

Kill 'Shabby'

The NLF leader, Ashabi, became a personal target for British troops in Aden. This was nothing to do with government orders. Mac and his counterparts decided this, and they concluded that the bastard must die before they left the place. This action was brought on by his openly gloating against the British to the printed press, radio, and television, and the fact that the bastard had been back to England and treated like a king by the stupid fucking Labour Government; especially Denis Healey, the two-faced lying bastard who started this bloody showdown in the first place.

Mohamed Farid, the Federation Foreign Minister from 1962 to 1967, stated that the Federation was completely betrayed by the British, and especially by Healey, who reneged on promises made by Duncan Sands at the 1964 Arab conference that the federation would have the protection of the Aden base at Kormaksa. Sands was furious.

Healey lied.

Many of the tricks that were used against the Arabs cannot obviously be disclosed, because the British are still using them in certain theatres of operations, and to tell them would be teaching the enemy tricks if they were spoken of openly. In those days, there were a certain amount of remote control explosive and detonator devices. Most of the equipment that was used relied on improvisation and tactics from weaponry used by Special Operations Executives and their equipment during the Second World War, and of course this equipment was had in plenty.

One of these pieces of equipment was called a 'trembler' device. It was simply a tube of plastic with a ball bearing inside and electrical contacts at each end leading to a detonator and explosive charge. One could place an explosive charge in a briefcase or tin or any type of container, connect everything up, and then place on either side of the ball bearing two knob pins to restrain the movement of the bearing. These devices could be left lying about. After pulling out the two restraining pins, the unit was armed and the ball bearing free to roll either way to make the electrical contact and initiate an explosion. Anyone picking up the case would set the ball bearing rolling to one end or the other, consequently making an electrical contact, which would set off the detonator and explosive charge.

The TWATT men held a Chinese court and decided that they could take out Ashabi by using a device with a trembler in it. It was obvious, because of his protection and his numerous bodyguards, that one could not go leaving an odd briefcase lying about in the hope that he might pick one up. It was necessary to use another tactic. Across from the NLF headquarters in Crater was a large shop, selling many varied items and a large range of briefcases. Somehow, if the team could get one of these items to him from this source, it would be less suspicious and might work. There were still problems arming the thing. The team could not leave anything in the shop armed so that might kill innocent people, although one of the ideas on the Chinese court was to plant a large suitcase full of explosives in the shop and blow the HQ up across the road, and bad luck to anybody caught in the blast.

It was pointless trying to break into the shop and leave a briefcase or other device lying about in the hope that Ashabi or some of his men came in to buy or 'appropriate' item. If this idea was used, the shopkeeper himself would be a problem; probably noticing the item was not one of his regular stocks.

Two methods were open to use. First, the team could put a man in the shop with a device waiting until the terrorist leader went into his headquarters. When this happened, he would then walk across to the Headquarters, pull out the two pins, arming the weapon on the doorstep, and make a pre-planned exit to join up with the others in case of pursuit or a fire fight. Secondly, the team would arrest the shopkeeper. Then they would make him write a letter to Ashabi's security men, instructing them that they should visit him in jail to collect the keys to his shop to pick up a matching set of luggage for

[252]

Ashabi to use on his forthcoming visit to Russia. The trembler position would be taped over and restraining pins put in through a strong adhesive.

When the luggage was unwrapped and the adhesive pulled off, the pins would be withdrawn with the tape and the weapon would explode when it was picked up.

Number two had the vote.

The plan was instantly put into action. A 'whirlwind' surprise raid on the street, which contained the headquarters and the shop, was organized. During this raid, the shopkeeper was arrested in a very high profile fashion. Not one of Ashabi's people could be in doubt that we had him in custody. Troops stayed in the shop, supposedly making intensive searches, and whilst this was happening, the people placed the matching luggage, ready for collection by the security men from across the road.

Everything went as planned. The security men fell for the luggage for Russia story, hook, line, and sinker. It was collected as planned and unwrapped in their HQ.

On the second of October 1967, the NLF headquarters in Crater exploded majestically. There were no survivors. However, Ashabi was not present. Oh well, you can't win them all, but it was a bloody good try. FLOSY were made the obvious scapegoats and blamed for the attack. Therefore, another set of tit for tat reprisals started between the two parties, thus resulting in them leaving the British alone.

There was another attempt to kill Ashabi, thanks to some SOE equipment and tactics used. This was a piece of equipment that exploded should there be a sudden and rapid change of light, for instance, it could be placed on a train and would not explode with a normal change from sunlight to darkness, but if a train entered a tunnel into sudden darkness, it would explode.

By this stage of the game the NLF was very clever at finding destructive devices and booby traps. Let's face it, they had plenty of experience. Mac and his crew felt that if they used the darkness to brightness method with the device, for instance, switching on a light to cause an explosion, the NLF would be suspicious at this time. The

[253]

British team themselves would expect a possible booby trap to detonate when a light was switched on, or a car engine, but not when it was switched off. Mac's idea was to modify this device and place it in one of their headquarters whilst the lights were on, then when the lights were switched off, the building, possibly weaponry and communication equipment inside, would be destroyed with minimal loss of life. It was, however, well known that the last man to leave from the Headquarters was very often Ashabi and his bodyguard. If he could be killed, it would be a bonus.

The plan went ahead with the assistance and expertise of the ATO branch. Three devices were modified to explode when a light was switched off. These devices were quite small, about the size of a packet of 500 sheets of A4 office paper. It had been observed that a continuous supply of paper reams was regularly delivered to all three NLF offices in the colony. Mac upped the ante and intended to blow up all three, increasing the odds of eliminating Ashabi. It was a simple procedure to infiltrate the paper supplier and include one of these new devices in an NLF office delivery, a patch of a clear freezer bag at the end base would allow the darkness to work on switch off. The plan was initiated and ready to go. After the previous suitcase explosion, the NLF occupied a new HQ. Mac decided to watch the newly commandeered NLF building in Crater himself. He felt this was the place they stood the best chance of killing Ashabi.

When he entered Crater over the Shamsan volcano rim, a major fire fight was taking place between elements of FLOSY, NLF and the Argyll and Southerland Islanders.

CHAPTER 22

Gerry AKC

Mac was pinned down behind a low wall, bullets were flying everywhere, but he felt pretty secure in the position he had managed to achieve. Once he had sorted himself out, he noticed that he was not alone. A rather rotund, friendly-faced, sunburned little chap was lying behind the wall with him.

In a rather quiet voice, his new companion said, "These are not very friendly people, are they? I doubt that anybody knows what they are shooting at. It's the same everywhere I have been today. Sheik Othman, El Mansoura, Little Aden - everywhere. The crazy bastards are at it all over the bloody place. It's a waste of time, don't you think?"

"What's a waste of time?" Mac asked this strange man.

"Television, mate. Film projectors and screens, photocopiers. I risk getting shot every day trying to retrieve these things from the military establishments we lent them to".

"What organisation do you work for?"

"The Army Kinema Corporation. Why, I wonder, is it so important to collect this stuff? I would have thought it expendable at this stage of the game, but it seems Gerry Prosser, yours truly, is the only thing that's expendable. I'm not worth nine hundred TV sets". Gerry explained.

Just then, about twenty machine gun bullets passed about three feet above his head and hit the wall on the opposite side of the road.

"I'd feel very inclined to tell your bosses to fuck off, if I was in your shoes. Why don't you?" Mac asked him.

"I have done so on many occasions. It's like hitting your head against a bloody brick wall. They need this equipment in the other Gulf stations rapidly, because of the increase in the number of troops that

[255]

are being stationed there. For instance, the ones being kicked out of Aden now are only moving up the Gulf. They're not homeward bound. Our lot should send a Hercules load of new gear for the Gulf Stations, but while they have a fool like me here, they will try to save money and kill me instead. It's hard to believe it, but the military police makes the job 50 times worse. They insist that when I go over The Causeway (a road running over Aden harbour) to the stations on the Little Aden side of the water, that I have a Military Police Land Rover escort. Now, imagine you are a terrorist on the other side of the causeway, you see a military police Land Rover followed by a military staff type car, and then another military police Land Rover following up in the rear. You'd think to yourself, 'It looks as if we have a prime target here with all these police escorts. Alert all sniper and machine guns. Let's kill everybody in the convoy, because we may as well have the military police scalps on our trophy wall, as well as the man riding in style in the car in the middle. He must be assumed to be a very important person. Let's hit him with rockets or machine gun fire.'

"This has happened to me on a number of occasions. I keep telling the military police I don't want an escort. The stupid idiots insist I have one. They're trying to fucking kill me themselves. What do you think? Do you think they're stupid?"

"I'm sure they are Gerry. I've never liked their calling, and they're always poking big noses into other people's business to justify their existence. I suppose we need them in a military organisation the same as they need police in Civvy Street, but I could never understand the mentality of a man joining any organisation who'll gain his promotion by fucking up other soldiers". As he was speaking, two loud bangs suggested the Dragoon Guards were entering the fray with their big stuff.

"Never mind. When I've finished here, I shall retire and buy a bar somewhere. Then I'll relax and take the piss out of old soldiers coming in for a drink and telling me their war stories. I've seen more fucking fighting in the last three months than most people saw in the whole of the last war". Gerry stated.

"Good idea. Let me know where you are, and I'll come and drink with you".

The fighting and sounds of gunfire had gradually died away, allowing Mac and his newfound associate, Gerry, to carry on with their business. Mac did find out that later, when serving in the Gulf, that Gerry of the AKC was awarded a very high civilian citation for his work in Aden. Much later, he found out that Gerry did retire, did achieve his bar ambition, and is still in the bar in a Mediterranean resort today.

Mac did not have to stay long in Crater to witness the results of the work and planning that he and his crew had put in. That night, at approximately 10:30 p.m., the NLF building exploded. There were numerous secondary explosions, suggesting that the weaponry contained within had also detonated. Later that evening, he received intelligence information that five people were killed in the building, but not Ashabi. He had been very prominent about the townships and in the media during that day, but Mac still had two devices in place to kill the bastard, hopefully that night.

'Shabby' was like the proverbial cat with nine lives. He had only just left, the Ma'alah Banda HQ by ten minutes when it blew sky high, but it did add six more to the terrorist body count. Mac was very pissed off with this close shave, but even more sickened when the third device blew up the stationary supplier's warehouse. The bomb had obviously not been delivered.

Personnel were now beginning to get their flight details or shipping times for the final movement from the Aden colony. The last people to leave were going to be the Royal Marine Commando perimeter protection forces and the Royal Air Force Police Customs and Air movements staff. These people would keep both the military and civilian air traffic under control until such times as the Arabs had qualified people to do the job. Of course, the British embassy would stay.

For a number of weeks now, an organisation called the NLFB had been pushing a load of anti-British propaganda over the Sanaa and Taiz radio waves from the Yemen, calling on the Arab nationalists to throw the British out of the whole of the Persian gulf and follow the good example set for them by their fine brave heroes and friends in South Yemen and Aden. Because of this development, it was decided that Mac should take all the captured terrorist equipment and booby traps that he had accumulated in Aden, and fly them up the Persian Gulf to give lectures to British forces stationed there and show them what had been used and how it had been used against the British forces in Aden and South Yemen. This, hopefully, would save lives if the NLF started to try to kill soldiers in the Persian Gulf, as their propaganda suggested.

This little task caused problems for a number of reasons. Physically, the Russian and Chinese grenades and explosive charges with their detonators were old, live, and sweating off volatile explosive inflammable fumes. Consequently, they were very unsafe to handle and move. At this time, there was no equipment available to steam out the explosives from these devices, nor could the men turn round and ask the Russians, Chinese, or the terrorists to give samples of demonstration equipment for training. These problems meant the stuff would have to fly in RAF aircraft to the Gulf stations. It would be too unstable and take too long by ship. The Royal Air Force would never agree to this, so once again, the goodies were packed in cases and labelled as MT spares.

Mac was to fly with them to help avoid causing suspicion amongst the Air movements and customs staff. Mac said afterward that he sat between two cases of his pet captured equipment for two and one half hours on board an Argosy flying to Bahrain.

He remarked, "Never mind the explosives sweating, I must have sweat away pounds upon bloody pounds, and every time the aircraft bounced in a thermal current I nearly shit myself. Everybody on that aircraft was happy to be leaving Aden, but if they had known what was in my cases, they would have jumped out of that fucking air taxi without a bloody parachute".

The safety of the forces left in the colony and the completion of the withdrawal was now firmly in the hands of Colonel Dai Morgan of 42 Commando Royal Marine. His barrier of 340 marines was now the complete airfield perimeter protection at Khormaksa.

Other units, such as the maintenance and servicing yards on the cemetery valley road and the garrison camps along the beach road, had all been closed and were now deserted of British troops, but were rapidly becoming Kochi townships for the Arabs. The beautiful football and sports stadium at Steamer Point was now full of corrugated iron and cardboard Kochi huts and open running sewage. It was hard to believe that not many weeks before, Mac had sat and watched sharks swimming around in the same place.

CHAPTER 23

The Final Humiliation

The first weeks of November were really the end of the end. The troops were moving out by aircraft on a continuous basis. Those who were going to the nearest coastal stations, such as Salahla and Masira, boarded ships for their Indian Ocean cruise, the lucky bastards. Those flying further up the Gulf to Sharja, Bahrain, Cyprus, and some for Malta, had all departed between the 10th of October and the 25th November 1967.

No farewell parades took part in the colony at all. The British literally sneaked out with their tails between their legs, something that has never happened on withdrawal from any other place in the world. Previously, any withdrawal was carried out with a feeling of nostalgia, the last post being played, and the flag would be lowered, then the new one raised. The enemies of the past shook hands and everyone promised the best for each other in the future. The Egyptians even laid on massive alcohol parties, which were against their religion, when the British handed over their bases on the Suez Canal before they took them back again in 1956. Not so with Aden. No parties there. The men expected to have to fight their way out at the bitter end.

Sir Humphrey Trevelyan took the final salute onboard HMS Intrepid to avoid any last minute terrorist show of force. It's hard to believe the troops were so humiliated that they couldn't carry out this ceremony on land. After so many men had died, and others maimed for life, not to mention the sweat and hardship went through with thousands of others, the British exit was a disgrace.

The soldiers should have had a parade the British way, and shot any bastard who tried to disrupt it, like they did when the Argyll's marched back into Crater after the mutiny.

CHAPTER 24

The Lessons

Looking back at our military achievements in Aden, one can see it was a valuable experience. The British learned a lot. The men learned a tremendous amount about Marxist terrorism and how the Chinese and the Russians were attempting to undermine everything that the Western and European powers did overseas. They also learned their weaponry. There was some very good insight gained into the psychological profile of terrorists. The British soldiers knew how and where they would use their equipment. The British also knew how to use their weapons and how to make them fail. They had learned how to keep the terrorists confused, unsure, frightened, and mostly ineffective and unsuccessful in urban attacks, and mountain work up country had also been good in the beginning.

Most importantly, the British tried and tested their own embryo equipment in an operational environment against a real enemy, giving them time to modify, adjust, re-design, and re-test to make them stronger. The British Military knew they could beat these communist trained terrorists anywhere in the world. This was proven in the Oman over the following few years, thanks to the British Aden learning curve.

Lt-Col Dai Morgan's Royal Marine Commando was lifted out of their defensive airfield protection positions at 2:00 p.m. on the 29th of November 1967. Dai flew around the perimeter, checking to ensure everything was cleared away before he left, and observing to make sure there were troop movements against the airfield. There was no enemy troop movement at all. The NLF threat of showing they could 'throw the British in the sea' to appease their people and prove that they could defeat the men in battle was one big load of bullshit.

Lt- Col Morgan finally left for HMS Bulwark at 3:00 p.m. on the 29th November 1967.

When asked by the media his thoughts on the situation, he said, "It's hard for a soldier to sit by and watch as civilian or uniformed men enter a building, and then hear gunshots and screams indicating damn well that people are being killed, and be unable to do anything about it because of orders and politics. Trained soldiers should never be placed in this type of no win situation".

Sources in the Commandos told Mac later that Colonel Morgan was deep in the shit with certain people, because of his very truthful professional soldier's comments.

Later, in the months of January and February 1968, Mac met members of the RAF Police travelling from Aden through Bahrain on their way home. They had stayed in Aden, running customs and air traffic. Apparently, all had a beautiful time. The NLF accommodated them in the best hotels, paid all their bills, gave out extra spending money on top of their British service wages, and generally wined and dined the lucky few, making the recipients of these favours feel very important and welcome. Some of the descriptions of favours given may well have been exaggerated, but who would believe that these people who were so generous to the British police were the same bastards who employed so many evil tactics trying to kill the soldiers a few months earlier?

If you ask Mac, he'll tell you he doubts he could have accepted their generosity, or if he had, he would have definitely ripped them off. The British Military Police were eventually relieved from their duties in Aden by Russian controllers.

Aden became the People's Republic of South Yemen, a Marxist state, and an ally of the Soviet Union. It is still a duty free port and the tourist trade is a continuous source of income, with cruise ships calling in for shopping tours nearly every day, plus a booming international trade in oil. Even though the place has wealth, it is still a very torn up area. Incidents arise daily, inter-tribal fighting is commonplace, the hill tribes are always at each other's throats, and they now have the added bonus of being able to travel over the mountains into what was known as the old Yemen and raid and loot. They've been fighting for centuries, why stop now?

Hostage taking is a favourite hobby and money-spinner with exorbitant ransom demands for the victims' release. Even in recent times we hear news that the British Embassy had been blown up in Sanaa in the Yemen, and a suicide bomber in a rubber dingy had seriously damaged an American warship in Aden harbour, killing six servicemen on board.

CHAPTER 25

Kidnapped

'The Bloody War of Aden' cannot be finished without writing about one of its humorous legacies sent up to the Gulf States.

Mac was well known by forces in Bahrain especially Jufair and Muharraq, because many of the men had come up from Aden, and had attended the Cemetery Valley ranges qualifying for the QGH 1, 2 or 3 Golliwog badge. It didn't take long for the RAF Regiment Ground Combat Training Section to start up the same competitions and awards. This unit also held the Mac and Buchan weaponry and ammunition that had been flown up from Aden, after being saved from a watery grave in Aden harbour. This meant that all of the Army, RAF, and Navy could fire modern weapons with as much ammunition as they needed. The SAS contingent based at Sharja ensured a continuous supply of ammunition, from where was not known.

It was at this time that Mac managed to get himself kidnapped. The friendly ship, HMS Eskimo, a Tribal Class frigate was in the harbour. These good men, one may remember, came to Aden to fire for their QGH, even bringing their own weapons and ammunition with them. Once they heard that Mac was in Bahrain, they headed for the 25 metre ranges at Muharraq to earn the coveted decoration once more. They duly fired the full range of weapons with great success, and then destroyed about ten cases of Stella beer in the target store behind the butts before returning back to the ship with Mac in tow. He had accepted an invitation to a King Prawn grilled dinner in the CPO's mess.

Mac had a great time, excellent food, copious supplies of booze, some bar games, including the single file hop around the deck with both hands on the shoulders of the man in front, and singing 'Hi Ho, Hi Ho, off to sea we go,' a famous melody in tune to the song sang by the seven dwarfs from Snow White. Mac realized he'd had enough to drink to last him a month and asked the ships Master at Arms to call him a taxi to take him home.

"No need, Mac. We have a liberty bus leaving in a couple of hours. You have a lie down on the night duty officer's bunk, and we'll give you a call when we're about to leave". Mac did so gratefully.

When he awoke from his obviously very deep beer induced slumbers, he was at a loss for a few moments as to his whereabouts. Gradually, slow recall became effective and he realized he was still on board ship. A glance at his watch brought him bolt upright, causing an excruciating headache. He had slept for five hours. There was a vague memory about a bus leaving in two hours, and somebody going to wake him, plus other confusing mixed up thoughts. He gave up trying to make heads or tails of events, because waves of nausea were sweeping over him. He then realized that the ship was swaying and rocking, and he could now hear what he assumed was the sound of water banging against the hull.

Gingerly, he managed to force himself off the bed, washed his face, and combed his hair. Feeling slightly better, he wandered through the CPO's Mess out onto the upper deck of the ship. He couldn't believe his eyes. There was water in every direction and not one speck of land in sight. Whilst he had been sleeping, the ship had put to sea. While he stood against the safety rail, contemplating his position, one of the CPO Mess Stewards came out in his white monkey jacket, carrying a tray with a large drink, which he presented to Mac with a flourish.

"The drink is Gin and Angostura bitters, Sir. Compliments of the Master at Arms. He will be along to see you shortly. If, in the meantime, you need anything, please ring the bell at the side of the door".

He indicated a triangular type of bell, often seen on films outside the cook house when they're calling the cowhands for meals.

The drink was a magic potion. After a few sips, Mac felt almost human again and actually began to enjoy himself.

"Mark Hudson! How are you?"

[265]

The rancheros stentorious greeting came from his friend, the Master at Arms. He slapped Mac on the back, in what he assumed was an affectionate manner, and nearly managed to cave in Mac's ribs during the process.

"You've surfaced at last. You looked so peaceful sleeping there, and you'd looked after us so marvellously that we thought we'd leave you alone to sleep the booze off, and then bring you as our guest on this little five day patrol".

"Look, you stupid Naval twat, I have lectures booked and people at the highest level of command to advise. I don't want to appear ungrateful, far from it, I'm very flattered by all this, but you must take me back".

"Sorry, me old mate, no can do. Even if we wanted to, this is a set series of routines we have to perform. We have to promote British goodwill, plus a strong presence in the area. We have to call in at certain places on a schedule. We have to deliver things to places at precisely set times. We have to collect certain items from places or risk political upheaval. Simply, we cannot renege on what we are doing, at the moment. We cannot lift you out by the helicopter, because it's fucking useless, and the mechanics are working on it now. On top of all that, we have already radioed Royal Air Force Muharraq for a ransom for your return".

"Thank you very much, you bastard. Well, I suppose if I've got to stay here, I might as well make the most of it. I'll have another gin and bitters. Incidentally, how much did you ask Muharraq to pay you for me?"

"Three hundred cases of Stella beer, five cases of whisky, five cases of rum, five cases of gin, five cases of vodka, five cases of mixed liqueurs, and after that supply being met, the WRAF contingent must bring them aboard and drink them with us on a gorgeous piss up on our return to Bahrain".

"You must be crazy man. There's no way the Royal Air Force is going to pay that much ransom for me. I'm not even stationed at Muharraq".

"That's what they said in as many words".

[266]

"What did they actually say to you then?"

"They told us to fuck off in no uncertain terms, and even said we should throw you overboard". He stated, seemingly in all seriousness.

"What happens if they refuse to meet your naval demands?" Mac asked.

"It looks like you have joined the Navy until they do", he laughed.

"Oh well, it could be worse. I might as well have a good time and enjoy myself. Is there anything you would like me to do on board ship?"

"No. Just have a good time, have plenty to drink, loads to eat, and mega amounts of sleep. You deserve it after your fucking job down in Aden. We'll keep updating you on the ransom stakes".

"That's fine by me. I'll have another gin and bitters, thank you".

That is just what happened. Mac had a great time. He was invited to drink in the Officers Mess, known as the Ward Room. He was drowned with drinks in the company of the men down below decks. He had drinks with the PO's in their mess, which doubled up as the CPO's mess at different times, and was given guided tours of all the various departments.

He calculated that if the RAF did pay any ransom, he would have drunk most of it during his forced holiday. On duty sailors showed him the work that had to do, but most of this important information went over his head, because he was too pissed to understand. On a few sober occasions, he conducted CQB, or close quarter battle training, and the men fired all weapons over the ship's stern. He gave a few lectures in the different mess decks on terrorist weapons and tactics as employed against the British down in Aden, but without the use of the sensitive training aids he had collected.

Every evening at about eight o'clock, he was awakened from his drunken slumbers by one of the CPO's, and went to their mess for his 'roster slot' evening meal and update on the ransom negotiations. He was not doing very well on the ransom stakes with the Royal Air Force or anyone else for that matter. They kept telling the Royal Navy, 'go fuck yourself,' and stated that they refused to pay anything at all. One telex even told the Navy to 'Throw him overboard bound and gagged.'

[267]

The Navy tried to ransom Mac to many places with the same results. Sharja said, "He's not one of ours. We only see him when he's down here practicing parachuting from helicopters with this new Para Commando chute".

Masira said, "The only time we see him is when he drops in trading 'blue films' and buying Crayfish from the locals".

Salalah said, "The only time we see him is when he calls in to sell us blue films and Crayfish, go fuck yourselves".

Time flew and before Mac realised it, they were on the last day at sea and docking at 8:00 a.m. the following morning. At this late stage, no ransom had been decided, and the last telex from the Royal Air Force made the situation quite clear that they would not give the Navy anything at all. Another message from the RAF Medical branch informed the Navy that on landing, Mac was to be put in animal quarantine on the docks and subjected to a barrage of tests to see what infectious diseases he'd picked up during his five days' exposure to the Navy.

Eskimo docked with all the non-working crew lining the ship's rail, looking resplendent in their white tropical uniforms. Certain rituals took place that involved a lot of to-ing and fro-ing by people in obvious positions of power and all accompanied by a cacophony of sound from penny whistles called 'pipes.'

Mac spotted a couple of Arabs and a large retinue of what one assumed were female harems coming onboard. This made Mac chuckle to himself when he thought about all these rampant Navy sex machines on the ship, all ogling this feast of womanhood trained to satisfy the needs of men in all their sexual fantasies, or so rumour had it.

Only one WRAF was in sight. She carried Warrant Officer rank and looked very smart in her KD tropical uniform. She was gray haired, granite faced, and managed to look extremely strict and pissed off at the same time; but the most intriguing thing about her was the lone case of Stella beer at her feet. This turned out to be the RAF full and final ransom payment for the return of Mark Hudson, and it was to be consumed by the WRAF representative and the ships Master at Arms,

[268]

before Mac was released to the lady's kindly care. The RAF had been generous and had forgone their quarantine demands.

No one came to welcome Mac back at all. As soon as the coast was clear of the dignitaries and the VIPs, the WRAF Warrant Officer made a beeline for the Master at Arms, clutching the case of beer to her bosom. Mac stood there, alone, like little orphan Annie. He noticed a Land Rover with the insignia of the 7th RHA on the side; he knew these were stationed at the Army Camp at Muharraq, so he scrounged a lift from the driver back to base.

On the way back to camp, the driver commented that the ship in the harbour, HMS Eskimo, had once captured a man accused of stealing weapons in Aden and took him out to sea and threw him overboard.

Wonder who that was?

Mac somehow had a feeling that the man was talking about him.

Back at Muharraq, things were as normal. Nobody said anything about his trip, welcomed him back, or asked about the ransom. It appeared to Mac that the whole exercise never happened.

One day, Mac was heard to say, "At least I know what my value is to people and especially to the Royal Air Force. Exactly fucking nothing," he laughed at his own comment.

Then he said, in a resigned sort of way, "I don't give a damn anyway".

CHAPTER 26

Nothing Can Go Wrong...Go Wrong

Another incident in the Gulf that is worth talking about again involved the Aden crews of adventurous souls.

Crayfish was in great demand in the Officers and Sergeant's Messes scattered around the Gulf area, especially for cold buffet type meals at dances. These types of activities still took place in the Gulf, because the married families and civilians working for the government had not been evacuated, as they had in Aden.

The greatest supply of Crayfish came from Masira, on the southeast tip of the landmass. 104 Argosy Squadron, called the Gulf Communications Squadron, based at Muharraq, were tasked to make the trip called the 'milk run' every day. This involved stopping at Sharjah, Abu Dhabi, Masira, and Salahla, delivering and collecting store's equipment and buying Crayfish at Masira to sell in the Messes on the way back. The sales goodies also included sexually orientated magazines and X-rated films by the hundreds made by the local Arabs. Everybody profited and was happy with these arrangements.

On odd occasions, the 'milk run' had to add an extra dimension to its normal task, mainly that of dropping paratroopers in the 'Golden Valley' dropping zone near Sharja. On one of these training descents the 7th Royal Horse Artillery (RHA), were heavy dropping their 105mm Pack Howitzers, and jumping themselves on a three day exercise. Nobby Hall, the RAF Parachute Jumping Instructor (PJI) attached to Muharraq and Mac, helped them out, jumped with them, and then lifted them back to Sharja by helicopter to continue the 'milk run.'

Everything went according to plan; the flight to Sharja was uneventful. The RHA managed their ground training - pre drop drills with additional RAF Instructors attached to the SAS at Sharja. The takeoff, flight, and drop went off without a snag. Within ten minutes of landing and wrapping up the parachutes, a helicopter of the Army Air Corps (AAC) picked up Mac and Nobby from the DZ and flew them back to the Sergeants Mess at Sharja, the agreed meeting point.

This is when things began to go wrong.

It was hot and sweaty, people had been involved in heavy stressful work, flying aircraft, parachuting, so a couple of cold drinks were in order and wouldn't do anybody any harm. After all, they were seasoned, operational, proven men, not a bunch of new recruits. Such was the thinking among them at the time. A happy half hour followed. Nobody consumed spirits, just ice cold lager, and this was drunk in small quantities, but it caused problems to both Load Masters. In this writing, we'll know them as S and G, for reasons that will become apparent.

When the crew arrived back at the aircraft, an air movement officer informed them that thirteen unexpected passengers were waiting on board to fly back to Muharraq, they only expected to fly freight, hence the little illegal drink in the Sergeants mess. Oh! Well, it would be okay, everybody was sober, the passengers just meant a little extra work looking after them on the two-hour flight, and everyone would have to behave seriously and not clown about, as was the norm on freight runs. Most crews used to do their own cabaret acts and impersonations of well-known artists to pass the time.

The pilot carried out his pre take off checks, whilst S re-stowed the cargo and G ensured the passengers were secure in the side nets (nets on the side of the aircraft that act as seats when carrying freight). The passengers were a mixed bag of different Regiments and ranks: an RAF Wing Commander Padre; a Wing Commander with pilot wings and many medals; a Blues and Royals Colonel; three Army nurses; four evil, dirty-looking bandits, covered in shit with no regiment or badges of rank symbols in sight. Looking at the passenger manifest, they had names, but no other information was offered. When it came to dishing out the plastic egg sandwiches, they wolfed them down like they were starving. They looked bloody menacing.

G took the tannoy microphone from its clip and began his pre-flight address to the captive audience seated before him. This was the

[271]

first indication that the drink had any effect on any of them, Mac included. Just imagine the passengers faces while they sat there, probably nervous, because the Argosy is a noisy, bumpy plane, and they heard this welcome:

"Good morning ladies and gentlemen. Welcome aboard the Gulf Communications Flight number thirteen, unlucky for some. I say unlucky for some, because we have had problems on flight thirteens before, and also when we have flown on the thirteenth day of the month. We shall be taking off shortly for our two-hour flight to Muharraq. That is, if the starboard outer engine manages to work properly. You may hear the pilot revving up the engine now to see if he can build up enough power for it to take off. We've had problems with the bloody thing for weeks, and the engineers that do our servicing have too much work to do. The ones we wanted to borrow from other aircraft that could manage to work for us have been sent off on leave. The Argosy aircraft is the workhorse of the Royal Air Force; it is powered by four Rolls Royce Dart engines, which are famous for being unreliable, especially in sandy desert conditions, such as we fly in. The filters and carburetors block up with sand, did you know?

"Unfortunately, the Royal Air Force cannot afford any better engines. There is not enough money in the coffers, hence, our grin and bear it brave attitude, and we settle for the tenth worst product on the market.

"One hour, forty minutes of our flight will be over the ocean. Normally, underneath your seat net, we keep a life jacket for the likely event of ditching in the sea. We do not bother to carry them with us now. The water that we fly over is infested with man-eating sharks. Tiger sharks, actually, for those of you that are interested. Therefore the life jacket would be of little use; it would only prolong the inevitable, horrible death that awaits us.

"Unfortunately, with this being a freight aircraft, we have no proper toilet facilities should you need to go to the toilet for either a number one or a number two, would you please go to the bucket situated to the rear of the aircraft".

[272]

With that statement, he pointed to a normal standard bucket without a seat positioned at the back end of the aircraft, just before the ramp and in full view of everybody on board.

The passengers looked a sickly white, tinged with shades of green. Some had blue streaks to the extremities of the body, ears, nose, and lips obviously caused by oxygen deficiency as a result of shock, and I feel it may be possible that some of the aircrew felt the same, not for their own fear, but for the effect on the passengers.

This little broadcast was not rehearsed and nobody, including the crew, had been informed that this narrative was about to be performed. It came on its way out of the blue. Now the gang was again surprised by a conclusion to the speech:

"I have just been talking to the pilot, ladies and gentlemen. He states that the starboard outer engine has not made its proper power output, and he intends to take off and fly the route on three engines. We should be okay, unless they start to overheat. Don't bother yourselves, this is something we do on many occasions, and all fail safe systems on this aircraft model are duplicated. It's very rare that anything ever goes wrong, goes wrong, goes wrong, goes wrong".

It sounded as though the tannoy had broken down and acted like a sticking gramophone record. Of course, it hadn't; it was all part of the passenger 'windup' and a good example how the 'supposed' fail safe systems didn't work. The Royal Air Force padre was openly praying by this time. The only people seemingly unconcerned about these goings-on were the dirty looking menacing bastards who were still eating plastic egg sandwiches. The nurses were holding hands. The RAF Wing Commander pilot had a notebook on his knee writing copious notes in a furiously frantic manner. All were to see that notebook again in less humorous circumstances. Unfortunately, for the passengers, it was a very bumpy flight. Even Mac felt slightly airsick. Combine this unfortunate situation with their detailed preflight briefing about the aircraft problem and one can see it wasn't a pleasant situation for them to be in.

During the course of the flight, the usual niceties were observed; tea or coffee was issued round, and of course, the proverbial plastic egg sandwiches. Strangely, on this flight, nobody seemed hungry, with the exception of the evil four.

Apart from the rough flight and the surplus of food, everything went according to plan, a normal flight, in fact, apart from G and his antics. GH bounced heavy on the tarmac at Muharraq, due to the strong crosswinds and turbulence, and this set the Wing Commander pilot off on another furious writing spree into his notebook. While the passengers thankfully disembarked, G was standing at the door wishing them 'bon voyage.' 'Hope you had enjoyed the flight,' and 'please come and fly with 104 Gulf Squadron again,' plus all the other things stewards and stewardesses say when one leaves an aircraft. Everybody smiles back and shakes hands with the people they've learned to love and trust during the few hours and minutes they've shared together. The noble people who have helped them put their feet on the ground again. Humans are grateful for little things provided by characters that they assume lead a glamorous, adventurous life, such as aircrew, for instance. This particular bunch of nervous wrecks did not exude this normal graciousness toward the aircraft staff.

The Wing Commander pilot turned out to hold the appointment of Wing Commander Administration at RAF Salahla and was making a journey on the 'milk run' to see his mate, the Station Commander, at Muharraq. Any complaint against an air crew by a character with that level of command and who can boast buddies on the same level is bound to be treated very seriously, even though he was scrounging a freebie flight at taxpayer's expense. Perhaps that's petty to say it that way, but necessary in order to relate how Mac and the crew felt when they told of their escapade, and how they scorned that individual, full of his own importance and obviously blinded with the abstract power reflected by his rank.

The disrespect for this individual by the crew was intense. They expected a rollicking, dressing down, or some sort of penury punishment, maybe an extra duty Officer or Sergeant. This man wanted them destroyed in the worst possible way for their high jinx and twisted aircrew type of humour. He was demanding disciplinary

[274]

charges, leading to boards of enquiry and court martial, and discharge from the service with ignominy, no less.

Mark Hudson and Bobby Hall were not included in this fiasco, because they were not officially the aircraft crew members. They, even though part of the Argosy operational task group, were classed as passengers. The danger they calculated was to be called as witnesses on any enquiry and have to tell the truth on oath against the rest of the jockey's team. The RAF could fetch them back from anywhere in the world for such an occasion, but Mac's idea was to be as far away as possible, in the hope that the powers that be wouldn't deem it worthwhile on such petty charges.

Mac organized, in double quick time, a trip to lecture on terrorist weapons and tactics to the British Army detachments and oil company workers based in Kuwait. He also gained permission for N to accompany him as an assistant. (A lot of heavy equipment to move about pays off sometimes.)

Disciplinary action against GH went ahead, because he was the aircraft pilot, and therefore, in command of the rest of the people involved. Even G, who had carried out the infamous cabaret speech and performance, (which was later mimicked at mess piss ups at stations around the world) was let off scot-free. GH was awarded a reprimand and this accompanied with one year's loss of seniority. Cheers to the RAF adjudicators, because GH only had eight months service left before retirement.

News soon filtered down to the troops that the rank happy miserable Wing Commander, who had insisted on the charges being filed, was berated in the Officers mess bar by his mate, the Station Commander. He was accused of being guilty of interference in the way things were run at Muharraq and "lowering the squadron aircrew morale, and trying to destroy the Battle of Britain camaraderie his chaps felt. A type of teamwork he had promoted and which was essential in that theatre of operations to help combat the stress and strain caused through long hours of flying that his men had to endure."

Well-done Station Commander! That interfering jerk really ended up with a dollop of plastic egg on his face.

Mac arrived back to the UK in May 1968, after blowing up his collection of goodies. They were too unstable to use anymore. Troops in the Oman were putting together another more transportable collection. These things, of course, would be of an updated variety for training the new arrivals out there in the 'Arsehole of South Arabia'.

Of the Aden Insurgency, Mac once said, "Let's always keep at least one hundred steps ahead of our enemies, and hopefully, out of his range, but ensure we keep him in ours".

That's good advice for military men wherever they serve.

BOOK FOUR _ THE AFRICAN AFFAIR

SECTION 1-Training
CHAPTER 1

Tanzanian Ranger Battalion

Mac and his men were now successfully out of the Arab desert sands, and as with any person employed as a military officer, after a round of rest and leave, he was sent on to other deployments. Jumping ahead in time, we will find Africa as the backdrop for this part of Maces story.

Mac's "Bastard Bush Bandits" or the 3-Bs as his Ranger battalion became known had been formed to deal with the increase in Ugandan insurgency raiding across the Tanzanian border in the mid-1970s, before the full war between the two countries had been declared. These raids were causing considerable damage to the small farms bordering the Great Lakes by crop burning, cattle and livestock theft, and murder of civilians.

Maces unit was divided into four groups. They were: Support Group for Fielding a Mortar Troupe, Heavy Machine Gun Troupe, Signals and Communication group, and Ground Infantry Companies with Attached Medical Support. The combat strength of the Rangers continually fluctuated, and, at any time, could number up to a maximum of 800 troops. It was estimated that approximately 10% of the Ranger battalion personnel were foreign volunteers; these men had served with experienced professionals in some of the world's finest forces. Many brought with them invaluable experiences of fighting African wars in countries that were supported by Soviet or

Chinese weapon supply, money and instructors, and on some occasions, as in Angola, front line troops.

These "Bush Bandits", as they were nicknamed, came from the disbanded Selous Scouts, the Rhodesian Light Infantry, and the South African Defense Forces with reconnaissance and fire fight incursions into Mozambique, Zambia, and Mau Mau in Kenya operations under their belts. No unit commanded by Mac Hudson would be complete without ex-members of the British Royal Marines, No. 9 Commandos, Paras, SAS veterans, ex-members of the United States Special Forces, and a few German mercenaries who had worked in the Congo with Mike Hoare and John Peters, plus worked the "boiling pots" of trouble in Zaire and South Sudan.

Although the Rangers were a small unit, they packed a powerful punch, with their collection of captured weapons, and they possessed a tough, aggressive spirit that counted for a high percentage of enemy casualties during the war. One prime example of this was an ambush staged during the early stages of the Ugandan aggression, when a forward operating base in Uganda gave warning of a company strength movement toward the southern infiltration route of the Great Lake near Bongo.

A ten-man, three section ambush was rapidly deployed, and in the ensuing firefight, the whole infiltration force was eliminated. Ugandan Army Company strength is usually 270 men and with attached supporting elements normally numbers 308 men, as in this case. The ambush party was free of any casualties, and total ammunition expenditure was 3 Claymore mines, 6x 3.5 inches "Bazooka" rockets, 36 HE grenades, 36 Phosphorous grenades, and 608 rounds of small arms ammunition, giving an average of 1 Claymore, 2 Bazooka, 12 HE, 12 Phosphorous grenades and 200 rounds of small arms per section. This was fantastically low ammunition expenditure for such devastating results. There were no survivors, because the African members of the ambush party exercised their right to disembowel the enemy to release their "warrior spirit" to their Gods.

Every morning when the "stand to" was called, normally by a whistle or siren, the effect was instantaneous. Men burst into action, clutching rifles and machine guns. All the men were clad in a variety of clothing. Many wore T-shirts, shorts, and trainers. A few were even barefooted after walking like that for years in the bush. Some sported weird mixtures of poor conditioned, faded camouflage suits. What bit of cash Mac had available was needed for weaponry. His men didn't need to look the part or to play the part; they were the part, for real. He wouldn't let them wear captured clothing, except footwear, in case his own men didn't recognize them. This would mean their instant death, because the teams worked under a strict shoot to kill policy.

During a stand to, the NCOs would rush around, signaling communications with their hands, but saying nothing. They had to do this in combat situations, so they did it all the time, even off duty. They were like an order of silent Monks that had vowed never to speak.

Approaching the group of huts, which was the headquarters area; the men slowed to walk and began to disperse to their respective places.

NCOs hurried away to the briefing on the opposite side of the chopper pens. The men relaxed, sitting or sprawling around while they waited for their squad boss to come back and "gen spew," which is what imparting information was called. It was not at all unusual at this stage for any operations or training to be cancelled. When this happened, a yell sign of "five finger widow time" echoed around the bush.

Most of the men carried whatever weapons came to hand. The shortage of weaponry was due to a serious lack of money in the coffers of the Tanzanian treasury. However, the Rangers could keep any weapons they "won" from a Ugandan terrorist. This gave the men a tremendous incentive to fight and kill. Men would bring diverse weapons back to their teammates who had not been included in a certain operation.

What's more, their webbing equipment was a strange mixture from different countries of origin, and years of manufacture. All ranged from standard British 44 pattern to all sorts of bastardized stitched up leather or webbing.

[279]

Civilian jackets with numerous pockets, but no webbing were also in vogue. Long shining belts of ammunition for the machine guns, and a further store of ammunition bulged out of the many pockets.

Pistols, machetes, and knives dangled from belts and shoulder straps. The NCOs came out of the briefing buildings and ordered that the men "Kit Up," in sign language, of course

It was a typical pattern of events on a counterinsurgency operations morning for the Rangers in the early stages of the war, when one of the eight man patrols had just turned up at the base camp after five days out in the bush, bringing back nine AK47 Kalashnikovs and a number of land mines and ammunition. This haul marked the success of the foray out to the "badlands" and meant nine more dead terrorists. One man had been shot in the thigh, the bullet passing straight through, so the wound had been left open and exposed to the flies and was crawling with maggots. This was a good thing, because the maggots kept the wound clean. They ate up any decomposing flesh and prevented gangrene setting in before the casualty could receive skilled attention at base camp.

In the makeshift base hospital tent, two British medical orderlies and a German doctor would deal with all manner of casualties and illnesses often performing surgery under Tilley lamps.

CHAPTER 2

The Enemy

The guerrillas came from operating bases in Uganda across the Great Lake, making hit-and-run raids against units in isolated areas. Such small incursions however, proved ineffective and costly. The Tanzania security forces were normally able to contain the problem.

During the mid to late 1970s, the picture changed quite drastically. Guerrilla activity in the combat zone became more organised, with direct support from units outside Uganda, mainly from Eastern bloc countries. Arms shipments and military advisors greatly contributed to the guerrillas fighting capability and training standards, and this increased their morale. Initially, the skirmishing had been concentrated on the Tanzanian side of the Great Lake, but eventually spread to the South and then the North of the country.

Mac knew that the Ugandans were being supported by Libya and by Robert "Piano Teeth" Mugabe, part of the ZANU organization from Zambia.

When the conflict escalated, Mac persuaded the Tanzanian forces to adopt an aggressive and preemptive approach to counterinsurgency, taking the war to the bastards who infiltrated their territory, as opposed to the passive strategy of sitting and waiting for attacks. This latter tactic had always been the Tanzanian way. They were too nice to be in any war, and frustrated the hell out of killing minded military trained professionals. Mac positioned a greater intelligence-gathering network in Uganda, (mainly ex Selous Scouts and ex SAS) and developed "Immediate Reaction" forces to deal aggressively with information gained from the new sources. Their job was simply to root out and destroy enemy units in the bush. Forces had to move very fast if they were to succeed in engaging enemy terrorists before they could melt away from the scene of any sightings.

High mobility, operational flexibility, combined with heavy firepower was the keys to success. Mac Hudson always preached to his patrol leaders, "It is quicker to Act then React."

CHAPTER 3

Patrol Activities

Sometime previously, under cover of atrocious weather, Mac's Rangers set up reconnaissance deep in the war zone, along the eastern border of Uganda. His men acted quickly and set up observation posts, under the very noses of Amin's Special Forces Camp, nicknamed "The Aids and HIV Development Center" by Mac's men. They then settled down to watch and wait for targets. The use of the SSE 707 night surveillance equipment (Artillery) was very advantageous at this time. It gave Mac's men twenty-four hours of daylight and made the poor Ugandan infiltrators into targets as easy as a fairground game of "Duck Shoot" during darkness.

The enemy had a small supply of individual night sights, mainly one to a squad, and had been commandeered by the patrol commander to find his route, but even if every man was in possession of these Russian units, they were very ineffective compared to the SSE. Their sights were rendered useless when a flare was fired. They "bloomed" out, and the poor bastard on the eyepiece was nearly blinded. Consequently, everyone was very reluctant to use them if they were near any lights at all, especially combat generated light.

As soon as the weather broke, reports of insurgent movements started flooding in from the observation posts. An operation was put in motion and a simple plan ensued: "Stop Groups" were flown into the enemies" return escape routes by helicopter, and then the Immediate Action Force (IAF) went into action, directly shooting at the first sign of an enemy sighting. Mac led this group himself, in case of bungled instructions and if difficulties arose. If this happened the Reserve Support Troop (RST) was called in. These would sweep through the area like beaters on a wild game shoot, and drive the guerrillas into the fire of the "Stop Groups."

The South African Army Puma helicopters had brought in the "Stop Groups" to the base of a large "gobo" (wood), a fair distance from where a bandit group sighting had been reported. They didn't want to draw enemy fire by landing too close. It was far better, and they were particularly effective when they were on the ground and could dish out maximum punishment. They spent the next two hours laboriously clambering over the slopes of a hill. Sweltering beneath the weight of their kit, peering cautiously into the bush, creeping steadily around boulders, they systematically operated a process that was now routine to most of them. Routine, but still nerve-wracking nonetheless.

A decomposed animal mutilated corpse was spotted by the patrol lying across the top of two medium-sized elephant tusks. From what was left of the body, it was assumed a lion, whose spoor was prominent in the area, had killed it. It also appeared others had accompanied him, because no weapons were located, and lions do not eat AK47 rifles. It was felt the poachers would return for the tusks. They had probably run away from the lions in fear and did not want to shoot weapons in case they gave themselves away to Mac's patrols. A quick ambush was set up, which hopefully would pay dividends, with probable captured weapons and more tusks, which Mac could trade for arms and ammunition. No one could know what a clump of bushes might hold, or where a desperate guerrilla might be laying concealed, sighting along an AK assault rifle, or worse still, an RPD machine gun or RPG rocket launcher.

The first kill occurred, as always, without warning. A fusillade of shots suddenly erupted, followed by shouts of warning. Orders passed up and down the sweep line and men ducked while rounds whined above their heads. Then it was over as suddenly as it had begun, and a very large but very dead buffalo lay in front of the sweep line. The "Return fire" had been the result of their ricochets. There was much laughter and embarrassed shrugs came from those responsible. They now, blushing at their show of unprofessional action in front of so many top class troops, rose to their feet, heads bowed in shame,

[284]

dusting themselves off. The sweep line carried on, knowing they could have steak for dinner that night.

High at the top of a "Kopje" (a large outcrop of rocks) a young Lieutenant commanding the ground troops called a halt for a few minutes rest. Most of the troops stood in silence, gazing at the magnificent panorama, when suddenly the sharp sound of gunfire exploded from the valley far below. It was easy to recognise the unmistakable intermittent crackle of the machine-gun automatic fire as a gunner cleared some bush. A vicious eruption of sound followed as the boom of the FNs on top of the machine gun fire all but drowned out the pop of the AK47 assault rifles. Green and red tracers arced skywards- signifying contact had been made. Mac heard the section commander Sgt Collins come over the radio:

"Contact, point (front man) pop red, (red smoke) tail (rear man) pop blue, (blue smoke) CAP (Combat Air Patrol) fly red to blue, ridge line right flank enemy, bush line 400 metres forward red, enemy machine guns concentration, Rocket weapon mix, copy?"

"Copy"

"The Puma's coming in!" someone exclaimed, their heads turned toward the sound of the helicopter as it came along the valley with its machine guns firing from both doors.

The South Africans had made many modifications to their Puma fleet, twin doors GPMG mounts, One 40mm rocket pod on a gimbal mount carrying 16 rockets, a 20mm rocket mount on the right with 24 rockets, and platform stabilization that would allow all rocket mixes to be fired simultaneously on a forward 180 degree arc. The machine guns had "taboo" arcs built in so they could not accidentally shoot any part of the aircraft, but could hit targets anywhere by instructing the pilot which manoeuvre to make. The "bird" came in low and fast with everything being let loose at once to help in clearing the substantial resistance they had encountered. An upward mushroom of orange flame erupted below it and behind it when it passed over the bush line, heralding the end of resistance from that area. The attack procedure was repeated. He strafed the target again just to make sure, and then landed a safe distance to the rear to "field" refuel and rearm, in case he was needed again.

Mac heard Collins laconic, "10 out of 10 CAP out, section two man skirmish teams. Go!"

The remainder of the patrol had a bird's eye view of the skirmishers rushing through the enemy positions using mutual supporting fire and movement and hearing intermittent bursts of fire while they finished off any enemy left.

The sweep then moved slowly down the side of the gobo, where they finally met up with the Stop Groups, who it transpired, had successfully killed seven guerrillas trying to run away from the fire fight and had taken one prisoner, a very rare occurrence but they needed information.

Mac heard Collins" crisp instructions over the airwaves, "Fire Group 1- locate and search for enemy dead and finish off any strays...Fire Group 2; move down into river bed with captive ahead of formation. Order him to call on any mates that are left to surrender or die, then kill them anyway. Out"

"Fire Group 1, copy. Out."

"Fire Group 2, copy. Out."

When the group wound its way round the bend in the river, all hell broke loose and another contact was initiated from Collins, "Contact, report in sitrep, all units."

"Search detail, gone to ground. Out."

"One skirmishing. Out."

"Two skirmishing. Out."

"Stop Group, we have business. Out"

One of the men, listening in on his radio set, gave a running commentary of the events up ahead for the benefit of his teammates. The shooting then ceased abruptly, plunging the bush into an eerie silence.

"Search Group, found four bodies. Out."

Mac: "Sunray, strip them of all weapons and ammo, bring hands back. Out."

[286]

The search group then proceeded to strip them of their weapons, among which them an RPG 7 rocket launcher with several 40mm rounds, and a Chinese made Tulare, eight round magazine Officers pistol, manufactured under license from Russia. The latter weapon promptly confirmed intelligence reports that the Eastern Bloc countries had a big finger in the trouble making pie, before the weapon disappeared into the radio operator's backpack.

Almost as an afterthought, the trooper bent down and removed several bracelets from one of the corpses, adding them to the others he already wore. The collection of such battle trophies was common practice among troopers, and many festooned themselves with African armlets, beads, and bangles. The victim"s hands were removed for fingerprinting; this was common practice if there were only a few casualties, if there were many, only the index finger was removed, to reduce weight.

Moving off, the search detail advanced cautiously along the riverbed, following the occasional bursts of gunfire and detonating grenades, while they relieved corpses of weapons and papers – mostly personal letters and the odd diary. Among the bodies found along the lower gorge were those of two white males and one female terrorist, no doubt mercenaries, many of which turned out to be disillusioned ex-British soldiers pissed off with playing "policeman" instead of soldier in Northern Ireland.

Brass cartridge and 16 gauge shot gun cases littered the bush, and huge sweeps of bush were on fire from the tracer shells fired into it. This, in turn, was cremating corpses. The acrid stench of cordite fumes and "kebab" flesh hung heavily in the air. The four "body search" troopers were quite alone now to continue with their unpleasant, yet necessary task, always some distance from the action up ahead, and occasionally being forced to seek shelter when the shooting became particularly vicious. They quickly sifted through the carnage wrought by the initial two sweeps, until finally, the search and destroy operation was tied up in that particular area.

The forces then linked up and continued to sweep down the remainder of the gobo until they arrived at a Kraal set in a clearing,

[287]

with its lone Acacia 'Thinking Tree" in the middle of the thorn bush circle, which surrounded the village to keep wild animals out.

Mac questioned the prisoner and discovered that this enemy incursion had come over the great lake at company strength. The total body count, so far in this operation, was 64 dead, one captive. This meant that over 100 enemies were still out there in the nearby vicinity. He also discovered that the unit had moved over the lake in flat-bottomed type barges, which had been given to Uganda as inshore fishing boats by a Swedish charity. These boats, 20 in total, had been modified and fitted with high powered outboard motors and used as fast patrol boats by the Ugandan Special Forces. All 20 craft had been used to bring the infiltration force over, so Mac immediately dispatched the Puma and sent an 8-man reconnaissance team to search the eastern shoreline of the lake for this transport. He figured the remaining Ugandans must be heading for home to escape.

Within 30 minutes, the Puma pilot was reporting in, "Found seven boats, all intact. Double fly by. Others have left. Over."

"Sunray, send craft found to Goanna on southern shore out of insurgents reach. Return and collect ambush party. Carry out complete refuel and fully rearm. You're going to Ugandan side of water. Out"

The men were now extremely aggressive and intent on destroying the enemy force that had so far managed to escape their clutches, and none of them were at all keen to return to base. The operation had been a success and they had suffered no serious casualties.

Suddenly, there was an excited yell and a flurry of movement while everyone dispersed, thinking they had come under attack. A Ranger appeared with three young Africans he had discovered hiding in a trench dug under a chicken pen behind one of the kraal-thatched huts. The Ranger had fired the thatched roof. Angry, but wary, soldiers then shouted questions at the suspects, repeating them in English and in Acholi, the captive's native language.

The terrified prisoners fervently denied any association with the "Mahayana," the terrorists, although minutes later the men scurried for cover when the air filled with exploding ammunition that had been

[288]

hidden in the thatched roof of the hut that the three had been found hiding behind, and was detonating in the heat and flames.

Then, in the midst of the confusion, four more terrorists were spotted in the bush only feet away from the main body of Mac's men. A heavy fuselage of shots and a brief moment of clinical killing ensued, and then it was all over. An AK47 and SKS carbine and two AK47s were added to the pile of captured weaponry.

The area was secured without further incident, and the remainder of the kraal was set on fire. While this was taking place, heavy small arms fire broke out to the rear, and Para illuminating flares went up just when the sudden African darkness fell.

"Ambush 1, two poachers arrived, both killed, three AK47 captured, plus four more ivory. Over."

"Sunray, come in, bring goods and hands, leave rest for lions, out."

With any immediate threat taken care of, the men took the opportunity to relax and await the helicopter to lift them out. It had been a long and active day, resulting in the death of 70 terrorists and the capture of four others. A lone "Stop" man, on the other side of the gobo had taken the final captive. At last the Pumas came in, flying low over the treetops. The Ugandan shore ambush parties climbed in, herding the captives between them. They would leave them in Uganda to tell other insurgents that they were on a fast road to death if they tried to cross the water into Tanzania.

The little huts slowly collapsed inward while they were consumed in the flames of the fire that was swirling in the downdraft of the rotors when the last helicopter lifted off, banked over on one side, and headed for the lake and the destruction of the remainder of the insurgents.

The team was in luck, because flying over the lake they found twelve of the missing boats full of soldiers making huge wakes as they sped back to Uganda. One boat was missing, so Mac radioed to ambush the ex-landing site on the Tanzanian side of the lake, in case any terrorists turned up, but for all he knew the boat could have sunk.

"Sunray, for CAP. Lay back off the boats. Wait until they are in shallow coast water, and then, on my word destroy all. We want water shallow to recover weapons. Copy?"

"Copy."

After some 20 minutes had passed, "Sunray for CAP. Destroy the Ugandan Navy and all the men. Copy?"

"Copy."

With that brief message, the 12 boats and all the occupants were sunk and killed by intense rocket and machine gun fire. Sgt Collins had taken a head count of the boat's occupants before the destruction started. Eight men to a boat, times twelve boats, equals 96 more dead. One operation equaled one enemy company of Special Forces destroyed and three Rangers slightly injured.

The actions had produced a large weapon haul, enough to arm another company. Once again Mac's tactics and training had paid off.

Mac was pleased with the Ranger's performance. At least he had the means to take pre-emptive action, and now he could kick arse.

CHAPTER 4

Tanzanian Intervention Force

If Mac's Rangers were his punch to knock out the Ugandan terrorists, his Intervention Force was his straight left to keep harassing and upsetting the guerrilla activity, and his powerful left hook if he could catch them when they infiltrated over the Great Lake and into Tanzania in their attempt to create havoc and cause morale failure among the Tanzanian populace. The Intervention Force led a very dangerous existence as opposed to the Rangers "go get them" system. The IF had to find an enemy infiltration by standard patrolling, an enemy who had the advantage of surprise and were expert at ambush. On one such standard "seek and destroy" patrol, Corporal Pete Higgins, a Mac-trained patrol commander and ex-Para Regiment was riding in the back of a Unicom truck, a heavy machine gun in the turret above him, and his standard-issue G3 assault rifle within easy reach. Although it was broad daylight, visibility was dreadfully poor in the sweltering teeming rain.

His driver shouted to him through the turret, "Can we put the fucking headlamps on, Corp? I can't see where we're going."

"Do it if necessary."

As the Unicom skirted around an area of swampy water, a whipping burst of fire from the right – a trap always feared by the Tanzanians by its surprise and ferocity, killed both Higgins's companions in the rear of the truck. Simultaneously, an explosion underneath the wheels at the front of the cab brought the truck to a halt and lying at a crazy angle, the upward blast severely wounded the two men in the cab and blew off the roof. Instinctively, Higgins started to use his rifle.

A grenade exploded at the rear of the truck, a fragment searing his back, neck, and upper thighs, while his face was creased by another fragment from one of the bullets sprayed into the back of the truck. Higgins went into automatic destruct mode. He grabbed his own satchel of grenades, a good mix of HE, Smoke, Impact, and Phosphorous and jumped down to take the fire fight to the enemy and try to gain some initiative that is always momentarily lost when you have to react to an enemy's" first move. He stormed the suspect firing position, firing all the way and lobbing grenades. When he suddenly burst out of the tall twitch grass, right before his eyes was the mortar position, which had obviously blown up the front of the truck. A phosphorous grenade instantly followed by an HE, and then a quick burst of fire over the parapet soon silenced this position. He could hear firing from back in the direction of the truck; obviously some of his men were still at work.

Retracing his steps, he came across two more enemies firing at the truck and killed them both by shooting them in the back. They were looking the other way, and he definitely wasn't going to invite them to turn around the same as the idiots one sees in the movies. Higgins's ammunition was expended and the pain from his wounds was becoming intense. He still remembered the machine gun and had to drag himself up to the bulletproof turret and began to swing the gun on its mounting. He had fired the first belt, when he finally realized there was nothing left of the enemy to shoot.

Four hours later, another patrol found Higgins, and the two from the back of the truck lying dead on the bush fringe, along with eight dead guerrillas. These types of infiltration patrols by the Ugandans were regular, and as the Tanzania patrols moved out to try to intercept them, they often entered into this type of ambush themselves.

CHAPTER 5

Terrain and Weather Problems

The landscape of mainland Tanzania is generally flat and low along the coast; a plateau at an average elevation of about 1,220m (4,000,03ft) constitutes the greater part of the country. Isolated mountain groups rise in the Northeast and Southwest. The volcanic Kilimanjaro (5,089 m/19,003ft), the highest mountain in Africa, is located near the Northeastern border.

Zanzibar is the largest coral island off the coast of Africa. Pemba, a second coral island, is some 40km (25 miles) northwest of Zanzibar. Both Pemba and Zanzibar are mostly low-lying, and are only mentioned in this narrative because Uganda was attempting to cause civil unrest through past religious hatred to assist in undermining mainland Tanzania.

Three of the great lakes of Africa lie on the borders of Tanzania or partially within it. Lake Tanganyika is located on the Western border, Lake Victoria in the Northwest, and the Lake Malawi in the Southwest. Lakes Malawi and Tanganyika lie in the Great Rift Valley, a tremendous geological fault system extending from the Middle East to Mozambique.

The climate of mainland Tanzania is more tropical on the coastal strip along the Indian Ocean, with temperatures averaging 27 degrees Celsius (81 degrees F) and rainfall varying from 1,016 to 1,930mm (40 to 76 inches). The inland plateau is hot and dry, with rainfall averaging 20 to 30 inches. The climate on the islands is generally tropical, but the heat is tempered by a sea-breeze throughout the year.

Deforestation has been a prime theme for foreign exchange in Tanzania, and this, of course, affected the patrol capabilities and sometimes caused patrol limitations in many areas. Because of this deforestation, many places suffered from soil loss and desertification.

In addition, vast regions were infested with the Tsetse fly, which transmits sleeping sickness, and the control programmes in force were controversial because they used pesticides that harmed wildlife.

The terrain in the various patrol areas remained a serious problem, especially because of poachers looking specifically for elephants ivory and rhinoceros horn. This, in itself, led to problems for patrol activity, because one would often find oneself in a firefight with poachers, rather than with the insurgents from Uganda the Rangers were looking for. These poachers were always well-armed with automatic weapons and intent on using them against any threat. They knew if they were caught they would die, and therefore they reacted accordingly.

Open and relatively dry forests and woodlands cover about a third of Tanzania. Wetlands, including coastal mangrove swamps, as well as inland systems, such as lakeshores, flood plains and swamps cover about 6% of the land.

Tanzania has a comparatively well-organised, protected land system, and it has received substantial foreign support and aid. The main elements are forest reserves, game reserves, and national parks, including Serengeti National Park. Two "Biosphere" reserves have been declared under the United Nations Educational, Scientific, and Cultural Organisation (UNESCO). Because of these many variations of terrain, patrol activity fluctuated accordingly and sometimes meant moving into the heavily wooded mountains of the northern borders.

Precise tactics were determined by the nature of the terrain in each sector, which varied from the mountain woodlands, flooded lakeside borders running many kilometres inland, to the open Savannas of the plains. One of the tasks against the growing infiltration was to seal off the border routes. To do this, the Tanzanian Intervention Groups usually divided geographic areas into sectors, and thus could operate in each sector as immediate reinforcements, specific task units, and escorts. All were similar mobile roles.

Much of the unit's effectiveness depended on the season. Some of the area was tropical, and difficult to work with the poor observation limits set by the undergrowth and heavy mud underfoot. Everything was really governed by the climatic cycle of cold nights and sweltering days of the dry seasons, and heavy mango rains, as well as the very heavy monsoon rains in which the enemy preferred to operate. Rainy months led to thick vegetation and limited activity from the air; the Tanzanians had air superiority until the Soviets introduced Surface to Air (SAMs) missiles in the mid-1970s, via Gaddafi in Libya. Air power opened up many windows of opportunity, such as attacking guerrilla infiltration routes, and providing a quick reaction to Intervention Unit's call for assistance. It also gave the units the extra aggressive capability to "go for the enemy" similar to the Rangers type of war.

CHAPTER 6

Alouette Tactics and Land Mines

The introduction of the Alouette helicopters in the late 1970s (The South African's Pumas were being used in Angola) changed the Tanzanian strategy; all teams now had far greater mobility, and could fly low and behind cover to defeat the enemy's use of SAMs. The arrival of the helicopters gave them the greater flexibility they needed. Each carried five men and was able to mount machine guns or a 20mm grenade launcher. The parties could now be dropped on guerrilla escape routes and in 1977-78 large scale operations against the infiltration of guerrillas became limited because of this essential new tactic.

Airborne operations were only part of the response to guerrilla activity. In other respects, technology was not of paramount importance to the Tanzanian counter insurgency units. This may sound hard to believe, but in the late 1970s, they used "Cavalry" very effectively, with three squadrons of mounted cavalry under the pay of the Tanzanian Peoples Defence Forces. The cavalry was used to protect the flanks of advancing troops in difficult terrain and, when supplied by helicopter, could mount extended patrols. It might be added that the horses acted as a good shock absorbers when the troops wandered into a minefield.

The mine was by far the most effective weapon of the guerrillas. In the mid to late 1970s, over 50% of the Tanzanian casualties were caused by mines. The newer and more sophisticated mines could not be located by mine detectors, few of which were even available, and so the troops resorted to the "pica," which was a sharpened stick.

Depending on the width of the track to be cleared, one or two men would lie on their stomachs and carefully poke at the ground to find soft areas that might indicate recent digging. If one was found, the "picadors" would then probe the area for the unmistakable hollow "clonk" of a mine. Other members of the patrol would remain vigilant, because this was often a setup for an ambush.

Having located a mine, the picadors would then ensure that no second mine was placed alongside it to trap the unwary.

The Tanzanians had improvised the use of special trucks with sandbagged floors and tires half filled with water to lead convoys and deflect mine blast, but in the long term, an extensive programme of road tarring was implemented to make it more difficult for the guerrillas to lay mines undetected. As stated earlier, there were not the many hard surfaced roads in Tanzania, but a real hard surfacing programme in Uganda had been completed over a distance of some 1,000 kilometres. The road building in Uganda far exceeded that by the British over a period of twelve years in Malaya or the United States of America in over six years in Vietnam.

Quite rightly, the Ugandan government was proud of their achievements, and it was commented in their government house that 'Revolt starts where the road ends".

CHAPTER 7

Improvisation

Other simple responses by the Tanzanians to their lack of technology included a ring of wire around their own positions from which hung empty beer cans and bottles, which was just as effective as sensors. The trouble with any form of "noise" or flare alert systems was the wild animals setting them off all the time.

Remember, there was a tremendous shortage of money and not much high tech equipment anywhere at that time, and certainly not in Tanzania. A standard anti-ambush drill was to hurl grenades into the bush when dismounting from vehicles under fire in case guerrillas were lying in ambush close to the road to catch the Tanzanians while they took cover. Apart from mines, the ambush was the most deadly weapon of the guerrillas. Frequent long range bombardment with mortars and 122mm rocket launchers were rarely effective. Ground, in the form of sand or swamp (changing by the season), with dense bush, absorbed most of the shrapnel from these types of weapons.

The Tanzanians discovered that small operations in the field offered far better chances of thoroughly disrupting enemy activities than large-scale raids, which only tended to shift the guerrillas somewhere else. An observer in the heavily patrolled mountain woodlands of northwest Tanzania found that units of about 30 men, on patrols of four or five day's duration, had become the most active and effective of all unit formations. All communications would be in sign language to maintain silence, metal parts of the uniforms and equipment were bound in cloth, and the footwear they managed to scrounge or steal, was normally covered in a linen wrap to minimise any sound when they walked over the rotting vegetation on the bush floor.

So effective were these precautions that the Ugandan guerrillas came to describe the Intervention Units as the "Ghost Walkers.' A variety of weapons would be carried; often three heavy machine guns and a Bazooka or mortar, or, alternatively, three mortars and a recoilless rifle. Those not responsible for the heavy weapons would carry ammunition, their rifles, and two bombs for the mortars or bazookas.

In eastern Uganda, a five-day patrol might cover as much as 100km, or further, in the open savanna. Tracks would not be used, if possible, to minimise the risk of booby traps, such as grenades attached to trip wires, or the Chinese anti-personnel mines, known by the American Vietnam war veterans as 'Dancing Betties", which would spin out of the earth to explode at groin height when men trod on their prongs.

Approaching a village where guerrillas might be encountered, scouts would be sent ahead to determine its size and approaches. The patrol, split into three sections would then go into the assault.

The men followed a pre-determined course over these four or five days, in order to avoid both their own minefields, and the possibility of attack by Tanzanian Air Sorties that had been planned for some time. Three walkie talkies were carried so they could call up air support if they needed it. Such patrolling became a deadly cat and mouse game, since Tanzanians and guerrillas tried to work out how to outwit the other in cunning ambushes.

Again, a patrol might return without having once made contact with the enemy. Mac himself was caught, in spite of his experience, he became stuck in a well hid, cleverly placed minefield, and in the subsequent hail of fire, Mac tried to throw a grenade. Another grenade exploded close by, and he slipped on the wet ground, dropping the grenade. He threw himself on the Russian F1 grenade to save his men. This was a modified grenade and it did not explode. They carefully checked out this modification so they could sabotage any other guerilla grenades they captured, and subsequently leave them for the enemy to use.

CHAPTER 8

Political Changes

Political events in Tanzania had radically changed the situation in the African state, with influxes of money and aid for the people being offered from many European states for the President to stop the war.

Fishing trawlers from Denmark and Iceland gave them the biggest fishing fleet in Africa. There were also donations of civilianized helicopters from France, office buildings, monuments, and theme parks from China (not finished when they found out the monuments were of Mao and Stalin), plus unlimited cash for game preservation and agricultural projects.

Unlike the old days when Mac had arrived in the country, cash was now pouring in. The President delayed his reply cleverly until Ida Big Dada was defeated at his northern bases and ran away from Ugandan soil. The use of the "Intervention Force" had been successful in carrying out its brief.

Tanzania claimed that less than two per cent of Tanzanian territory was controlled by the guerillas in 1978-79 as compared to about forty percent in the mid-1970s. When the Tanzanians went on the offensive on the Ranger type operations, the guerrilla losses were extremely high and vastly outnumbered those of the Tanzanians. The Tanzanians proved, with their tactics, that they were a far superior force than the Ugandan Army, with all its outside support, and they had won the war against insurgency across their borders.

Mac proved to his Rangers and Intervention Force that these tactics worked, and also to the government. Again, he was confident of overall victory once he had finished his logistic buildup, and was ready to attack mainland Uganda. The stepping stone of Entebbe airport was already in his sights, and his forward reconnaissance units were now firmly established at key points in Uganda.

This operation was not to be long in taking place.

SECTION 2 – Overthrowing Big Dada Amin
CHAPTER 9

Dar-es-Salaam, Tanzania, East Africa

The VC10 slowly banked to the left, lining up for its final approach. 'Fasten Seat Belts' and 'No Smoking' lights came on the console above the row of seats in front of Mac. Out of the window, he could see dusty spirals of sand making small whirlwinds, or wind devils as they were commonly called. These natural rotavators were breaking up the arid, reddish looking ground, stirring up the local terrain and spiraling high into the air, thousands of feet, carrying with them razor sharp grains of sand, and causing turbulence that made landing an aircraft at Dar-es-Salaam a tricky business.

Sometimes these genie columns hid the few scattered roundavals (local houses) that could normally be seen on the landing approach. Small matchstick sized men and boys made a perfect Loury scene, while they tended the cattle herds that seem to wander aimlessly about, yet, as one knew, they were purposely heading toward water and the sparse overnight growth of grass.

There were not any permanent buildings in evidence, or anything else to suggest in any shape or form the hustle and bustle of the sprawling Tanzanian capital city five miles away.

Dar-es-Salaam, here we come again.

Mac stretched to ease cramped muscles. An uneventful trip, this one, compared to some others; just a small hiccup at Rome airport when the service crew found a panel missing from the plane's fuselage. Not having a spare one in stock at Rome, plus a pilot who refused to fly without it, gave all passengers and crew a 24-hour delay while the missing piece was flown from British Airway's base at Heathrow.

Now, when a man with the willpower of a louse finds himself with an unexpected stay in Italy, with plenty of money in his pocket, and placed in the famous Nova hotel in the centre of the City of Rome itself, one is going to have a ball, especially when a war between Tanzania and Idi Amin's Uganda is waiting for him at the other end of the journey. So, ball was the name of the game, all night and most of the morning.

The resultant hangover was crippling, hate filling his heart for everybody, especially Idi Dada Bloody Amin, self-appointed VC and Macar, George Medal, 5 DSOs and 32 Mentioned in dispatches, American Legion of Honor and more. Hate for him was easy to find. Now, Mac was in a good frame of mind to pick up his duties as Field Operations Advisor to President Nyerere and General Twalipo in Tanzania.

A rolling, weaving approach and a tremendous banging and bumping indicated the big plane had touched down, and it played havoc with Mac's hung over thick head. As usual, the tannoy announcement requesting that people remain seated until the plane had stopped moving signified most people jump to their feet to fight to be first out, whilst rescuing their baggage out of the overhead lockers. Some of the passengers would have shit in their trousers had they known what merchandise had been carried in the hold of the plane for the Tanzanian war effort, especially after that terrible landing.

Labelled in boxes, addressed to Mark Hudson, described as a mining Engineer/Surveyor, were a number of cases containing items described as underground surveying equipment supplied by Rank Pullin Instruments of Stepney, London. These containers held SSE 707 Night Surveillance Artillery Ranging Equipment, one per box. Packed in with them were five 66mm LAWs, (Light Anti-tank Weapons), disposable single-man operated rockets, held in place by an assortment of rather dubious anti-personnel grenades of different origins, ages, and stability. Twenty boxes in all. The Tanzanians would be very worried themselves, knowing that these goodies were on a plane with wrong descriptions and false end user certificates, plus a 24-hour delay in arriving.

[303]

Mac's head was still crippling him. He would need all of his patience and resolve to be kind and friendly with Major Awouley waiting for him on the tarmac with his army working party to secret the stuff out of the airport. Such was the return of Mac to Tanzania.

TPDF HQ or Tanzania People's Defence Force Headquarters was a dirty stinking hole of a military camp. It consisted of derelict buildings, litter, rusty equipment, and a wide variety of evil smells; signs hanging off posts and structures, and fallen huts. It was hard to believe this filthy place could be so important. The place stood right in the middle of DAR, surrounded by the embassies of about thirty countries.

According to Colonel Ricky Lakongo, the camp's Commanding Officer, the condition of the garrison was in that disgusting state on purpose. The aim being to mislead spies on the ground in knowing it's true function and importance, therefore avoiding sabotage attempts and preventing the enemy, Uganda, from acquiring information to supply aircraft with a bombing target.

African bullshit.

After a while, one got used to hearing the most amazing stories from the Africans, all of them said with very sincere facial expressions and in a serious manner. It was very hard to tell if they were taking the piss out of you, or deadly serious. Mac had learned to use a half-sincere and studious, bemused, yet attentive look, and said very little when these yarns unfolded. His method seemed to be more than acceptable to them, and they seemed to make a beeline for him if they had heard something new or had a rumour to pass on.

Mac's services were often requested by unit commanders through TPDF to train their troops. It's hard to believe some of the crazy things that happened during this phase of his work, so daft in fact, many people would think he was making it up.

He was not.

The Tanzanians always showed the greatest respect toward Mac, sometimes far more than was ever expected or wanted. Mac had to be careful that they were aware their dependence on him was not the complete answer to all their problems, because many of their actions deserved to fail, and when this happened, they had to take some responsibility instead of turning to him. Teaching meant talking a lot, making up for his previous reticence to speak. He also made his verbal output related to the "Bushman" Swahili method of description, using native wild animal behavior as examples of what he expected students to know, and help them understand the purpose behind it.

The funny outcome from this was the mimicking that followed. When he arrived at a confirmation stage of a lecture or lesson and especially in question and answer phase, the student's return observation was often said in a very good imitation of his own voice, and sharing his own mannerisms. Good fun really, but it did not make them good soldiers. Only lots of patience and hard work helped in that outcome.

Major Pasco Awouley was waiting on the tarmac when Mac finally de-bussed after letting the crowd disperse. Pasco walked over, arms outstretched in a very positive gesture of welcome, his giant grin spreading from ear to ear. This action caused a large number of fellow passengers to look and whisper amongst themselves. This was the last reaction Pasco should have wanted from people, considering the covert munitions in the hold of the aircraft. Anyway, not to mind, Mac knew it was the Tanzanian way of doing things. They were paying him very well for his part in their little war, so why worry? He would create waves about most things if the military protocol was not followed, but thought it would be taking things too far to chastise the Major on exuding a very genuine welcome on his return to the country.

Arrangements had been made for the customs at Dar to pay a lot of attention to the passengers on the aircraft, and to ignore Mac and Pascoe's troops unloading and moving equipment straight off the aircraft into army lorries and driving away. Pascoe himself was driving Mac in his Land Rover, specially armored with extra steel plating on the floor and sides up to shoulder height and triangular barbed wiring stakes, welded as upright wire cutters on the forward edges of the windscreen. All the vehicles in Dar were fitted with this local produced armour, but they never managed to modify the vehicles involved in the fighting in Uganda. Mac always believed this ballsup was deliberate to impress the Tanzanian people how good and well equipped they were, typical African propaganda. This vehicle was fitted with a TCS 13 radio unit, complete from command down to small unit communication level channel selection boxes. Well done, to the British Government, the only known source of supply, legally. Who else may be doing things out here illegally?

Get to know, Mac thought, in this game one needs to know all the niggers in the woodpile.

The act of driving in Tanzania was supposed to adhere to British rules.

No way.

Africa was a novel experience when it came to driving any type of vehicle, because no rules of any sort were in existence. The African always sat sideways in the vehicle, with his arm hanging outside, in a nonchalant manner as he once saw on a film somewhere. He knows how to press down an accelerator. The brake and clutch were normally out of order, therefore surplus to requirement. Gear boxes were ruined daily and repaired with old tins, aluminium dinner plates, and any other form of metal that could be moulded with the black man's super-dexterous hands.

Fortunately, 95% of the vehicles on the road were knackered in some way, many in more ways than one. Few had any suspension. With the exception of a few miles, there were no hard surfaced roads, and the earth scrapes the Tanzanians called roads, were always in different states of repair, depending on the season; the amount of rain fall, or severity of a drought.

Travel was very slow, many breakdowns were in evidence, and if a vehicle was left by the road unguarded for more than a few minutes, it was stripped down to its shell for spare parts. All types of vehicle parts were in desperate short supply throughout the country, not just DAR itself. In a good Land Rover, the journey from the Airport to TPDF would take about fifteen minutes with no problems.

At the TPDF Ricky afforded Mac the same welcome as had Pasco. This time, without the presence of civilians, his reserve fell away, and allowed him to respond more openly to Ricky and his theatrics. Both Ricky and Pascoe were full time, regular soldiers, which meant a far higher training standard than the normal short-term and voluntary reserve officers that formed the bulk of TPDF, and of course with most African armies.

The British Officer Training School at Sandhurst was the ultimate course for which to be selected. Any student passing the grades in all their various shapes and form became the backbone of the nation's Army and held in high respect among the people. Training at Sandhurst also meant they were assured of a good future on returning to their own country.

Ricky and Pasco were both Sandhurst men, and with that qualification, held very high military appointments, with far more decision making power than their rank suggested. Pasco was Director of Arms Procurement. Ricky was Commander of TPDF HQ, and Director of All Arms Training. In their own spheres, they were both the top men within TPDF and therefore, the two men with whom Maces work was most closely linked, although he could report directly to the President, Minister of Defence, and Joint Services Chief Of Staff.

Ricky greeted Mac in his usual fashion. "Hello and welcome back you English bastard! We thought you'd deserted us. Where have you been?"

"Hi, Ricky, you black bastard, mind your own business."

These insults about colour were used only in a retaliatory form. After they threw some sort of slang at him, they expected it. He was

[307]

sure if they didn't hear this sort of reply, they would think he was upset in some way.

"Screwing about in Italy, I suppose, you bastard." Ricky's English carried a strong Yorkshire accent, a result of his long relationship with a sweet Yorkshire belle, whom he met when he was a student in England.

Instantly, the most lurid story you could imagine came out, invented by Mac, spontaneously, about his stay in the Nova, and the three (imagined) young, nubile Italian girls with which he'd had to perform.

This imagined tale took about half an hour to recount while drinking a bottle of White Cap Brandy, and six Kalka soft drinks, a drink made in Tanzania and similar to Coca Cola.

With this hair of the dog, Mac's hangover started to fade away. Should anyone have attempted that type of bullshit with British troops, they would have been booed out of the room in twenty seconds. Ricky, Pasco, and Augustan's eyes reflected their belief in his fantastic mental creation. Strangely, they always believed him. They sometimes worried Mac with their trust.

Augustine, a Sudanese Lt attached to TPDF was Ricky's adjudant, six feet three inches tall, and as thin as a latt. His one wish in life was to make love to a white woman who loved him.

"It would not be good to rape. I want some woman like the Maraline Monroe for to love me as I need to love."

Quite novel thoughts coming from a Sudanese. After about one hour of loose talk, and questions to and fro to bring everyone up to date on each other's activities, they finally settled down to decide a plan of immediate action. Mac was accommodated in Government rooms in the Kilimanjaro Hotel, his usual quarters when in Dar, which was not very often. He spent most of his time out in the bush, where good authentic training was achieved.

[308]

CHAPTER 10

Accommodation

The rooms numbered 402 and 403 were normal hotel rooms, two single bedrooms with an adjoining door, and refurbished to make one sitting room and one bedroom. Standard type hotel rooms one finds anywhere in the world, following one design. They appear to all be made from the same set of architect's drawings. Through the entrance, then immediately off to one side the toilet, bath, shower, hand basin, and a razor point that never worked. The room itself boasted a single bed and headboard, containing a bedside locker each side of the bed, with one drawer, a bedside lamp, a Bible, coffee table, settee, two easy chairs, built in wardrobe, small set of drawers and the fridge. Fridges were always kept full of beer, spirits, soft drinks and water.

In Mac's rooms, the sitting room acted as a briefing room, and secret drinking room for the TPDF Officer's White Cap parties. Both rooms had patio doors leading to balconies overlooking Dar harbour, a fantastic view.

As they were situated on the fourth floor, the rooms had an unrestricted view of the mangrove bordered twisting waterway, leading to the sea. Oyster Bay, with its pure white sands, looked like a huge ivory boomerang.

It looked like a holiday brochure paradise, but one was likely to be mugged, robbed, raped, or even killed if they went there for a swim or any other reason. The locals will kill to steal a wristwatch to sell or barter for food.

Tonight, a special party had been arranged for the TPDF Officer corps and some civilian Ministry of Defence personnel. Included in this jamboree were a number of local traders and some visiting company representatives who were staying at the Kilimanjaro. Another reason for this function was to see the Officer's wives and girlfriends dressed up. Before returning to England to do the business on night sights, orders for clothing and other goods were listed for Mac to purchase on, mostly for goods unobtainable in Dar.

Nearly every Officer's wife was about to receive a dress. Ricky and Pasco were coming to Mac's rooms that afternoon to collect the clothing and accessories he had brought back with him. These would then be delivered to the ladies in time for them to try them on, and make any corrections and alterations should they be required, before the ball. This meant a tremendous belly laugh was in store for most people on this coming night. Dresses were something Mac was not very clued up about, so when it came to buying the presents for his African Army buddies, he designated responsibility and a payment to a British Army friend's sixteen-year-old daughter and her gaggle of mates.

Mrs. Lecanto gave Mac the list for the dresses and jeans they needed. No sizes, just a woman's name.

For example:

Mrs. Likongo - Red short dress, low cut neck, belted waist.

Mrs. Awouly - Yellow dress, flared at the bottom, look like a bell shape to shoulder.

Mrs. Termini- Blue dress, no sleeves, easy to lift for Captain Termini.

A simple rule of thumb became the method to solve dress size problems. Firstly, forget the length. No one would complain if they found a dress too short. They could call the style youthful. If a dress was too long, it could be shortened, so only bust and backside estimates were left to make.

Western cultures seem to have a theory that the nearer the bone, the sweeter the meat when it makes an image of attractiveness. Our catwalk queens on television advertisements show slim women in profusion. Not so for the African men - they love larger fat women (to marry anyway). They find big, square shaped backsides are a most attractive attribute in a woman. To address somebody as "mataka maqumba sanna" which is colloquial Swahili for "big fat arse" is one of

[310]

the highest compliments you can bestow on a person. Mac's own radio call sign during operations was that statement of affection.

Back to the sizes, keeping the breasts and backsides as the datum point, categories were as follows: Big, (no one was normal) very big, huge, gigantic and monstrous. Big became a large fitting, very big, and huge rated extra large, with monstrous and gigantic claiming the highest accolade of extra, extra large. It was in this atmosphere of pleasant, frumpy, silly nonsense that the foreign troops and the Tanzanians together fought their war with Idi Amin Big Dada.

CHAPTER 11

Idi Amin

Most people are aware of the brief history of this evil, black African dictator who thought he was God, because of his widely televised deeds. Idi was an ogre of a man who killed hundreds of thousands of his own Ugandan people in a very short time period, and then left his country ruined financially and its reputation on the international scene in ruins. A slightly more detailed resume of this most horrible buffoon of a man will help readers to understand some of the deep hatred behind the drive of most Tanzanians to defeat him in every way possible.

Amin's father was a policeman, therefore his childhood days carried some forms of discipline. Tribal wars in Northern Uganda prevailed at that time, and these skirmishes shaped his wishes for the future. He wanted to be a soldier. An active boy and youth, with the discipline induced by his father, he made a good candidate for the British Military, who were recruiting in Africa, and at the age of eighteen he joined the African Rifles.

Loyal, smart, a good shot and good at sports, he became well-liked by his British Officers, who loved someone who can win their companies shields and trophies, and at the same time, enhance their own reputation as good leaders and commanders.

At six feet four inches tall and the Ugandan heavyweight boxing champion, Amin didn't need much leadership ability. He could bully, if need be, but his huge size made that unnecessary. Most troops liked him. Therefore, he received rapid promotion, becoming a Sergeant Major (equivalent to Warrant Officer Two) at thirty years of age, the highest rank an African national could achieve, even if they held high educational qualifications, which Amin didn't.

Following his upbringing on a menu of tribal raids and skirmishes, Amin hungered for war. In 1953, his wishes came true with the Mau Mau terrorist campaign in Kenya. This insurrection, aimed at the British and anyone who supported them, was full of extremely bloodthirsty terrorist incidents. Amin, with his brutal nature, showed his opponents no mercy, gaining for himself even more praise and fame amongst the British Officers.

Ugandan Independence became a fact during 1961, and policy changes meant that African Officers were now needed in the Army. Amin became the first Ugandan Officer within these changes, due to British recommendations, even though he could still not read or write.

As soon as the Despot received and tasted the abstract power of an Officer Commission, he abused it. When some cattle rustlers were caught in the north of the country, Amin murdered them in cold blood, without trial. No action was taken against Amin by the then President Obote, and this seemed to give a seal of approval for further murders in the name of government. During the independence year the country was rife with dissention and unrest. The different tribal factions were ready for civil war, with Amin at the centre.

President Obote wanted to get rid of the Kabaka, via Amin's resources. In the ensuing battle with the Kabaka guards well outnumbered, over two thousand were killed. The majority was thrown alive into the Nile River to feed the crocodiles, and the Nile croc is a very big croc indeed. If they tried to climb out of the water they were not shot, they were cut to draw blood then thrown back in, the "blooding" was to attract the crocodiles, but really wasn't needed, because the river ran red with blood for miles. The only reason some victims managed to climb out was because the crocodiles had so much food and were unable to deal with everyone at once.

[313]

The carnage was similar as shown in the television portrayals of the Wildebeest and Zebra, crossing the Mara River on their bi-annual migrations.

Democracy didn't exist in Uganda anymore, law and order could be summarized as execution without trial. Obote was a dictator and Amin was his tool to carry out his will. Amin's soldiers, even though frightened of him, worshipped him in a "feared" way. He tried to put them first, as the British had taught him. Israel funded Amin in these early years and helped launch his political career. He became known as "The man of the people."

Obote feared Amin and saw in him as a serious threat to his presidency. In a 1970 showdown, Obote issued orders to have Amin arrested, however, whilst Obote was in Singapore on a state visit, his secretary informed Amin's secretary of the plot. Amin then pulled off a successful military coup, with his soldiers taking Kampala, the capital.

At first the people loved him, and women in bright coloured dresses would line the streets, dancing suggestive African style sex gyrations when he drove down any road. He often jumped out of his vehicle to join them.

Dissenters against him had to flee or die.

CHAPTER 12

The Exiles

Many of these "unwanted" people went into exile in Tanzania, setting up interim government departments in preparation for the time when Amin's reign of terror came to an end. Mac met most of the exiles, and they were a valuable source of intelligence to help defeat Amin in the Tanzania Uganda war.

Some of the stories told to his organisation by the exiles, and often supported by documents and pictures, confirmed what a hell of a place Uganda had become under Amin's dictatorship. Amin must have realised the job was above him and beyond his abilities. He had no concept of how to run a country; he closed Parliament, and the terrible killing he engaged in became apparent and abhorrent soon after he came to power.

He was a big, blustering baboon of a man, and foreign newspaper reporters loved him, because of his showmanship. They always managed a story out of this childish killer, and he thrived on praise he received from any quarter. He would perform like a monkey to receive acclaim from the media.

Amin was often described as "Twinkle Toes", because he was very light on his feet for his huge bulk, and when he was touring around the country, he would dance with his people, waving his Field Marshall baton in time to the Bongo Drum's rhythm. This comical and entertaining behavior hid the evil goings-on in his country, and for a long time the International press was oblivious to his true character.

One of his main opponents was his own personal physician, who in the end was so depressed with Amin's treacherous behavior; he tried to denounce him to the outside press. Unfortunately for him, before he could leave the country, Amin's henchmen caught him in a lift as he was coming out of his hospital. They had waited for him in the lift, turning other users away. When he entered they stabbed him in the stomach, bundled the body in the boot of his car, drove the remains to the River Nile, and fed it to the crocodiles.

Amin's new personal doctor was called to treat his wife for a high-temperature. The doctor went to the fridge in Amin's kitchen to collect some ice to attempt to lower the woman's fever. On opening the fridge, he found two human heads in the deep freeze compartment, much to his shock. Amin came up behind him just when he was standing transfixed, staring at the heads.

"Ah! You are admiring my trophies doctor. When we have war, heads will roll. Ha-Ha. You like my very good humour, yes? Thank you very much."

That was one of Amin's characteristics. He said, "Thank you very much," nearly every time he saw somebody or said something. "Thank you very much" would pass his lips at least one hundred times per day. He even said, "Thank you very much," when he shot somebody or passed a death sentence.

An exile from Uganda had an amazing story to tell of a very lucky escape. He came and offered his services to help defeat Amin, so when Mac spoke to him one night in Tanzania, he began to go through the interrogation procedure.

"Why do you want to help us? How and why did you manage to escape from Uganda?" Mac asked him his reasons for wanting to help, along with many other things, which are standard in such circumstances. Intelligence Office (IO) was cautious not to recruit people who may be agents for Amin and trying to infiltrate their setup. Ugandan IO had tried this before and succeeded early on, but Amin was now so hated, few would risk themselves to support him.

The man answered, "One night in Kampala, myself and three friends were in a coffee bar playing cards. A fight broke out in the bar involving another four men, and it soon spread outside, into the street. A lorry with Amin's soldiers pulled up outside and clubbed the men, throwing them into the truck. They then came in the bar and beat us into the truck, even though the owner was telling them we were innocent. They drove to a clearing in the bush and tied us to a cow-counting fence. They lay on the ground, took aim and shot us

[316]

with Kalishnikoffs rifles on automatic fire. This was an execution. No trial, no disciplined firing squad, pure, cold-blooded murder of innocent people, and it's happening everywhere, which is why I want to help.

"I was hit in the shoulder, and it spun me round and over the cow fence. I was still hanging from it with one wrist tied. I must have lapsed into unconsciousness. When I came round, I was smothered in blood. I think a lot of it came from a man draped across me. The soldiers must have thought I was dead. The soldiers were still about, so I stayed perfectly still, I hardly dared to breathe, my chest hurt badly, but my shoulder was very numb, and I could hardly feel it.

"After the soldiers left I managed to dress my wounds and stopped any bleeding by using the other victim's clothes for bandages, and also to wear in the cold nights. I searched their pockets for identities, but the soldiers must have taken every bit of evidence, except the bodies. The nightly hyenas would scavenge these.

"I could walk, with difficulty, and headed for a little village I knew very well on the shores of the Great Lake. Friends I have known for years and trusted in their hate for Amin protected and helped me until my wound was much better. These good people, at great risk to them, managed to procure a boat and row me over the Great Lake to Tanzania. A border patrol brought me to you." He finished his story.

He took a deep breath and asked, "Can I be of any service?"

"We will check your papers, attempt to corroborate your story, which shouldn't be difficult, because we have arrivals from the escape route every day, and then, when we are happy, we will contact you. If your story doesn't prove correct, you will have wished you'd stayed with Amin. Understood?" IO always threw in frighteners; it often made people start talking again about things they'd "conveniently" forgotten.

"Yes, Sir. I understand well."

[317]

CHAPTER 13

Astles

Amin's right-hand man and so called "advisor" was Bob Astles, another bloody maniac and a perfect foil for the buffoon. Both men were egotistical, self-centred and perfect partners in crime. Astles was an ex-British spy in the intelligence service, who mysteriously came out of the military under some sort of cloud (the details of which are not known). He married a Ugandan and took out Ugandan citizenship and used this to great effect in the field of procurement of military stores, switching his nationality flag between British and Ugandan, depending on the type of deal he was involved in.

One deal he made for his big leader was to procure 200,000 name tags, supposedly fire proof and blast proof, to hang around the soldier's necks for identification. The tags he bought were made of cheap tin, but the same price as the NATO standard tags. He and Amin pocketed the difference in UK Sterling, deposited in England by the company that supplied the crap and provided inflated invoices.

Astles was the man behind a £50,000 price on David Martin's head, the author who wrote the book "Amin." David, at the time, was a foreign correspondent for a famous and well-known British newspaper; The Observer, and was exiled from Uganda to Tanzania, because he was the only correspondent, along with lecturer and author Denis Hills, to write about Amin and the situation in Uganda as it really was. David slated Astles and his two-faced, wicked double-dealing ways in no uncertain manner, so the bastard persuaded Amin to put out a contract on Martin's head.

Amin was furious at reports that stories were being written about him in a publication by Denis Hills, a British author. Hills had lectured at the Makerere University in Uganda since 1963, and stayed on in the country after Amin seized power eight years later. He had intended to leave the country well before his book, The White Pumpkin, was published, as it revealed what was really going on with regards to the atrocities performed by Amin and his sidekick, Astles. Needless to say, these stories were not showing Amin in a very good light. In actual fact, Denis was doing the same as David Martin and simply telling the truth. He was reporting in print what was happening in Uganda at the time. The British High Commissioner asked Dennis to renounce his documents as "fabrications" for his own protection and the safety of people around him, knowing, of course, how vindictive and malevolent Amin could be against anybody who upset him.

Denis Hills refused, and two of his manuscripts had already been sent back to England, so to renounce them now would be too late. Denis Hills was arrested and thrown into jail without charges being made against him or trial. The British Commissioner went to see Amin and asked for Hill"s release, but all he received for his trouble was an onslaught of abuse.

Amin called him the pretending "Lawrence of Africa" and barraged him with personal insults, insults against his wife and family, insults against the British government. He threatened to declare war on Britain if the "shit" country thought they had a harder, good enough Army to fight him, Idi Big Dada. Amin said the only way he would set Hills free was if Her Majesty the Queen came from England to see him personally and begged him on her knees for Hill's release. He was finally released after the British Prime Minister, Harold Wilson, wrote an apology. The Queen sent Amin a personal appeal to spare Hill's life.

CHAPTER 14

Russian Exodus

It was at about this time that foreign journalists began to realise they were being seduced by Amin, and at great risk to themselves, began to tell the world what was happening in the former lovely country often called "The Jewel of Africa." One of the top journalistic coups of this new open style of reporting was Amin's "sacking" of the large Russian element of diplomats and engineers who were helping him in many technical ways.

"Ambassador, I want you and your lazy pheasant Russians out of my country in twenty-four hours, because you are idle and you cheat me, your best friend and protector, out of my supplies."

He repeated these words to the press conference, and embroidered on them as to how the Russians were lazy and no good. Amin was in the swimming pool with his eight female swimming partners (if one tried to get out of the pool, soldiers threw her back in, screaming; some drowned) when Astles told him the Russians were actually leaving.

Amin rushed to the airport to beg the Russians to stay. They left, saying they needed advice from higher authority in Moscow. When they moved to the aircraft, Amin played the "Volga Boatmen" on his little hand accordion, to give them a musical send off. He made a big political play about throwing out the Russian delegation, portraying himself as the strong man of Africa, who could humiliate major powers. He had a large barbeque party organised at the residency, inviting all the foreign embassy staff as a celebration of the Russians departure.

He had his Gate Guards hold six of these staff at the residency gates, and when he arrived, the six were forced to carry him, shoulder high, into the party on a litter. He was humiliating them verbally while they performed this task.

[320]

During this same party, he took a fancy to one of the guests wives. He danced with her, telling his henchmen to remove her husband from the scene. The poor man was taken to the lakeside and beaten unconscious. Amin then took the woman into the residency on the ploy that he was delivering her to meet her husband. He threw her on a bed to rape her. Rather than go through with it, she somehow managed to stab herself in the stomach. In his anger at her, he was screaming at his staff to throw her over the balcony and clean his room, claiming the ungrateful woman was staining his sheets with peasant blood.

Whilst this party was in progress, Amin's car was blown up on the front of the residency lawn. For some reason, which is still a mystery, he blamed the sabotage on the Roman Catholic community and confiscated the Roman Catholic churches and turned them into Mosques to please the Arabs and Islam. He was immediately offered arms from the Arab states, above all from Gaddafi in Libya.

CHAPTER 15

The Rally

Russian money was now in serious doubt, so Amin went to the Central Bank and demanded one million dollars in cash, immediately, to build a special car to enter in the Ugandan Rally. He would drive it himself and win international recognition for his great Ugandan Nation.

The head of the bank told him that no money was available. He would love to oblige, but just couldn't drag money out of thin air. Amin ordered him to "print some." The poor manager nearly went blue in the face trying to explain to Amin that they couldn't just print foreign exchange. For his efforts, Amin's henchmen dragged him outside and beat him up.

The next day, the manager was dragged out of his car, in front of his daughter who he was driving to school, and savagely beaten, and then thrown into the boot of his Citroen and driven to jail. His wife went to see the Minister for Justice to beg for her husband's release. The Minister promised to help her, and issued an execution order. Her husband was then executed by shooting without trial, because she had begged the Minister for his freedom.

The Minister of Justice told her, "I have kept my word, now he has been released forever."

Amin did take part in that farce of a Rally; he drove a Toyota provided by the firm. He had an escort car, and armed Land Rovers at staging posts to offer him protection.

At the start gate, he noticed an attractive, young woman in the crowd. He called her over, much to the annoyance of the starters who were trying to keep things moving to the timetable.

"Hello, my pretty lady. You like to speak to your kind President, yes?

"Yes, your Excellency" she mumbled shyly.

"Would you like to ride with me as my co-driver?

"I would, your Excellency, if I knew how."

"Come, my little cherub. Your kind President will teach you everything you need to know. Come and climb in next to me, my darling."

By this time, the starters were getting extremely nervous. The girl nonchalantly strode round to the passenger side, and Amin ordered his son (his co-driver) out of the car.

"Climb in, my darling. That's it. Make yourself comfortable. Pull your dress up, because the engine is hot and will make your legs hot and sweaty. That's right. There's a good girl, and off we go, thank you very much."

Amin drove about six miles, and then entered a dead end sand track and stopped to screw the girl for at least one hour. His escort cars were waiting for him and led him back to the finish, whilst his Land Rover cronies at the checkpoints held everybody up, until it was announced on radio that Amin had won.

CHAPTER 16

The Underground

An underground movement was now forming, mostly involving escaped soldiers or "deserters and traitors," as Amin had labeled them. Mac was instrumental in arranging the training, clandestine operations, and tactical target planning for this group.

They set an aim to destroy the Ugandan economy as the quickest way to oust Amin, even though he was making a fairly good job of doing just that of his own accord. The second alternative was to assassinate the Dictator. This was easier said than done. Amin was a clever snake in the grass. Rumours of his whereabouts were freely circulated, and the snipers or bombers could be waiting for him. The only problem was that he had a dozen or so look-alikes, all dressed in his uniforms and medals, making visits to different places at diverse times.

Mac trained his snipers to go for the Big Dada target first, then, anyone on the podium who tried to help him or shield him. This tactic would remove a lot of his secret service bodyguards from the order of battle. To Mac's knowledge, sixty-four innocent Ugandans were killed by this subterfuge on the dictator's part.

Amin ordered his army to execute anybody, on the spot, if they "thought" the person was against his rule. It was now free licence for soldiers to kill anybody they didn't like and pay back old grudges. It was anarchy.

A gang of twenty soldiers loaded a lorry with bodies from the prison and drove them to a mass grave in a clearing. When the soldiers threw the last bodies in the grave, Amin's bodyguard shot the soldiers and threw them in the same grave. This was done to prevent an outsider of Amin's circle to know the grave's location.

An indication of Amin's mental state now was his visit to a witch doctor, taking a live chicken as a sacrifice. The witch doctor warned of a gloomy future. Amin did not agree with him and had him executed on the spot, and then cut the chicken's neck and bled it over the body. Amin kept his Army together by promises of new arms and profits from the disposal of other National's assets. He endeavored to procure arms from Britain, and when he was refused, he sought to get his own back by launching the process of kicking the Ugandan Asians holding British passports out of Uganda, seizing their assets, and in doing so, keeping face with his soldiers.

Canada offered to take one thousand Asian deportees, but needed Amin to free the Asians enough assets to pay for their air tickets in foreign exchange, because the airlines refused to take Ugandan Shillings as payment. This request was denied, so Canada used their own planes to make the evacuation, as did other countries. Amin charged them exorbitant landing fees and refueling costs, and raised a heavy airport tax.

CHAPTER 17

The War

Amin ordered his Chief of Staff to take a body of men in Tanzanian uniforms to the Tanzanian/Ugandan border and assassinate a few thousand of his own people, burn down their villages, commit a few atrocities, rape a few women, and drive the livestock over the border into Tanzanian. He could then blame Tanzania for the raid and justify his war with them. He remembered "his friend Hitler" doing the same thing against Poland. This would also help him in his bid to procure arms, he hoped.

Eventually, President Nyerere of Tanzania declared war on Uganda in 1978. The Tanzanian Army was a good army by African standards; 30,000 strong, with light tanks, armoured cars and a small but effective Air Force. They had decent artillery, with a usable range of weaponry and some 122mm heavy pieces. They had the latest second-generation night surveillance equipment and knew how to use them to maximum effect, thanks to Mac.

One of the memorable things that happened around this time was when Amin flew to England, unannounced, on his weapon chase. He was invited to meet the Queen, who asked him, "To what do we owe this pleasant surprise?"

"I cannot find the size fourteen shoes in Uganda, so I buy them in England and help your country's exports."

In fact, Amin was in the UK attempt to procure tanks, arms and ammo for his army. As news of his outrages was beginning to filter through, by now, he was denied.

As previously stated, he did not in fact need to obtain weapons from the British. He acquired them from Gaddafi in Libya, proclaiming he was Islamic and his country would embrace Islam. Backing up this weapon loan meant kicking out the Israelis, who, up until now, had been one of his few backers, because he had adopted his false anti-Arab/Islam stance, now he chose to show the opposite face. No one really understood what the man was up to from one day to the next. He was emphatically crazy. A total of 50,000 Asian refugees were sent to England and Ugandans were given their various businesses. Within a matter of months, every business collapsed, because the Ugandans did not have the faintest idea how to run them. Because of this, Ugandans no longer had access to everyday necessities, and slowly began to become malnourished and starve. Amin's reaction was to increase suppression, and even more people were murdered as they tried to procure supplies to prevent dehydration and starvation.

At 47, Amin had turned a nation into his private kingdom. People were turning against him, and he, a megalomaniac, showed off his boisterous magnetic personality by awarding himself other country's top medals. For example the British Victoria Cross, the George Medal, the American Legion of Honor, and numerous others.

CHAPTER 18

Entebbe

Amin's major downfall came after June 1976 when a hijacked aircraft landed at Entebbe airport with many Jewish passengers aboard. Amin said he would help the hostages, but fooled about posing as a great mediator, negotiator and benefactor, until the Israelis had had enough and forcefully rescued the hostages, except one, Mrs. Dora Bloch, who had been taken to hospital and was never seen again. Hospital staff witnesses confirmed after Amin's defeat that she had been dragged screaming from the hospital by Amin's household guards, who told the doctors they were working under Amin's direct orders.

Elisa, one of Amin's regular bedmates, told Mac that Amin was in bed with her and a girl called Mandy when the Israelis landed. When Amin became aware of the sound of gunfire, he jumped out of bed and hid himself in the bedroom wardrobe until the firing stopped. When he later found out who had made the attack, he threatened to invade Israel and wipe it off the face of the earth, for the cause of Islam.

It was a brilliant rescue by Israel, right from under Amin's put out nose. His blunder at Entebbe sowed the seeds of his own destruction. Humiliated in front of the whole world, he went on a killing spree. One assumes he was trying to boost his own shattered ego.

Many Army men of different tribes were slaughtered. He used a Catholic school as his killing base. One group of soldiers had been complaining about the conditions they had to put up with at Jinja barracks: stale, polluted water, poor meals, hardly any medical facilities, bad food and more.

Amin labeled them dissidents and enemies of the state. The soldiers were told they could have a posting and told to fall in on parade for a roll call to establish who wanted a posting, and where they would like to go.

When they formed up in three ranks, vehicles around the parade ground had the tarpaulin covered backs thrown open, exposing machine guns. All the soldiers on parade, a reported total of thirty-one were shot.

He was reported to have said that his friend Hitler had done the same thing to American spies.

One cannot help but think of the Malmedy Massacre and the American POW executions.

CHAPTER 19

The Press Murders

Journalists, trying to report on this massacre were arrested, and two American reporters were escorted in their own Volkswagen Beetle onto a mountain road, machine gunned in their car, and pushed over the cliff where the car burst into flames. Amin told the Judge in charge of the arrested reporter's trial that all the "criminal propagandists" arrested were to be found guilty at their trial and given severe sentences. The Judge, tongue-in-cheek, said he would do as he was ordered.

At the trial, the Judge found the reporters 'not guilty' and dismissed of all charges as they had arisen, because of the "military overstepping its authority." The Judge was arrested as a traitor and executed on Amin's orders. Amin then went to see the Judge's body in the mortuary, ordering the doctor out, and he sliced a piece of meat off the Judges breast and ate it, muttering tribal incantations. The doctor said Amin was eating raw meat when he left the room, and he found the wound on the Judges breast still bleeding.

The Judge's head was removed and placed in Amin's deep freeze, amongst his other trophies. This head was scorned, even after death, because it was often taken out and positioned on Amin's office desk, where it was given a scolding for "forcing Amin to kill him."

CHAPTER 20

Clergy Murder

Amin invited the Archbishop of Uganda to his residency and had a series of photographs taken with him by the World's Press. He then took the Archbishop inside the residency and berated him about not praising Amin from the pulpit, put his silver plated Browning pistol in the man of God's mouth, and shot him.

Murder in cold blood meant nothing to the Despot.

He then told Astles to stage the murder to look like a car accident. Two cars were crashed on a bend of a mountain road, with the Archbishop's body in one of them. While this was being set up, Amin was flying round above the site in his Army light aircraft, choreographing the scene. The pilot of this aircraft defected shortly after this incident to Mac's team in Tanzania. The aircraft and all the flight photographs went with him.

The Archbishop's head ended up in the freezer, and it was still there when the residency was captured.

Mac saw the results himself, of one of Amin's more well-documented killing techniques.

Men stood in a straight line; the second man in the line was given a fourteen pound hammer and crushed the skull of the first man. He then handed the hammer to the next man who crushed his skull and so on, until the last man, who was then shot in the head.

Another often-used favourite of Amin was the rat. This consisted of a victim being staked out on the ground, bound with his arms and feet, and a Peak Freen Biscuit tin turned upside down on his stomach, with a large, black Ugandan sewer rat inside the tin. The only way out of the tin for the rat was to eat its way through the man's stomach. This process took hours and hours, and the victim was showered with water to keep him awake and stop him lapsing into shock-induced unconsciousness.

[331]

Another slow torture Mac witnessed was a staked out victim with honey in his eyes, nose, mouth, rectum, and penis to attract large half-inch long black ants. The victim would be slowly eaten away.

CHAPTER 21

Amin's Final Fall

As 1979 arrived, Amin was an International embarrassment. The war against Julius Nyerere's Tanzanian Army had been lost, but Amin managed to escape by helicopter from Jinja barracks, where his career had begun thirty years before. His eight years of rule was over. He went to Libya for asylum and left behind a country in ruins.

When the torture chambers were opened, international observers were appalled at what had taken place.

Mac's IO party opened the chambers during the battle for Kampala, weeks before. Over 200,000 Ugandans died at Amin's hands. A sad legacy still left behind in Uganda is that the British helped make him what he was.

In 1980, Amin was given sanctuary in Saudi Arabia, because of his stout service to the Islamic faith. Astles tried to escape through Kenya but Mac's team captured the bastard three miles over the border. He tried to tell Mac's crew he was English and that they should let him go. He was the worst type of Ugandan, a crazy white one.

Mac toyed with the idea of executing him out in the bush, but decided he should stay alive and suffer the same as his victims. He took him back to Kampala prison and locked him in a cell, which was still covered in blood from Astles' previous victims, with orders that he should "never to be released until death."

Godfrey Binaisa became temporary President and Attorney General. Binaisa was a corporate lawyer, with a practice in the United States, whom Mac knew well from his last visit to Tanzania. He had last met Binaisa at Dar-es-Salaam airport, when the former was desperately trying to take part in the government formative conference in Arusha, and then Arua in Northern Tanzania.

[333]

At that particular time, he had been "frozen out" of the conference by other members.

Binaisa released Astles, because he thought Mac was being too brutal, and it was time to rebuild for the future. Mac was furious and to this day berates himself for not killing the son of a bitch when he had the chance.

Other well-known exiles took positions of high office in the new Uganda. Among them were Muwanga, Bannanuka, Salamba, and many others who shared the same outlook as Binaisa. Mac couldn't believe or understand it, and knew the new government would terminate his and his men's contracts.

He had been very instrumental in winning the war, but now felt insecure and very doubtful about his crew's future value in the new setup. His experience of Africa was generating a gut feeling that said "Get out. Now!"

His predictions proved correct.

CHAPTER 22

The War Final Stages

Assessment of a war situation and its development is not always easy. A cut-and-dried set of circumstances that can state clearly, that one is winning or losing do not exist. They overlap, and a crystal ball is needed to decide in which way a situation will develop.

The Tanzanian/Ugandan war assessment problem was the same. There were few casualties on each side, because Amin fought a fighting retreat, slowing Mac down with skirmishing forces. He was intent on stretching the Tanzanian lines of supply and communication to a point where they could have severe difficulty to maintain them. Intelligence sources told Mac that Big Dada was preaching "Montgomery of Alamain" tactics, and that he would use the same tactics. This gave Mac a crushing victory over Amin near his main garrison at Jinja in North Uganda.

The intelligence information decided the tactics: a slow, careful advance, using light weaponry, so as not to damage the country infrastructure or cause unnecessary civilian casualties. There was little point in shelling with 122mm artillery when the enemy was running away. Save it and the ammunition until the big battle to come.

Every small piece of logistic supply was hoarded, when that was possible, including nearly two million pounds worth of glass to replace windows shot out during the attack. That is why the first major objective had been Entebbe airport. This vital link in the supply chain was captured after eight hours of fighting with light weapons, so new equipment could be bought in to establish the logistic train.

A well-organised transport system was evolved and supplies were soon flowing in by Army Air Corps Buffalo aircraft, by two chartered Hercules transports with Israeli aircrew. As soon as goods arrived at the airfield they were moved to tactical storage and distribution harbours en route to Kampala, the next objective.

By doing this, troops were avoiding bomb damage to stores and saving last minute motor transport requirements to move the equipment. Overall, this gave a slow, careful buildup of everything needed and available on the way to the target. These tactical reasons meant the buildup took rather a long time, and some Tanzanian Officers wanted to speed up the process, mainly General Twalipo and his cronies. He reminded Mac on a number of occasions that he was a Sandhurst trained student and he carried seniority.

Mac had to tell the pompous bastard in very forceful language that, "All the students that have crossed my path from African and Middle Eastern states were paid for by their governments to attend Sandhurst. I have never met one who has passed on their own merit; I was a Sandhurst Instructor, and we had to pass students so the government would think they'd received their money's worth. If you think you're so fucking good, why have I been brought in to advise? Go and tell the President that I have relieved you of command, as of now! You're nothing but a big, posing, pain in the arse. I'll win your war for you. You just sit back, pick up the medals and promotions, but keep out of my fucking way."

Twalipo got the message. He was himself a big hulk of a baboon, like Amin, believing he was Africa's General Patton, and always sported two pearl-handled 38mm Smith and Wesson revolvers on his hips. No one had ever seen him without a stupid looking tiny pimple of a red beret on his head. His promotions came from having a good education and his stint at Sandhurst, his only attribute over and above Amin. This made him dangerous and forced Mac to take more care and watch his skin. A stray bullet in the back was easy to come by over there.

Generally, things went well in the buildup, and after three weeks the attack on Kampala was feasible with light weapons, although the latest intelligence confirmed that 2,000 Libyan conscripts were in defence, not that they bothered Mac unduly, because the Libyans

[336]

were useless fighters at the best of times. He had met them, fought them, and won before, without any unforeseen problems.

These poor soldiers were conscripts and didn't even know they were in a war. They had been told they were on a training exercise. However, Twalipo nearly fucked it up.

Just prior to the Kampala attack, which had been delayed nearly three weeks to ensure the correct Logistics and Command and Control was in place, Twalipo decided to talk to the troops waiting at the start line, ready to go. The buildup had been clever and secretive, placing the men at the start line without the enemy being aware of their presence. This was until Twalipo did his "Patton" bit in front of the eight hundred men of the Ranger Battalion, who was to spearhead the ground assault.

He stood on a lorry bonnet, with his big gut sticking out, the red pimple beret balanced on his head, and his pearl handled Smith and Wesson's with the butts pointing forward, as though he were some Western cross draw merchant, and said in a deep drawl of a voice, "Where are we going?" and then stamped his foot on the bonnet in the typical Masai stomp.

The Rangers shuffled their feet in embarrassment, knowing that they should be quiet before they attacked.

Again, "Where are we going? We are going to Kampala!"

Another foot stomp, but louder this time.

His voice volume increased tenfold, "Where are we going? Tell me. Where are we going? Kampala."

This time followed by a crescendo of foot stomps, while the confused Rangers started to join in his mesmerising mental conditioning.

Before long, every man was stamping his feet chanting "Kampala" at the top of their voices in time to Tallapoosa's (as he was called) fucking orchestration and conducting. Some even started to fire weapons in the air.

Mac, in desperation and being aware he couldn't stop this, blew his three blasts on the whistle, and fired the green signal flares that were the agreed signal to start the attack. Fortunately, everyone started to run, screaming toward Kampala for the assault and left Tallapoosa standing on the vehicle bonnet like a spare prick at a wedding.

It was amazing that anything constructive came out of this at all. All the detailed, careful weeks of planning and supply structuring had nearly gone out of the picture in one foul, egoistical swoop by the degenerate imbecile, Tallapoosa.

The worst was yet to come.

The Rangers eliminated the opposition in a matter of three hours, but then the problem started. Tribal beliefs came to the front, and if you are a good soldier and fight bravely in your defence or attack position, your spirit must be presented with honour and respect to your God. This means your conquering soldier releases your warrior spirit from your now defunct body. Your now non-operating lump of body is disemboweled to clean it, and release its old warrior spirit to the Gods, regardless of whether the unfortunate soul is dead or alive. No agreement or acceptance is needed; it just doesn't matter. It is a custom carried on from centuries of tribal warfare, and you will conform. It's not as though a man is in a position to stop someone disemboweling him if he's severely wounded or unconscious.

The press had a field day. The major newspapers around the world carried stories such as "The Despot" and likened the situation to a Concentration Camp Commander selecting the people for the gas chambers, and, of course, Mac's name became "Eichmann the Second" as a pet media phrase. Mac was taking a slating by International media, but didn't have time to hang about to give his side of the story.

The Ugandan Army had broken up and was fleeing north toward Jinja. They were throwing away weapons and equipment, and they were completely disoriented and demoralized. Mac had to immediately exploit the situation, and he smashed through them to the Dams in the North to defuse the bombs already laid by Dada to destroy these vital parts of the Ugandan infrastructure. Had he not managed to do so, the effect would be devastating to the Ugandan economy. They would have lost the Hydro Electric Power Grid, thousands of acres of crop irrigation, jobs for thousands of people, and very much more.

After a hectic, crazy drive, and a few firefights and expending approximately 20,00 rounds of ammunition from the twin 50 calibre machine guns mounted, front and rear mountings on the jeeps and Land Rovers, they drove on to the dams just in time. The Ugandan Engineers were putting the final touches to the explosives but ran away when Mac's jeeps rushed across the top of the dam service roads, blasting away at everything that moved. Not many escaped, but the place was safe. Tanzanian Rangers secured the area, disarming anybody who was still alive.

Big Dada escaped by his private helicopter. Astles was caught trying to escape in his boat in Kenya. It was over. The war was won.

Twalipo received his promotion to Minister of Defence, and Mac found out (as he suspected) that he had become a prime target and had to escape as his life would now be in danger. To do this successfully, he needed to make his move unannounced, and quickly, even at the expense of losing his pay.

SECTION 3 – After Amin's Exile
CHAPTER 66

The Baboons

The Tanzanian Uganda War, as an operation, had been a complete success in most ways until the battles were over and the new political masters started vying with each other for power. This had led to Mac's present predicament, hiding under an outcrop of rock on an escarpment in Northwestern Uganda, keeping company with a small troupe of baboons. It was here he had to camp out to prevent Twalipo's soldiers on the plain below from finding him and killing him.

Turnbull the Crap Hat had decided to stay in Kampala, in spite of Maces warnings. While he let his mind wander over recent events that had led to his present situation, Mac wondered what had made him accept a military overseas job with an ex-RAF pilot. His guard had slipped badly.

Turnbull and Mac had worked together before in the Trucial Oman and Aden. On those two occasions, Turnbull had been flying CAP (Combat Air Patrol) and Mac had been the FAC (Forward Air Controller) on the ground. This had worked well and many a camel convoy of arms had been wiped out by precisely placed Napalm, much to the great surprise of the Arabs who thought the British had eyes everywhere by day and night.

Flying on one of these missions, Turnbull received a number of hits by ground fire, and, as he climbed out of the attack, all he said to Mac on the air to ground radio was, "Cunt."

Turnbull managed to fly the Hunter back to Khormaksar but, on landing the badly damaged aircraft, the nose wheel collapsed and Turnbull's forearm smashed through his upper arm and finished his flying career. It was this accident that put Turnbull in the ground role operating Instructor Teams in the Middle East and Africa.

He recruited older retired British soldiers, mainly Special Forces, to do the work he had contracted for with people he had known as a pilot, hence Mac's instructor position.

Involvement with the East Africans in any deals was a dangerous affair. The Governments were unstable. A war was taking place in South Sudan between the northern Muslims against the Christians. There was a civil war in Eritrea. Mozambique was at war in dozens of different directions between the "War Lords" and Tanzania was in a flux of civil disturbance, because the people were starving. There was hardly any work available, and inflation was sky high. If people found work, the money paid was worth practically nothing.

Of course, Mac had just finished his war against Uganda's Big Dada. It was in this turmoil that Turnbull accepted to supply Night Surveillance Equipment and train the Army in its use.

The money was good, if they paid. Jan Leclerc, an ex-French Foreign Legion Colonel who had worked with Mac before, had told him that the Tanzanian Government always found the money to pay for arms, even if the people were starving. So Mac, against his inner instincts, accepted the offer to "do the business."

Training was conducted at the Tanzanian Peoples Defence Force, just on the Embassy outskirts of Dar-es- Salaam, and all went as planned for the first few months. Then, after the battles took place, new politicians were in power. Money was owed to the team and Mac decided they would not be paid, especially since he had made enemies with some high-powered people. More than likely, they would meet with a "timely accident," instead of the new Government paying up - a common practice within African states.

His experience told him to "get to hell out of there," so he laid his plans to do just that, and quickly. Over the weeks, he had been thinking about just such an eventuality. Despite his advice to the rest of the team, they decided to stay, and died in a Brant Blindside rocket explosion four days after Mac left.

Maces plan was simple, steal a well-serviced Land Rover and fill it with as much water and petrol as possible. Make sure he had a good quantity of grenades and ammunition and, at last light, when, unlike the British, the Tanzanians reduced patrol activity, he would head for the Democratic Republic of Congo Zaire border, and eventually get to Kinshasa and hitch a plane ride from the French Foreign Legion based there.

He took a small amount of concentrated food. His intention for food was to shoot an impala and make biltong. Mac headed South, to lay a false trail of sightings, and then swung around Northwest, as fast as possible, so he could lay up and camp up to avoid helicopter spotters at first light.

During the first night, he covered approximately two hundred and twenty kilometres, pulling off the main road on four occasions to avoid enemy convoys. His movement from now on would be slower, because he must come off the main road and head across country, northwest, to avoid all enemy activity if humanly possible. If this could not be achieved, the intent was to fight, and with the arsenal of weapons he'd brought with him, and the fact that he was a marksman on all of them, meant a lot of Tanzanians would likely die before they took him out. That frame of mind stayed in place throughout the journey.

That first day he camped up at first light, as planned, in a small copse, less than twenty metres from the road, so as not to give himself a major task of rubbing out tyre tracks, which would be seen by helicopters. This area also gave him plenty of camouflage material, and good surveillance of any increased troop movement. This would indicate that he was the target and a fast route out if he was compromised in any way. All in all, he was happy with the situation, and after a while, he went on a catnap spree until last light, when his journey continued.

Mac's one regret was that he had failed to put his hands on one of the small section signals sets used by the Tanzanian army. Made in Japan, they were small and compact, but would have let him know the state of play by listening to the enemy. Their signal personnel spoke in English when on the radio. He decided that should a firefight occur, he would kill the signaler and steal his set.

[342]

Movement was slow. He was proceeding down a single road sand track with high twitch grass on both side and stopping every one hundred yards to observe his next bound through the SSE 707. It turned out to be a good move, because, after some twenty kilometers, he spotted a roadblock about eight hundred metres ahead.

Shit, he thought.

Giving even more close scrutiny to the problem, he could not exit the road anywhere, and the twitch grass was impenetrable. The roadblock consisted of two Armoured Personnel Carriers and three men to each. If he stayed where he was, someone could come up behind him and he would be trapped between two groups. He could take them out by LAW, but that would tell people where he was.

He decided to take them out, and then double back northeast. Hopefully, follow up troops would hunt for him Southwest. This would also give him a chance to get that radio.

Decision made, let's do it, he mumbled under his breath.

He slowly moved the Land Rover toward the target, night sighting all the time. He knew they could not see him, but they might hear him.

At approximately 400 metres, he switched off the engine and breathed a great sigh of relief when he heard them running up their engines, probably recharging radio batteries. He now moved boldly. He knew well the devastating effect of his LAWS. He prepared two; opening up both rear-arming slides, and made sure the two hundred metre sight arch was clear and unobstructed. He checked the two fragmentation grenades were armed and ready. Finally, he set the SSE 404 night sight range graticule at 200 metres, and then, confirming the APC engines were still running, he drove to the point of contact.

At just under 200 metres, he stopped, collected his equipment, and walked a further 100 metres and hit both APCs in quick succession. French Panhards are famous for burning. Grenades and bullets were not required. Both APCs exploded in flames, and the scene was made more devastating when fuel and ammunition went up. The vehicles seemed to be throbbing in and out with the inferno-taking place within them.

Mac walked around the position. Only one man was outside the vehicles, and he was on fire and screaming. Mac gave him one shot to put him out of his misery. The pungent smell of burning flesh and cooking metal was a memory jogger for him from previous operations, where he had not considered his enemy with such kindness.

Alas, no radio. He had hoped they had used the small one outside, as nothing would survive the heat inside.

Fine, he thought, let's get out of here.

He followed his deception plan and was 20 kilometres north and in a camouflaged lager by dawn. Helicopters full of troops passed overhead, heading south like he thought they would. He remained unobserved; the enemy was searching for him forty km away. He catnapped all day until night came to urge him on his way.

Two LAW, he thought. At this rate I could fight the whole bloody army and win.

Over the next three days, he followed his plan. He moved at night and lay up during daylight. Progress was slow, but it was still progress in the right direction. Then, a problem arose. The Land Rover drive shaft fractured. He had no spares and nowhere for hundreds of miles to steal one from. He still had forty kilometres before the border.

One good night's romp, he thought.

However, the immediate problem was to ditch the Land Rover and find a place of safety for the day. He unloaded weaponry and water and thought about using petrol to burn the vehicle. This idea was cancelled, because the burning vehicle would attract a helicopter full of troops. After about an hour of very strenuous exertion, he managed to push the Rover over a small, dried-up riverbed bank and climbed down after it to camouflage as best he could in the short time available before daylight.

A safe place for the day was the next task. As dawn was breaking, he noticed a kopje (escarpment), a huge outcrop of rocks quite common in Africa. On the plateau, he noticed five of these geological wonders, but the one he liked most had a troupe of baboons in residence.

Now Africans are shit scared of baboons. In the local Kraals, if somebody is ill or frail, or often a girl child at birth, the people would leave them out at night for the wildlife to eat. They believe that the deceased body takes the form of a baboon and are therefore frightened to go anywhere near them. Mac knew of this superstition and decided to move in with these "ghosts."

Quickly, he manhandled weaponry and water, hiding it behind a large rock at the base of the hill, and then, taking his G3 and ammo, started to climb the hill to a vantage observation point. This was when the trouble started in the shape of the huge male baboon, a beautiful specimen. This animal had a large, long face, broad back, big chest, and was covered by a coat of long, shaggy black hair, with a gray mantle around his shoulders. When he rushed down the hill toward Mac, this lovely coat stuck straight out, making him look monstrous in size, but the most striking feature were his fangs, especially his incisors. They were gigantic, full six inches in length, top and bottom. These ivory tusks were mounted in bright red gleaming gums and looked awesome.

Some bloody ghost this one, thought Mac.

When this creature arrived about ten feet from Mac it stopped, stood on its back legs, and threw a stone at this intruder in his territory. Now baboons are inarticulate when the art of cricket and throwing are concerned. They throw from the wrist and have no power in the shot. The stone barely reached over the ten feet distance to Mac.

Thank the lord, thought Mac.

He did not want to shoot the animal, because it was a noble beast and also a shot may give his position away. However, neither did he want to tangle with those fangs, and the beast wanted to play cricket with him anyway. Now Mac used to play the game at school, in fact, he bowled fast for the school team.

So, the dual began, strictly to Queensbury rules, one shot each, and may the best man win. Mac let the baboon have a second throw in case the first one had slipped.

It hadn't.

The next one was just as pathetic.

"Now it's my turn, Mister Baboon", and with that, promptly smacked the cock of the roost right in his teeth with a large brick, traveling at a very fast rate of knots. A look of complete surprise mixed with pain crossed the animal's face and blood spurted from those lovely teeth.

"Want any more, Mate?" shouted Mac at the great beast.

It must have taken this roar as a serious challenge, and it didn't want any more of those bricks, so he turned around and ran up the hill to sit on an outcrop of rock, sulking and looking very sorry for himself.

Come forth the second contenders: four young males rushed, but as a gang - not solo as the brave old man had done. Just like young men in Civvy Street, as a gang all-brave, screaming, egging each other on, and a load of yellow cowards when they are on their own.

Mac enjoyed himself. He went into automatic destruction mode, taking them all out with a barrage of well-placed shots in very private places, even hitting them in the balls when they ran away to join the prime male in a sulking session.

All this dramatic activity had been closely watched by a group of females and their baby baboons. These offered no objection when Mac climbed the hill and found a good comfortable observation point in the shade under a protruding ledge. From this position, he could rest and observe the plateau below. He had water and weapons, plus vegetable concentrate for which he added water for a wholesome meal. He felt good. A nice rest today and a forced march tonight would see him home and dry.

It didn't quite work out that way.

At approximately two o'clock in the afternoon, a troop-carrying helicopter landed on the plateau between Mac and his way out to freedom. Eight fully armed troops dismounted. At first, Mac thought they had seen the Land Rover poorly camouflaged in the riverbed, but soon realised the helicopter had a problem when the aircrew dismounted and opened up the engine cowling and started work underneath. Fifty minutes later, a second helicopter arrived, obviously called up by the first one, and another eight armed troops debussed,

[346]

and the second aircrew began to work with the first crew. All this activity by 20 men in the path of Mac's way home was very frustrating.

Never mind; he was in good shape, and another day's rest would not go amiss. He decided to stay overnight, and the next day, and be really well primed for the 40km forced march the following night.

It was at this point that he noticed a baby baboon rush across and touch his boot, and then scurry away back to its mother. She said something to the baby in baboon language, and the baby came back and sat on Mac's foot and started to groom the hairs on his legs. A strange situation developed quickly, inside half an hour he had six babies grooming him and inspecting everything about his anatomy, lifting and feeling inside the legs of his shorts. When they found something they was interesting, they would scurry back to their mother and tell her the news and she would then come and have a look or a feel for herself. It was obvious that Mac was now the prime male of the troupe. The females had seen him defeat the other males in battle; he was kind to the babies, so he was number one, and two, three, and four.

This was confirmed when the females went foraging for food and brought him back presents of shit beetles, grubs, cockroaches, young birds, cashew nuts and various forms of other food they had found. He could live forever on these tokens of allegiance, because they were A1 protein. If he stayed there too long, he would put on weight. Mac felt quite proud, in a way. His brain and knowledge of African customs was keeping him safe from an enemy, and now, by popular choice, he was a tribal chief with a ready-made family of six women and six children. Not bad going, he thought, as he turned over to sleep for the night, protected by his own sentries.

He slept the long sleep of a contented man, free from worry, and woke up to the large bright red African morning sun climbing its weary way up the heavy sky until it changed colour to yellow, then white, for the duration of the day. Looking down at the plateau, he could see the enemies were still in attendance, but he decided that if they didn't move today, he would go tonight anyway. His baboons went foraging again and brought him another batch of protein. He liked the shit beetles best, because they were big and full of healthy, juicy meat, which tasted like smoked chicken.

It was at this stage he was to learn he was expected to earn his keep and had certain duties to perform. One of the female baboons had come on heat and needed servicing, and as he was the alpha prime male, he was expected to do it. The baboon's rear end had swollen and turned bright red and she insisted on sticking it in his face and turning her head to look at him. She growled, showing horrifying four-inch long incisors, as if saying "Screw me, you bastard, or I'll rip your throat out." It was very rare that Mac found it difficult to make decisions, but this lustful program confused the hell out of him. He hadn't much experience with women anyway; Mac had married at a young age, but due to his way of life, the marriage was doomed from the start; he was a man's man, and the few women he had since grown close to, he tended to treat with an almost awe-like respect, dating back to his upbringing with a very strict and proper mother.

This thing in his face and the turning head with the big fangs flummoxed him. To say she fancied him would be the understatement of the year. His reputation as a cool professional killer and operator fascinated a lot of women, but this one was seemed considerably more interested than any previous companion.

Now he had a serious problem. As the day progressed, she got randier and more insistent. Her bright red, noisy, squelching rear-end was hardly ever out of his face, and she was snuffling and nuzzling him, as though trying to kiss him, and the more he refused, the closer those lethal fangs came to his throat. He could not escape. The enemy was on the lower slopes, and if he tried to move he was dead. If he didn't shag this baboon, he was dead. He had to make a decision to die or stay alive.

He decided to stay alive.

Within a few hours, one helicopter flew off, lowering the odds against him, so he decided to head out on his journey. Ten well-placed shots got rid of the eight soldiers and two aircrew. He took out the aircrew first, so signals could not be passed, nor could they follow him. The poor soldiers could not understand why they were being picked off so easily in pitch-black darkness. They had never been introduced to night vision instruments, and of course, to Mac, it was like a duck shoot, only easier.

He did not bother to set fire to the helicopter, but put a few bullets in the cockpit dash board and kept his sense of humour and fair play by leaving an invoice for £35,000 pinned to the dashboard and wrote on it "Paid in full, thank you."

Mac managed to arrive in Kinshasa and locate the French Foreign Legion. After taking a detailed debrief, feeding him, and clothing him, they put him on a Nor Atlas troop transport aircraft and flew him to Istres in France, where he caught an aircraft to the UK.

On arrival at Turnbull's office in Ebury Street London, he cleared out the safe. He found an irrevocable letter of credit to draw on Chase Manhattan Bank for £35,000 Sterling, from the deposed Tanzanian Government they had originally contracted to, plus with loose petty cash, he drew nearly thirty nine thousand. He went to London Zoo to see the captive baboons, and not being impressed, he made a donation of nine thousand pounds to the zoo to make a bigger baboon compound with more activity toys for them to play with.

It was good to finally be home, Mac thought.

Yet, even with that thought, Mac knew himself well enough to know he would not stay in one place for too long. With his lifestyle, and lust for adrenaline, Mac could not stay in one place, living the 'normal' life, for very long.

Soon, Mark 'Mac' Hudson would once again be off on an adventure.

CONCLUSION

Sometimes allowing life to continue, sometimes taking life, the soldier moves through his life one day at a time. From the shores of Britain to the mountains of the Mediterranean, to the desert sands of the Middle East, Mark "Mac" Hudson took the journey through a lifetime of service. In thought and deed, laughter and anger, confidence and confusion, the true life of the dedicated soldier is displayed on the pages of the four books in this series "British Post World War II Military Campaigns.".

The reader of this collection of encounters might well ask if the story ends here. Of course, it does not.

After years of life devoted to service, Mark Hudson formally left the British Military on a "special release". The conditions of this release included his becoming a Private Field Operations Officer to various Middle Eastern countries on behalf of the British Government. The details of his duties during that period of his life are not those of the type that can be disclosed here.

What can be said is this: The operations Mac became involved in fall under the classification of "dirty work" campaigns. Private Field Operations Officers were used in certain deployment situations where the British Government preferred to adhere to a public policy of "disavowal" of any knowledge or connection to the operations.

During this new stage of his life, Mac was involved in many behind the scenes type of exploits. Among others, he carried out surveillance operations, sabotage, and "government eliminations". One daring, but successful coup was made against the oil revenues of Saddam Hussein in the El Sheba region. Mac played his own special role in causing the despotic leader to suffer.

Due to the nature of his operational involvement with these Middle Eastern Countries, Mark Hudson has lived the remainder of his days with a price on his head. Earlier pages in the book mentioned that some of the tactics used in Maces career are still in use today. As such, the details cannot be divulged in order to ensure the continued safety and effectiveness of the men that follow in the footsteps of the amazing legacy left by their predecessors.

Mark Hudson left the services of the British Government for good in 1985. He started yet another lifetime of service, this time in the role of a college teacher and lecturer in the North of England. With a special focus on Military History Tactics, Mark was able to breathe a force into the subject from the point of one who had lived it. Self-defense and personal protection were added to his repertoire of knowledge that he shared with both individual students and military units.

At the time of this writing, Mac would be an elderly man, with a history of experience and adventure, which has been poured into the pages of these books. It is the legacy of a soldier, and a glimpse into the life of a man dedicated to the ideals of a country he served well for many years.

Mac went missing somewhere in the Middle East about seven years ago and nobody has heard a thing about him, or from him since.

He was once rumoured to have said that when age caught up with him (if he managed to achieve old age) he would retire to a nice, quiet place, somewhere in the sun, and write a book about the wars in which he had been involved.

So now, one shall wonder if he is doing that very thing somewhere, right now.

Printed in Great Britain
by Amazon